Glowing Comments from Leaders About...

No Excuse! I'm Doing It

Jay Rifenbary

"We love your new book, *No Excuse!* We implemented your new philosophy company-wide and achieved a 30% increase in sales volume. You can take this book directly to the bottom line. There is No Excuse! for not reading it today."

—Kenneth J. Burgess Jr.
Former President, Morgan Hill, Inc.

"Jay Rifenbary has found the key to personal power, internal motivation, and individual excellence! This book gives a simple, practical blueprint for outstanding performance. Everyone needs to read it."

—Brian Tracy
Author of *Something for Nothing*

"I read your book! Exciting! Filled with good stuff. Have quoted you in two speeches and two TV shows this week."

—Ty Boyd, CSP, CPAE
Founder, Executive Learning Systems, Inc.
Speaker and Consultant

"I am very impressed with the book *No Excuse!* You have gathered a wealth of knowledge and compiled it into a simple, clear, concise volume. I hope its circulation will spread far and wide."

—Robert A. Rohm, Ph.D.
President, Personality Insights, Inc.
Author of *Who Do You Think You Are Anyway?*

"Well done...*No Excuse!* is a tough but caring view of the mission of our lives...read it and use the principles. I recommend it whole-heartedly."

—Larry Wilson, CPAE
Founder of Wilson Learning and Pecos River Learning Center
Co-Author of *The One Minute Salesperson* and *Play to Win*

D1051855

No Excuse!
I'm Doing It

Jay Rifenbary

Copyright © 2008 Jay Rifenbary

ISBN 10: 0-938716-34-4
ISBN 13: 978-0-938716-34-1

Published by
Possibility Press
www.possibilitypress.com

1   2   3   4   5   6   7   8   9   10

All rights reserved, including the right to reproduce this book or portions thereof in any form or any means, electronic or mechanical, including photocopying, recording, or by information storage retrieval system without written permission from the publisher, except for the inclusion of brief quotations in a review. All rights are also reserved for translation into foreign languages. No liability is assumed with respect to use of the information herein.

Manufactured in the United States of America

DEDICATION

To my beloved wife, Noni, and my children, Nicole and Jared, for their patience, love, and understanding of their adventurous spouse and dad.

To my mother, Dorothy, for her lifelong love, patience, and untiring desire to be the best parent possible, which she accomplished.

To my sister, Deborah, for her expertise in language and life.

To my Uncle, T.J., for the love and support he gave me in all that I strived for in my life.

To my dad, George, for the spirit of what he was and what he gave.

Tribute: To all contributors of knowledge, hope, common sense, and love, and all those who strive to make a difference.

A LETTER TO MY FATHER

January 1, 1995

Dear Dad,

This is the first letter I have ever written to you. As you know, I was only eleven when you died, but I never had a need to write to you until now. I am thirty-eight now, and a lot has happened in my life that I know you would be proud of.

I just want to tell you how much I have missed you and how much I have desired your words of approval and reassurance. There were many times in my life that your being there would have meant the world to me. It certainly would have made life's trials more bearable.

The simple hug or touch a father shares with his son I will never feel again, yet I now have the wonderful opportunity to share that with my own children. It took many years for me to become satisfied with me and what I have to offer others around me. I know that while you were here you gave me everything you felt was best, with honesty and sincerity.

I truly love you and ask for your blessing. I ask for your spirit of strength for my family and me. Thank you for helping me find peace within myself and to feel the satisfaction of giving to other people.

Your loving son,

Jay

CONTENTS

PROLOGUE

I'm twelve hundred and fifty feet above the earth. My parachute hasn't snapped me out of my fall. I can't look up to see what's going on. My head is caught in a vise of tangled lines and my chin is hammered into my chest. Instinct and images recalled from training films tell me my parachute is trailing above me like a ribbon. The world around me appears chaotic and unconcerned about my dilemma. The drone of the plane above is gone. The sound of the wind and my awareness of the earth and sky is lost as I shut down and shut out. I can hear only my thoughts and feel my pounding heart.

I had only myself and my pack when our Airborne training unit boarded the C-130 Hercules transport plane for our *first* jump. As I stood in the belly of the plane, I felt all alone. All I had was on me and within me. Suddenly I was standing in the open door. I would be the first to fling a half-yearning, half-reluctant body out into space. "Go!" was the final word I heard from the Jump Master. The rush of wind, when it seems to pull you out the door, is the greatest thrill. All of a sudden you're suspended in mid-air, but only for an instant. As you start to fall, nature instantly measures your mass and determines your destiny according to its laws.

My parachute was carefully packed...or was it? It's supposed to blossom and save me from falling to certain death. The laws of aerodynamics and physics are crucial. I knew this intuitively and through my education. They need to become allies. If not, my twisted lines will hold me hostage until I die!

"No excuse, sir!" I thought back to my West Point training. No whining. No complaining. No blaming. Get on with it! Accept responsibility. I wanted to be Airborne, and was I ever. All I wanted now was a safe landing. I just wanted a chance to achieve what I desired in life. I wanted a successful military and business career; I wanted to be a loving husband and father; I wanted to be a leader who makes a difference in the lives of others. The future I dreamed about was instantly being tested by my willingness to risk.

My survival was at stake. I had animal instinct and past experiences to rely on...my study of yesterday's pre-jump instructions...the academic, physical, emotional and spiritual discipline that got me into and through the United States Military Academy...my studies in nuclear physics, chosen because it was the toughest subject...my ninth-grade determination in swimming that formed championship proportions and drew me into poised, playful, social proficiency...my triumph in overcoming the humiliation I felt at having to repeat 7th grade...my mother's dauntless conviction that her only son, fatherless from age 11, would be a man of excellence. Finally, I had my father's heroic stature, his too frequent absences while he was alive, and his achingly illusive presence since his death.

"No excuse, sir! No! Whose fault is this, anyway? Did someone pack this parachute incorrectly? Did someone...did I...slipup in putting it on? Who's going to be in trouble for this mistake?

No excuse! Cut through the garbage. *My lines are twisted.* Do something!

"If the Lines Become Twisted...Bicycle!" All at once, my legs and brain remember. My feet are in heavy combat boots, never intended for flying or pedaling, but they must be put into motion. Miraculously...in action, the laws of physics are wonderful...the lines untwist. Like a newborn coming from the womb, whose lungs fill with that first breath of air, the parachute "explodes," forming a beautiful floating canopy. It jerks my freed head upward to behold the wonder. It gives me life and time to enjoy the glory of the world waiting for my touchdown.

If my mind drifted, even for an instant, to make an excuse, it would have fatally distracted me from the enormity of my predicament. I would not have reacted fast enough to remedy the situation.

Is this what we want when we jump into LIFE? Are we looking to explore new sensations...to push at the borders of our experience? Do we want to harness the forces that would control us? Do we want to grow and become better people? Do we want greater capacity for life and a deeper understanding of nature and other people?

Like an opened, gliding parachute, *No Excuse!* can help carry you over whatever thresholds you choose to cross. *No Excuse!* can help give your life a whole new meaning. *No Excuse!* can help you lead a successful, happy, fulfilling life of personal growth. *No Excuse!* can help you grow and become the best you can be, and make a difference. You can feel as if you are special and valuable...because you are!

ARE YOU SICK AND TIRED OF PEOPLE WHINING?

The principles in *No Excuse!* have given me the understanding to reach heights I hadn't dreamed of. They can do the same for you when you put them in place and use them. They'll give you the tools to scale any mountain. At first they'll assist you like excited, new-found companions met at the start of an adventure. With time and practice, they'll be your reliable, comforting friends, always ready to help you handle challenges. These principles can lead you to true wealth, which is so much more than just money. They can help you change untapped ambition into success.

I have put together the *No Excuse!* principles based on my own experiences. I have drawn particularly from my years at West Point and my Airborne Ranger experiences. My years as a military officer, corporate executive, business owner, lecturer, and motivational speaker, as well as a spouse and parent, have been invaluable in creating the *No Excuse!* philosophy.

Fundamental to the philosophy is that people need the dignity of satisfying work to make their lives and the lives of others better. B.C. Forbes, founder of *Forbes Magazine* and author of several books, suggested that, "Whether we find pleasure in our work or whether we find it a bore depends entirely upon our mental attitude toward it, not upon the task itself." *Whenever we combine labor and love, true success follows*. That's what the foundation of *No Excuse!* is all about. It can guide you to work smart at a life you love living.

Guard against drudgery and discouragement in everything you do. Know that your work contributes to your well-being, as well as that of others. It is absolutely essential to your personal and professional development to understand that, *anything you let get in the way of applying yourself to your goals is only an excuse!*

No Excuse! is designed for people who want to make life better for themselves and others. They also need to be humble enough to be guided and encouraged to do so. *No Excuse!* is designed for people who want to lead fulfilled lives. It's for those who are willing to accept responsibility for their own success, as well as play a responsible role in the success of others.

No Excuse! is designed for people who grow to understand and accept that success and failure are simply the outcomes of their behavior. Failure is a lesson to prepare us to achieve the outcomes we want. It's a stepping stone.

For many, it's not easy to accept success for themselves. They see success only in the lives of others, which can cause them to develop apathetic, defeatist attitudes.

It's difficult to recognize our own success if we're caught in a web of negative thinking. *No Excuse!* means we accept responsibility for thinking positive. Dwelling on failure holds us back from having the results we want. Once we learn the lessons from them, we can let go of our failures and mistakes. *No Excuse!* is designed for people willing to eliminate the negative thinking that thwarts and overburdens their efforts. *No Excuse!* supports your efforts to identify, work toward, and achieve your dreams and goals.

The exercises in this book are meant to challenge you to explore your own thoughts, feelings, and perceptions. They are particularly meant to challenge your hidden thoughts so you can realize wisdom, strength, and goodness. More of your energies can then be used to serve others while achieving your dreams and goals.

What's your reward for this challenging work? How about getting rid of the fears of rejection and failure so you can move on? Many of us carry around excess baggage, full of excuses. They may always be there, ready to keep you in "safe" and sorry places when you fear failure and rejection. As you begin living a *No Excuse!* life, you'll have less room for excuses.

By using *No Excuse!* principles, you'll come to the day when you can honestly say *No Excuse!* because you won't need any. You'll eliminate that bad habit. You'll learn how to truly define success for yourself. You'll learn from your experiences that there is *No Excuse!* for you not to be successful.

When I devoted myself to developing and living out *No Excuse!,* I made a personal and professional decision to walk away from what I thought was security. I would risk everything I had accumulated and have no one to blame, not even myself, if I failed. I had to realize that blaming myself would only be another way of defeating myself. This helped me remember my formal introduction to the *No Excuse!* philosophy.

I entered West Point in July of 1976. It's a place where the phrase "No excuse, sir!" is uttered by cadets every day. It's one of the four answers a plebe (freshman) may give when addressed by an upperclassman. The others are "Yes, sir;" "No, sir;" and "Sir, I do not understand." In 1976, when I was 19, "No excuse, sir!" meant no more to me than a way to end an uncomfortable one-sided conversation. I was too frightened and intimidated to understand why such rigid limitations were part of military training.

Thirteen years later, on a night in 1989, I had a powerful insight: *No excuse, sir!"* was a basic statement that left nowhere to hide. It had played a vital role in my development as a thinker and a doer. *No Excuse!* thinking was basic training. It was "Achievement 101." With every repetition, the *No Excuse!* response emphasized the benefits of cleaning the slate and getting on with the search for solutions. There was no time to waste in unproductive excuse-making.

I was standing alone in my office, alone in the hush following a grand opening party for the business I had just started. For years I had dreamed of doing this, and I seized the moment. To get there, I had let go of a secure, flourishing career where I was methodically making my way to the top.

It was a difficult decision, about as hard as deciding not to make the military my career. I was driven by the desire for a different life. Fortunately, I was blessed with my wife's encouragement and support as I wrestled with decisions and made them.

I was happy about how I had gotten to where I was that night. But when the celebration was over and the hundreds of friends and supporters had gone, why did I stand there feeling so alone and frightened? When opening my own business was a dream come true, something most people only fantasize about, why did I feel so unaccomplished and unhappy?

I was filled with a rush of longing for my dad. I had never missed him so much; I never wanted his touch and approval as much as I did then. A yearning for what might have been surged through my heart. It was as though I was faltering on the edge of a cliff. I stood there until a peace came over me, as I sadly acknowledged it was time to let go of my father's death. It could not serve me as a reason or an excuse for making future decisions. It could never be an excuse for not attempting anything. His approval could not serve as motivation for attempting anything either. This would be true even if he were alive.

I realized I was now an adult, moving on to create the life I wanted for myself and my family. What I accomplished was achieved through honesty, sincerity, and commitment. It was also the result of vigorous effort in partnership with people I respected and loved.

In this moment I began my life as a self-responsible person. It's incredibly important to release the need for approval when we begin traveling on the road to fulfillment. I realized, for the first time in my life, how crucial it is to create a life based on our own expectations. *In general, the real or imagined expectations of others simply don't matter.* Of course, if you are in a job situation, you may need to align some of your personal expectations with those of your boss. But be careful that your actions are in line with your value system and what you know to be right.

While feeling the great emptiness of my father's absence, I understood what was needed to begin living a full, mature *No Excuse!* life: self-respect, self-responsibility, and self-acceptance.

No Excuse! was born that night. It meant more freedom and power over my own destiny than I had ever known. Up to that point, all my achievements had only been on loan to me. Now I finally owned them and could benefit more fully from the lessons learned along the way.

I committed to moving on. I felt secure in my ability to produce. I believed in the Golden Rule (Do unto others as you would have them do unto you.) and my ability to live and prosper by it. I was grateful for the love and support of significant people in my life. I was especially thankful for Noni, my loving wife, best friend, and business partner. Once I had made the decision, tremendous relief and exhilaration replaced the anxiety I'd been living with for so long. I could now experience the power of the growth that occurs from responsibly crossing the threshold into new maturity and awareness.

Your Life Is in Your Hands

High on a hilltop overlooking a beautiful city lived a wise old man. The local children were taught to seek his guidance and respect his teachings.

One day, two boys devised a plan to confuse the old man. They caught a small bird and headed for the hilltop. As they approached the seated figure, one of the boys held the little bird cupped in his hands.

"Wise old man," the boy said, "Can you tell me if the bird I have in my hands is dead or alive?"

The old man gazed silently at the two boys, and then said: "If I tell you the bird locked in your hands is alive, you will close your hands and crush the life from it. If I tell you the bird is dead, you will open your hands and it will fly away to freedom.

"Son, in your hands you hold the power of life and death. You have the power to choose destruction and the end of a spirit and a song. Or you can choose to free the bird so it has a future, with all its potential. You are wise to know you can choose between life and death.

"If you allow my answer to determine whether the bird lives or dies, you'll have given away your power. You'll have also given away your responsibility to make the correct choice, and to rejoice in your own strength and wisdom."

The boys came down that hill a bit wiser. The old man, in respecting their desire to test themselves and his authority, proved to be a leader and a teacher. He perceived their rebelliousness as an underlying desire to relinquish their self-responsibility. By refusing to cooperate, he contributed to their self-awareness and growth.

We Are the Decision Makers—*The Choice Is Yours*

You and I need to be the decision makers in our own lives and careers. It is also our responsibility to allow and encourage others to do the same. We all have the power to choose, and our accumulated choices largely structure the lives we lead. *Acknowledging we have choices is a first step toward accepting self-responsibility.* Choosing to exercise our personal power by making choices is a challenge and joy in and of itself.

Children are exposed to society's expectations every day, through their parents/caretakers and other family members; in our places of worship; through their peers and schools; and through movies, television, books, and music, to name a few influencing factors. Some of the expectations are positive and some are negative.

How often are children taught that their first responsibility is to reflect on whether a certain direction is right for them? Did anyone ever tell you that? If so, when did you start doing it? Did you stop? Did anyone ever teach you how to think? Or were you, like many of us, taught to listen to parents and others without thinking for yourself?

This book will help you discover the power within yourself—the power to choose and act. It's a message meant to reach you where you think and feel, in your mind and in your heart, where it really counts. I hope *No Excuse!* will serve you, just as the wise man's words served the boys. I hope you will acknowledge your power and use it for the good of all. When you use your power to obtain something truly in your best interest, as long as you aren't causing harm, it's also in the best interest of others.

Use the principles explained here to make choices that are in your own and others' best interests. Your alternative would be to adopt the behavior patterns of many who blindly follow the dictates of society and others, or blindly rebel against them. Either extreme is equally self-destructive and not self-responsible. Just the fact that you are reading this book is a strong indicator that you are doing your best to make wise choices.

The outcomes we experience in life are largely dependent on our choices and actions. The lessons I learned that night have been confirmed every day since. *Our actions, based on clear self-awareness, accompanied by self-responsibility, can create turning points in our lives.*

When you live a *No Excuse!* life, you'll never again allow yourself to be pushed by circumstances or other people's desires that aren't in your best interest. You'll clearly see where and when it's your opportunity and responsibility to make a decision. You'll accept responsibility for the actions you take that contribute to your failures and successes. You won't blame anyone else for your failures, nor be self-centered regarding your successes. You'll always be aware of the part you played in both. You'll rejoice in your successes and view your failures as learning experiences. When you live a *No Excuse!* life you'll be drawn toward your dreams.

The *THESAURUS Factor* and the *Staircase of Success*

The principles you find in this book constitute the treasury of my life. It is a treasury that increases every day and each time it is used. It contains truths that are essential to live a happy, fulfilled life. As you use these ideas, they will help you increase your understanding of life, giving you the opportunity to increase your prosperity in all areas.

Why was the idea of *No Excuse!* and building *a Staircase of Success* developed? To organize the principles of success so they are easy to understand and apply. I wanted to create a method everyone could use to make a difference in their lives and the lives of others.

Why are success principles so important? They're similar to the fluids in a car. You could have the fastest car on the track, but if you neglect the fundamentals, you won't even finish the race. Things like gas, oil, and water, while simple, are vitally important.

You can be on the fast track of success, but if you neglect the fundamentals you won't even be able to finish the greatest race of all, let alone win. Concern yourself with things like honesty, integrity, purpose, desire, and letting go of the past. Do you ever think about them? Most people are so concerned with the challenges of daily living, they rarely or never stop to think about the essential ingredients of success.

I wanted to find a synonym for success I felt would be appropriate to use as an acronym. I pulled out a thesaurus, but couldn't find a word I liked. I started thinking, "What does *THESAURUS* mean?" I went to a dictionary and found that it means "a treasury of ideas; a treasury of knowledge."

That's when I decided *THESAURUS* was a great word to describe the treasury of ideas on success that I wanted to share. And that's exactly what the *Staircase* is built on. Your *Staircase of Success,* the *THESAURUS Factor,* takes each letter in the word *THESAURUS* and uses it as a step.

First, we'll cover the foundation of success—self-responsibility, purpose, and integrity. This'll prepare you for your journey along the *Staircase of Success,* which is explained in-depth starting with Chapter Four. Keep an open mind and have fun. It's going to be an exciting journey!

Chapter 1
SELF-RESPONSIBILITY
The Basis of a No Excuse! *Life*

Attenn…TION! At ease. You may have picked up this book to learn what a more successful life is all about and how to achieve it. In the simplest sense, the answers lie in the title—*No Excuse!* Once you become alert to the opportunity to make a productive decision, and are willing to take responsibility for it, the payoff can be a happy, fulfilling life.

I could tell you to go no further than that and be on your way. I could tell you to read no more, close this book, and start living the life you want. Well, it doesn't work quite like that.

As Ben Sweetland said, "Success is a journey, not a destination." It's also a learning process. Therefore, it is often helpful to learn about the experiences of someone else who has overcome obstacles that may be similar to yours. Perhaps some of the experiences I've had in learning to live a *No Excuse!* life can help motivate you toward living the life *you* want.

When I aspired to write this book, I had to get through all the roadblocks, all the really "good" excuses not to do it. I had to avoid distractions like raking the leaves, making more coffee, and the multitude of other things I could do to avoid it. I had to imagine you starting here and getting inspired and instructed along the way.

What an important combination—*inspiration and instruction.* They're tools that can help you achieve more and live your dreams. Whatever your dreams and goals may be, inspiration and instruction are key components in beginning your journey toward the life you want.

Maybe you're not sure about what you want out of life. You might be emotionally reluctant to admit it. That's okay. Many people have been beat up and put down so many times that they've given up on their dreams. My suggestion is to do whatever it takes to—*Snap out of it!* You can do it.

I've set and achieved some extraordinary goals by living a *No Excuse!* life. I'm not saying this to brag. I just want you to know that you, too, can do the same, using the ideas in this book. When everyone feels free enough and is encouraged enough to achieve their goals, this will be a better world. So I've taken the challenge and set the goal to let others know that it feels good to be self-responsible.

I encourage and challenge you to make the commitment *now* to do whatever it takes to live your dreams. The time is now! The missing link may simply be that nobody ever told you how exhilarating it is to assume responsibility for your own life, dreams, and goals.

With this part of the book, you'll start mastering the basics of *No Excuse!* You'll build self-confidence as you develop a life plan to guide you. You'll envision the success you've always wanted. As you later move through the steps of the *THESAURUS Factor*, your *Staircase of Success*, you'll learn everything you need to accomplish your goals. Best of all, you'll experience more control over your life than ever before. This will lead to reduced stress and a gratifying sense of accomplishment.

Of course, it's likely that you're going to need to make some changes. As you might expect from a book titled *No Excuse!*, *if you want some things to change in your life, you need to change some things in your life.* After all, insanity could be defined as "doing the same thing and expecting *a different* result!" If you're waiting for your life to change, guess what? It waits! It is highly unlikely that someone will come to your door and offer you an exciting life.

Applying the principles in this book will give you the opportunity to eliminate the negative thinking that has formed seemingly insurmountable obstacles. Start believing your dreams are attainable.

As you apply the principles of *No Excuse!* and discover you can reach your dreams and goals, you'll realize that you can be happy, successful, and fulfilled in all areas of your life. Grow and become whatever you want to be. Assume self-responsibility and take appropriate action.

If you have a healthy desire to be successful, then you're ready for *No Excuse!* living. You're then ready to make the most of yourself and your opportunities. If your patterns of personal management are crippled by ignorance and self-doubt, I suggest you prepare to let them go. From now on, you'll have the opportunity to live your life with new understanding.

Before we get to the *THESAURUS Factor* in Part II, let's put the cornerstone of your new *No Excuse!* life in place. Let's begin with the fundamentals. Consider starting to build your success by making self-responsibility one of your greatest strengths.

From Roadblocks to Enrichment

Responsible parents want their children to have a healthy respect for life. Yet the warnings, advice, and encouragement we receive as children sometimes defeat that intent. In some instances, the message gets so serious that happy feelings seem wrong and inappropriate. Being good begins to be frightening. Do we believe being responsible isn't any fun? Have you ever felt that way? *No Excuse!* can help you change your mind. Living responsibly can be *great* fun! Few things will lift your mood and strengthen your confidence as much. The pleasure of self-responsibility expands dramatically as you live it.

Does that mean it's easy? No, not necessarily. But it is simple. Clearing a space for a self-responsible act can be challenging. Once you've done it, however, it gets easier. Euphoria creates energy. Your determination grows with every experience of mature, decisive action. Whether it leads to success or failure, a self-responsible act increases your power to move on. You are gathering momentum toward the life you want.

This book includes mental exercises that will challenge your thinking and cause you to explore your inner feelings. It will help you identify the obstacles that have stopped you from achieving your goals. Maybe you let inexperience or a difficult experience hold you back. Perhaps, for the first time, you'll understand what happened and why.

Look for other things too. Most of all, watch for signs of the strength, courage, wisdom, and inner beauty you already possess. These are the foundation blocks for you to build your future on. A greater understanding of the excellent qualities you have to offer is part of what's in the pot at the end of the rainbow! What about the baggage you're carrying as you travel toward it? Every time you rid yourself of an excuse, your load gets lighter. You have more room for the useful things you need for the journey. Every time you work to remove a roadblock, every time you see an excuse and allow it to evaporate, the qualities you value are enhanced. Your life is enriched.

No Excuse! teaches you to recognize your fears, without letting them stop you. You'll use them as a resource to point the way to your heart's desire—the direction in which your greatest successes lie. *Whenever you sense a fear of failure or rejection, realize that you are getting closer to your heart's desire.* Let it be a sign to you that opportunity is near, and it's time for you to call on the inspiration and instruction of *No Excuse!* Challenge the cloudy and often deceptive nature of the excuses that seem to protect you from failure and rejection, at the cost of success and triumph. Get ready to cross new thresholds with a greater sense of who you are and what you are capable of doing.

My decision to leave the corporate life to launch a business is one example of how adding challenges brought unexpected growth. I carefully calculated the costs and benefits. At that time, I couldn't imagine that the *No Excuse!* philosophy would emerge. I gained a greater understanding of something that had always troubled me: Why do some people reach for and attain fullness of life, while most don't? Most people make excuses!

They excuse themselves from living a better life. Don't be one of them.

Getting Your Wheels Turning

Do you remember the times you surprised yourself, and perhaps others, by taking charge of a risky situation and bringing it to a successful resolution? I hope you've had experiences like that because they help you develop a confident maturity. Recall a moment from your past when you felt exhilarated by success, perhaps a moment when you achieved a goal. Stop here and don't go on until you do. Dwell on that memory. How sweet it is!

The memory of your past successful performance plays an important part in how you mold *No Excuse!* for your own needs. I'll prompt it by recalling one of my own experiences. It's an almost universal memory for Americans who grew up in the Twentieth Century.

You are sitting on a hard triangular seat, but it's not on your trusty tricycle. You're up on a two-wheeler, wobbly, legs dangling. Your feet are slipping from the pedals, toeing the ground right and left to keep yourself from losing balance and tipping over.

A parent's hand grabs the seat, balancing you until you're moving fast enough. Remember how they kept pace with your fledgling efforts? They were more confident than you that you could do it.

Remember the exhilaration you felt when you could finally ride and control the bike? The laws of physics formed a network of support. They enabled you to succeed at something that had seemed scary before.

Let's go back to why you wanted to ride a two-wheeler. Remember how great your tricycle was? When you were on it, you didn't even have to think about it. You could go backward and forward or turn, and not fall! Why were you choosing a wobbly bicycle over a stable tricycle?

Did you outgrow the tricycle? Had your knees started hitting the handlebars? Had you begun compensating with an awkward legs-akimbo style of riding? Try to remember. What told you it was time to move on to a new challenge? Were there people helping you explore options and consider alternatives? A larger tricycle? A pedal car? Why were the right decisions, the right size bicycle, the level terrain, the guiding hand that knew *just* when to let go, provided for you?

Pedal Power

Before we examine these questions, and explore how the physical, mental, and spiritual components of life work together to help you overcome each obstacle, it's time for some sheer pleasure. *Feel it.* Feel it happening. *Your face parts the air. The wind whispers, gently passing by your ears. Your arms and hands loosely guide your direction, confident and comfortable on the ringed ridges of handlebar guards. Your feet press the pedals, pumping and coasting in natural rhythms of motion. You're excited and free!*

This is the feeling *No Excuse!* gives you. It's exhilarating and freeing. It's the feeling of honest personal power—the power to choose and act. Self-responsibility is the key.

We could also examine the moment you mastered your tricycle. It's important to recapture a moment of self-responsibility. Recall the pedals responding to your legs. Recall the forces of nature brought into play by your ability to coordinate your effort. Recall pushing the pedals and turning the big front wheel.

Pushing pedals! Turning a wheel! Going from stop to start! Did you go backward or forward your first time? It doesn't matter. You were in motion, turning at will. Your mind communicated the idea of "leaning in the direction you wanted to turn" as your arms and hands ever so slightly moved the handle bars in a moment of almost miraculous coordination.

Would you like to experience that feeling of mastery again and again? Well, you can! The choices you make as an adult living a *No Excuse!* life can be more thrilling and fulfilling than any childhood challenge ever was.

Be the Hero in Your Own Life

Were you taught that life is a struggle? This perception causes a lot of unhappiness. To struggle implies you are in a negative, no-win state. This dim view of life acts as a self-fulfilling prophecy and leads to negative results. It's an attitude of defeat. This is not to say that life isn't challenging. Without challenges your life would be boring; you would experience little, if any, personal growth. Challenges test you and help you stretch to new levels of achievement. As you incorporate *No Excuse!* into your life, you'll find that doing it without a struggle mentality is more effective, just plain easier, and a lot more fun.

Strive for the excitement and joy self-responsibility brings when you accomplish a goal. If you are reluctant to leave the comfort zone of hiding in shadowy fears, that's where you'll stay! It's your decision when to step out. The choice is yours.

It's a wonderful feeling when you understand and accept that outcomes depend on actions. This is the cause-and-effect principle. Even if you choose to stay in the shadows of your fears and you accept responsibility for it, you have reached a level of awareness that most people will never know.

You can be a hero in your own life story. Whether or not this is apparent to anyone else is irrelevant. It is only important that you have reached this fundamental realization; it's essential for any meaningful accomplishment. Although your decision-making process can be influenced by others and the environment, it is ultimately *your* decision to act or not to act. *The actions you take largely determine how you live your life.*

A Knight to Remember

The Knight in Rusty Armor is a favorite story of mine that I'd like you to have as a traveling companion on your *No Excuse!* journey.

In the opening pages of Robert Fisher's symbolic book, we meet a knight at the top of his career. No other knight had rescued more damsels in distress. No other knight had slain more dragons or ridden off in as many directions looking for the latest crusade. This knight was also famous for his armor. Its brilliance told the world (and reassured him too) that he was *the* example of a good, kind, and loving knight. That's what he wanted to be, and that's what he happily thought he was.

His wife Juliet and son Christopher, however, were not so happy about him. It seems the armor never came off anymore; a knight needs to be everready for battle, and never let his fans or his guard down. Christopher didn't know what his father really looked like, or felt like, and Juliet couldn't remember. She had experienced enough of a life reduced to rigid and unfeeling embraces. She delivered an ultimatum: The armor gets hung in a closet, and the knight spends more time with her and Christopher, or else.

Was Juliet the damsel he once rescued? The knight pondered his predicament. He began to suspect getting the armor off would be a problem. He woke up to the fact, thanks to his wife, that he had lost himself in his own foundry-wear. What he didn't know, and she didn't either, was how he could get it off. When even the best efforts of his bully blacksmith failed, the knight started out on a journey for help.

First, he made the trip to bid farewell to a king he had worked for in the past. The king wasn't available, so the knight spoke to his jester about his dilemma. The man scoffed at the knight's notion that his situation was unique. "We all get trapped in our own defenses from time to time," he assured him, and he gave him the magic word. Merlin was the "can opener" the knight needed.

In the lonely woods, the knight eventually met Merlin, but was too weakened by his wandering to run from the truth. However, Merlin's observations didn't sit well with the knight. "Perhaps you've always taken the truth as an insult," Merlin responded to the knight's indignation.

The knight's rehabilitation began. In the company of a squirrel and pigeon, who supported and cheered him, he would travel on the Path of Truth. He would enter three castles along the way: the Castle of Silence, the Castle of Knowledge, and the Castle of Will and Daring. He would leave each of them remarkably changed within and without.

His armor would gradually fall off. Each life-changing experience was accompanied by torrents of tears that rusted the armor in critical places. Each insightful moment was followed by a piece of rusted armor falling from the knight's face, head, arms, and hands. Increasingly less burdened, the knight was better able to climb the steep mountain slopes toward his goal.

The lesson the knight learns from the animals is *acceptance*. "When you learn to *accept* instead of *expect*, you'll have fewer disappointments," Rebecca, the pigeon, tells the knight, as he stands at the door of the Castle of Silence. At the Castle of Knowledge, the knight learned the difference between expectations and ambition. Merlin then reappeared and said, "Ambition that comes from the mind can get you nice castles and fine horses. However, only ambition that comes from the heart can bring happiness.

"Ambition from the heart is pure. It competes with no one and harms no one. In fact, it works in such a way that it serves others at the same time."

With each successful lesson learned, the knight found himself again on the Path of Truth. Each time he was encumbered by less and less of his armor. His insights, which were lessons in self-knowledge, continued to bring tears of recognition, remorse, and relief...as chunks of armor continued to rust and fall from him.

At the third and final castle, only his breastplate remained as the unlikely trio faced the dragon guarding the Castle of Will and Daring. The knight advanced bravely toward the dragon because he believed that fear and doubt were illusions. As the knight's fear and doubt grew less and less, the dragon grew smaller and smaller, and finally disappeared.

Once again on the Path of Truth, he was within sight of the mountaintop. Hand over hand he pulled himself toward his final goal. He clung fiercely to the rocky surface, only to learn that his last challenge would be...*to let go*. He fell into the abyss of his own past. He recognized fully, for the first time, the responsibility he bore for his own life. He realized the necessity of shedding judgments that others are to blame for his mistakes and failures.

Faster and faster he dropped, giddy as his mind descended into his heart. Then, for the first time, he saw his life clearly—without judgment or excuses. In that instant he accepted full responsibility for his life, for the influence that he allowed other people to have on it, and for the events that he had permitted to shape it.

From this moment on, he would no longer blame his mistakes and misfortunes on anyone or anything outside himself. The recognition that he was the cause, not the effect, gave him a new feeling of power.

He began to "fall" *upward,* as if the force of gravity was reversed, and found himself standing on the mountaintop. His tears of gratitude for life and the lessons he learned brought him to his knees. The tears were extraordinarily hot because they came so fully from his heart. They melted the last of his armor, the breastplate.

The brilliant splendor once lent him by the armor has not been diminished. Now, because he is healed, he shines with an inner radiance more beautiful than reflected glory.

Like the knight, we can all get trapped in our own armor at times. But once we learn to shed society's expectations and realize the importance of our own expectations, we too can have our place in the sun.

"Brains in Your Head and Feet in Your Shoes"

In Dr. Seuss's final published work before his death, *Oh, The Places You'll Go,* he wrote, "You have brains in your head, you have feet in your shoes, you can steer yourself any direction you choose."

Follow the teachings of Dr. Suess's small verse and act on your decisions with honesty, integrity, and selflessness; the world will be your oyster. Every day you'll witness new pearls. You possess the unique talents and resources that will help you put yourself on the *Staircase of Success.* Of course, it is necessary that you first learn to take full responsibility for the decisions you make. The following list of questions will help you open your eyes to the excuse-making that may exist in your own life today. HOW GOOD ARE YOU AT MAKING EXCUSES? *Read these questions out loud so you can hear your own voice.* This will make it easier for you to be truthful with yourself.

- Do I say, "The dog ate it"?
- Do I blame tardiness on "an alarm that didn't go off"?
- Do I use the words "can't," or "couldn't," when actually I "won't" or "wouldn't" is the truth?
- Do I procrastinate and leave a mountain of work unfinished because "After all, I'm only human"?
- Do I avoid doing new things because I'm "too old," "too young," or "too tired"?

- Do I accept defeat, convinced that "nice guys finish last"?
- Do I excuse myself from blame for a wrongdoing because "I was only following orders"?
- Do I fail to return phone calls or reply to emails because I "forget" to do so or I'm "too busy?"
- Do I overeat because "I simply can't help myself"?
- Do I cheat on exams because "everyone else does"?
- Do I blame my career or business stagnation on my boss or the economy?
- Do I neglect my family because I "can't find the time"?
- Do I say, "I don't have time," to avoid doing the necessary tasks to become more successful in life?
- Do I say, "It's not my cup of tea," when I am objecting to an idea, instead of stating the real reason?
- Do I say, "I don't have the money," when it's not true?
- Do I say, "It's in the mail," when it's not?
- Do I say, "I'd do it, but…" when I'm about to offer an excuse?

If you answered these questions honestly and, like many people, said yes to some of them, you are well on your way to eliminating excuses from your life. You are on the road to living a life of self-responsibility.

What are some of the decisions you are preparing to make this week, month, or year? Which will have the most impact on your personal life and professional career? Are those decisions personal, financial, educational, familial, or spiritual? Are you willing to make the decisions necessary and take action to move forward? Are you willing to accept responsibility for the outcomes of those decisions?

Be courageous. Get a clean sheet of paper and write down a list of the decisions you will soon be making that will impact your life and the lives of people around you. This heightens your awareness of the excuses you may have frequently used to either avoid facing decisions or taking responsibility for the results.

Take a Brave New Look at Your Thinking

Benjamin Franklin said, "He who is good at making excuses is seldom good at anything else." So how do we eliminate excuses? The first step toward becoming good at anything is to realize you may own a storehouse of self-imposed burdens. They're called excuses!

What if you see the need for self-responsibility one moment, then see yourself slip back into an old excuse the next? It's better to see it all happening than to be blind, or pretend to be blind, to what's going on. Opportunities for courage are everywhere, and your brave moments will accumulate as you practice *No Excuse!* You'll become aware of your own excuse-making. A part of you will start peeking out from under the blindfold you've made for yourself and say, "Uh-oh, I did it again." Every time you say that to yourself, it's a self-responsible moment.

It can feel as good as the wind parting in front of your face on your first all-by-yourself bicycle ride. Remember, being alone is part of the glory. If it feels a bit lonely, that's okay. It's going to be challenging and rewarding.

So out with the old way of thinking and in with the new. Excuses can have a root in reality, and at one time every excuse may have been a real reason. For example, at one point it was true that you couldn't ride that bicycle because you weren't big enough, old enough, or ready enough. When old reality, however, turns into a permanent excuse, trouble sets in. "I'll never be big enough or old enough"; "I'll never be able to ride a two-wheeler. I'm just one of those people who was born not knowing how." Sure you are...you and everybody else! *Whenever you find yourself looking for an excuse, change your thinking.* That's what this book is all about helping you do.

How to Keep Excuses in Check

We all live largely by behavioral patterns and habits. They are practical solutions to our need to have ready responses to everyday situations. They are necessary and, for the most part, serve us well. In certain circumstances, however, our logic can falter. We may fall back on excuses to explain a failure, justify a fault, or quit on ourselves.

Keep these things in mind:

- Initially, the challenges of living *No Excuse!* are just that...challenges. Relinquishing excuses requires effort.
- What's true for you is true for me. We all face problems that have a certain degree of sameness. We all need reasons to live, people to love, work to do, and joy to share. We all have sorrow and disappointment to bear.
- We're all better off when we're on the path of self-responsibility and action. Most of us are immobilized by the habits of blaming and excuse-making to one degree or another.

Will you grow rich with *No Excuse!* living? Yes! Rich may or may not include more money. That depends on you. However, *No Excuse!* living will enable you to:

- Enrich your life.
- Enrich the lives of the people you love.
- Enrich the lives of the people you work with.
- Give you the elements to create the success you want for yourself and your family.
- Help yourself begin with a self-responsible act: Accept that time is what you're born with, and life is, for the most part, what you make it.

A Lesson in Human Behavior

How you live your life is largely determined by how much you are willing to accept responsibility for shaping it. For too many people, time is what they are given...period. They never design a life. They look at what they have and what someone else has and make a judgment. Either they say, "I don't have it so bad, I've got more than the other guy." Or they say, "That other guy is so lucky. If I had what he's got, I'd be all set." Whichever determination comes up, their evaluation of their own life is based on another person's acquisitions and accomplishments. With *No Excuse!* living, you are freed from the bind of comparison. All you are concerned with is how to get started and stay on the path to the life *you* want.

Some people tend to get caught in the status quo of their circumstances. But remember, life is meant to be more than the nine-to-five...or whatever routine or rut we may have created. *The challenges and stresses we encounter every day are not normally caused by nature. Most of them are the result of the unmet expectations that arise from our thinking.* Most of them are not original, but are the result of what we've been taught by our elders, observations, or experiences. In most cases, your thinking determines your life. The good news is, *you can change your life by changing your thinking.*

Few young people reach adolescence without discovering that a good excuse will probably help them out of a tough spot. However, we are not born with this thinking. It's learned behavior. Most often it is learned by example and tested by experience. The more tough spots a kid gets into, the more excuse-making could become a habit.

What happens here? If a child's inappropriate behavior is not corrected, the opportunity for him or her to explore other behaviors may be lost. More importantly, the young person's insights into the part he or she actually plays in creating the tough situation becomes clouded. The truths of self-responsibility actually become hidden or lost to that individual. What kind of energy or motivation would a person have left to correct nonproductive behavior if the constant strain of coming up with a good excuse was always the first priority?

Three Little Words that Changed My Life

I arrived at West Point in July 1976 for seven weeks of Basic Training. We called it "Beast Barracks." By then, I had learned the value of having a good excuse. Whenever circumstances warranted, and I wanted someone or something to blame for an unwanted result, I thought a good excuse would benefit me. I guess I was pretty average in that regard, much like my fellow plebes. Then, too, we were all achievers or we wouldn't even be at West Point. Nevertheless, we were all going to be amazed at how difficult it was to be deprived of the opportunity to excuse our way out of a situation.

Excuse-making was forbidden! We weren't allowed to give the upperclassmen reasons for our mistake(s) or failure(s), regardless of whether we were involved individually or collectively. Because of this rule, we were frequently going to hear ourselves and other plebes say three little but powerful words—"No excuse, sir!" Here's the full paragraph given to excuses in *Bugle Notes,* the Fourth Class System Handbook:

> *Cadets cultivate the habit of not offering excuses. There is no place in the military profession for an excuse for failure. Extenuating circumstances may be explained and submitted, but, even if accepted such explanations are never considered excuses.*
> *—BUGLE NOTES, Cultivating the Soldierly Habit*

The idea of self-responsibility was enforced right from the start of the West Point experience. This excerpt from *Bugle Notes* illustrates its importance:

> *The first seven weeks of a cadet's life at West Point are devoted to intensive military training. During this period the entering class of cadets are equipped and given the preliminary training necessary before they join the Corps. Here, entering civilians undergo the stressful socialization process which produces a well-disciplined motivated class, prepared for acceptance into the Corps of Cadets as fourth classmen. It consists of training characterized by clear, careful, thorough instruction of individuals; exactness of execution; strict but just discipline; immediate response to correction; development of willing compliance to*

directives, careful physical hardening, and begins the process of culti-
vation of the soldierly habit. The new cadet's waking hours are
completely controlled. Every activity is carefully supervised. Attention
to detail and flawless appearance become second nature to him.
        —*BUGLE NOTES,* 1976-1980, p. 53-54

At the successful conclusion of Cadet Basic Training, I was accepted into the Corps of Cadets as a fourth classman. The Fourth Class System is administered by the upper classes and supervised by the Commandant of Cadets. This system is in place to achieve very specific objectives. One is to teach the customs, traditions, and heritage of the United States Military Academy to new arrivals. The system is also meant to generate a controlled, stressful, military environment. Cadets who cannot function under stress, or who cannot otherwise meet the standards of the military profession, are identified.

Completion of Cadet Basic Training coincides with the return of the three upper classes during the last week in August. For the first time, the upperclassmen have an opportunity to observe the new Fourth Class as they stride confidently to the stirring notes of "The Official West Point March."

This is a moment of high exhilaration. Inevitably, thoughts turn to the men of honor who passed this way before. Foremost on my mind on the day I joined the ranks of "The Long Grey Line," was General Douglas MacArthur.

Bugle Notes, the handbook quoted from earlier is the plebe's "bible." It contains everything he needs to know for survival in the world of West Point. *Bugle Notes* is essential, because survival is truly a plebe's major concern.

Cadets without the capability or desire to perform to the standards of the Academy simply leave. Sometimes, they are there one day and gone the next. So it's only natural to look for inspiration from the remarkable people who persevered and made it.

Words to Live By from a Leader's Leader

General MacArthur was one of West Point's finest sons. The inspirational speech he gave as he accepted the Thayer Award in May 1962 was reprinted in the plebe's handbook. In his speech, he pointed to the motto "Duty, Honor, Country," inscribed on the Military Academy's Crest:

...Those three hallowed words...make you strong enough to know
when you are weak; and brave enough to face yourself when you are
afraid.... They teach you to be proud and unbending in honest failure,

but humble and gentle in success; not to substitute words for actions, nor to seek the path of comfort, but to face the stress and spur of difficulty and challenge; to learn to stand up in the storm but to have compassion on those who fall; to master yourself before you seek to master others.... They create in your heart the sense of wonder, the unfailing hope of what is next, and the joy and inspiration of life. They teach you in this way to be an officer and a gentleman.

—BUGLE NOTES, p. 31-32

In my first days at West Point, I was too frightened and intimidated to understand that "No excuse, sir!" was a response required to encourage plebes to be strong and self-responsible. This fact became clear to me later on.

"No excuse, sir!" I can still hear the trembling quality of those words. It was scary trying them out under the stern and unrelenting, often glaring, gaze of a questioning upperclassman. Gradually, "No excuse, sir!" came out stronger, even assertively. What had seemed a natural inclination to find excuses, gave way to a new pattern of thinking: Cut through to a simple statement of fact and address the situation. Whether or not reasons are given or even known, consequences need to be dealt with when something's done incorrectly or left undone.

The Story of My Success

With each passing year, I have reaped lessons from my West Point training, and I expect that to continue for the rest of my life. Military training was designed to encourage healthy self-reflection. In fact, the need to examine personal behavior was emphasized. I developed the habit of correcting patterns that were not producing desired results.

The lesson of the "No excuse, sir!" response soon became clear...healthy self-reflection does not lead to excuse-making. To this day, when I find myself dwelling on past achievements or failures, I think of the words No excuse, sir!" This snaps me out of self-congratulatory or self-pitying traps.

Saying "No excuse!" will help you to be stronger, particularly when you've taken a leap into the unknown, and find your belief in yourself faltering. Critical times are like the moment a trapeze artist hangs in midair. Will his timing be right as he releases his hold on one bar and waits for another to swing into his grip? I've felt that way many times: on the edge. How about you?

My arrival at West Point was one of those times of uncertainty. I felt like I was hanging in midair. Every new arrival had overcome some obstacles just to be admitted. We all had other options, yet we chose this one and we were now facing the consequences.

In entirely different circumstances, thirteen years later, I felt equally challenged. By 1989 I had experienced a successful career at West Point, in the military, and in corporate America. Those years had been full of challenges and achievement. Nothing, however, matched the thrill I felt while standing in the office area of my own business for the first time.

I was alone. The grand-opening party was over; the crowd of supporters and well-wishers had departed; my wife had taken the children home. I was enjoying the calm solitude as I walked through the store preparing to lock up and go home. I appraised, with pleasure, the retail operation my desire and efforts had put in place. I had a resource center for personal and professional enrichment. I was elated. And suddenly, I was scared.

"No excuse, sir!" The words were in my mind. I had risked everything in this venture and there would be no excuse if it failed. For the first time it hit me: I wanted my father to be with me so very much.

I had not experienced a feeling this strong since his death. It had so suddenly interrupted the life of this vital, active man, that we didn't even have a chance to say goodbye. He was an established dentist and an accomplished amateur golfer. We (my father, mother, sister, and I) lived in the small city of Kingston, New York, where he had been born and raised. He was gone in one shocking moment. His heart stopped beating one sunny day on the patio of our home, while he was sitting with my sister and her friend.

The day he was buried was sunny as well. I can still see myself as an 11-year-old boy. There I was, standing by my mother's side, saying over and over to myself, "I will survive, I will survive."

From that moment on, I looked to my father's memory for strength and encouragement. He had shown me how he felt life was meant to be lived. I wanted to fulfill his expectations for his only son. But they had never been spoken, so they could only be imagined. I developed unrealistic expectations of myself as a substitute for his. I exaggerated the demands he might have placed on me. I tried to live up to my memory of him, which was distorted by my longing.

I wanted to please him and my mother. She has always been an encourager in my life, consistently supporting me and my efforts. Beginning with my six-weeks premature birth with collapsed lungs, and those first days of "hanging on for dear life," she led me into a strong and healthy manhood. However unrealistic my expectations of myself had been, she spurred me on to achieve some ambitious goals. They might not have been realized without my single-minded determination to keep my father's death from being an obstacle to my becoming a man of whom he'd be proud.

As I stood in the offices of my new business that night, I continued to reflect on my thoughts and feelings. I had deliberately separated myself from the hierarchical, paternalistic organizations where I had achieved success. I now felt as if I was face to face with my father's memory in a way I had never experienced before. I had never before acknowledged or sensed so fully, my longing for his presence and approval.

"No excuse, sir!" I was speaking to him, as well as myself. Something profoundly lonely had me in its grip. His death had deprived me of his loving presence, but had also been the catalyst for my will to succeed.

At that moment, I knew I was letting go of the hold I had allowed the past to have on me. I accepted that not even my father's death could be used as an excuse. It couldn't keep me from moving on.

I knew I was ready to stand alone. I realized that my expectations, and not his, would be enough to keep me going toward my dreams and goals. I no longer needed to please him or anyone. I also knew I no longer needed his approval; all I needed was my own. In this moment of open longing and new understanding, I accepted that I was alone, and it was okay.

I had the memory of my father's love for me. I was also aware that we both had met success through honesty, sincerity and commitment.

They Conquer Who Believe They Can

Create your life based on your own expectations and not the expectations of those around you. We all have the ability to accept or not accept who and what we are. Think about it. How often do we try to mold ourselves to someone else's expectations to please them? If we do, we will probably suffer, in silence or denial, the tragedy of not accepting ourselves and what we choose to do. Owning your life means having the courage to face up to such truths. It means risking, and maybe even taking a relationship to the edge in order to assert yourself. You're likely to generate more respect from others as well.

Becoming self-responsible is a process. As you practice *No Excuse!*, your self-responsible experiences accumulate and can then positively contribute to structuring a life that is more reflective of who you are. You can become a whole person incrementally. If you believe you're whole already—balanced and developed in the seven key areas of life (to be explained more later)—you're further along than many. You grow with every mature decision and the understanding that you alone accept responsibility for your actions.

You may have already noticed that your need for recognition from oth-

ers has been inversely proportional to how much you were at peace with yourself. To a point, it may be appropriate to seek advice from or model your behavior after a few select people whom you respect—people whose lives are worthy of emulating. It's only human nature to desire acceptance from others. However, it is wise to be selective. Focus only on those people who have your best interests at heart, whose value system is admirable to you, and who love and support you. Then there are times when it is important to stand apart from even these people. It's essential to examine your life and discover whether you like where you're headed. Do you need to change your course in some areas of your life? Are you receiving the outcomes you want?

Practicing *No Excuse!* principles can enhance your feelings of self-worth, self-love, and self-esteem. You'll learn to let go of people you may be using as protection from the fear of rejection. You'll learn how to create new relationships and live life on your own terms. *As you let go of beloved people and stop hiding behind them, you and they will experience a freedom to love each other beyond anything you've ever known.*

You will experience life more fully when you realize that *you* determine your future. With *No Excuse!* thinking, you no longer blame events or other people for your shortcomings, failures, or timidity. You will have the opportunity to lay the foundation for a future of living life to the fullest.

You may want to ask the questions that anyone on a new path might ask: Am I ready for this? Am I self-responsible enough? Am I capable of dealing with success? Am I capable of dealing with failure? Am I prepared to accept the impact my new-found self-responsibility will have on my family and friends? Am I willing to take responsibility for my actions when things don't go my way? Am I willing to stop weaving an intricate tale of so-called inescapable coincidences to tell the world how everything conspired against me? Am I willing to say "No Excuse!"?

Long ago, I knew a man who took responsibility for his actions; he didn't make excuses. For example, if he was late for dinner, he would say to his wife, "My dear, I didn't leave the office on time." Even when I was a youngster, I liked that fellow. I now believe his words had an early influence on the *No Excuse!* approach to life. He accepted full responsibility and wasted no time inventing excuses. Excuses would have been useless and wouldn't have helped the situation.

A Labor of Love

As you accept responsibility for your actions, you will likely live life with a lighter heart. Knowing you have deliberately decided not to blame others for your actions, you will feel stronger, less alone, and less frightened of the consequences. The fear of rejection and failure that once crippled or handicapped your efforts, will diminish. You are taking charge. The likelihood that you'll let fear control or paralyze your actions will be reduced. Your sense of self-responsibility can develop as you grow personally and as your life becomes more expansive.

As my business grew, it became clearer that I was headed toward another career decision. I began to realize what I loved to do most, which you need to do whenever you consider changing careers. Throughout my life I've always been sociable. I'm eager to communicate with others. My enthusiasm often carried me into new situations where I quickly became acquainted with new groups of people. I particularly enjoyed public speaking while I was in school, in the military, and during my years as a businessman. I learned how important it was for organizations to utilize outside resources to help them meet their motivational and training needs.

The information provided by a third party is often considered more credible and is more readily received. I decided my niche was being that third party. I started corporate training, speaking to small groups and large organizations. My objective was to help them better understand the relationship between self-responsibility and personal and professional success, thus increasing their productivity.

My retail store was full of inspirational and motivational materials. I read all of it voraciously and gained new insights into their valuable messages. I devoured the works of Dale Carnegie, Norman Vincent Peale, Napoleon Hill, W. Clement Stone, and Earl Nightingale, to name a few giants of the past. I also studied the books of such modern day authors as Harvey Mackay, Dr. Susan Jeffers, Stephen Covey, Dr. Robert Schuller, Larry Wilson, Tom Peters, M. Scott Peck, and more.

Self-responsibility is a critical part of all their messages. Nonetheless, many individuals have difficulty putting it into practice. Developing self-responsibility, to the degree necessary to attain notable personal and professional success, requires great courage, maturity, and the support of like-minded people.

I felt confident I could structure an approach to *No Excuse!* that would give people practical guidelines to living self-responsibly. I knew this approach could help people counteract personal and professional stagnation and mediocrity. It dawned on me I was the person to do it because my life had been lived the *No Excuse!* way. My objective is for these insights to benefit you. That would be very rewarding for me.

Nothing has given me more pleasure and satisfaction than bringing *No*

Excuse! into reality. It's for groups of three or four in boardrooms. It's for large corporations and small. It's for traditional sales and marketing organizations and network marketing groups. It's for government employees. It's for you and your family, friends, co-workers, business associates, and acquaintances. And finally, it's for anyone who will read this book.

I have the hard evidence that proves people have made their lives easier and more productive by using these principles. People with unsuspected potential have discovered themselves through *No Excuse!* They harnessed their emotion, ambition, and talents to benefit others, their organization, and, of course, themselves.

It's up to you to change your life. Through *No Excuse!,* you will have resources and mechanisms to help you make positive changes. You'll have a chance to relate differently to the people around you and be a positive influence on their lives. It can spark in you a new zest for living, a new zest for accomplishing dreams you once thought were impossible.

Good Work—*Congratulations!*

You're not at the mercy of circumstances. You're the master of your own destiny, if you choose to be. Congratulations! Y*ou've been empowered to take greater charge of your life!*

At this point it is likely that you have one foot firmly planted in the *No Excuse!* grounds of success. Step by step, you'll learn how to be committed to yourself and your personal action plan, which will lead you to accomplishing your life's goals. You'll discover that, as you gain a clearer sense of purpose, you'll be better able to direct your energies precisely where they belong. With your new focus, you'll be able to achieve your success with an ease and swiftness you've never dreamed possible.

Now that you have had an opportunity to equip yourself with a new sense of self-responsibility, are you ready for the next part of your success training? You'll discover why you might want to channel your newfound energies in a certain direction and how to do so. The time is ripe for you to arrive at your own resolve.

Chapter 2
THE POWER OF PURPOSE
Your Definition of Success

Before you can begin thinking about becoming a success, you need to define what success is for you. Know what you want to reach for and believe you can attain it.

Take the example of General George S. Patton. Even as a boy of barely seven, young George had a purpose as clearly defined as the edge of a saber. It was, pure and simple, to become a Brigadier General. He was so committed to this that, like any model soldier, he stood at attention and saluted his father every morning.

As Patton grew through his teen years, he continued to "do his damnedest always" to achieve his purpose in life as only he could define it. He avidly read stories of the great military men of history. He studied Persian, Greek, and Roman Generals, battle formations, and medieval wars. His class reports featured themes of fame, glory, and heroism.

Self-responsible to a fault, Patton learned early on that prizes in life were earned through persistent effort. It was sheer hard work that helped him overcome dyslexia and graduate from West Point. Likewise, through the course of his historic rise to fame, culminating in his promotion to full General of the United States Army, he rode on no one's coattails. It was his honest, all-out effort that saw him to his end purpose every time.

As a plebe at West Point, he scribbled in his personal notebook the credo that would eventually help him achieve his greatest purpose, his Generalship:

> *Do everything with all the snap and power you possess.... When ordered to do a thing, carry out the spirit as well as the letter. Do all you can do, not only all you have to do.*

Everyone who knew George Patton, or who has read about his life, has their own opinion of him. However, I believe they would all agree that Patton was, above all, a man of purpose. He reached out and embraced history. In this sense, he fulfilled the destiny about which he often talked:

> *You have to turn around and know who (destiny) is when she taps you on the shoulder, because she will. It happens to every man, but damned few times in his life. Then you must decide to follow where she*

points. You have to be single-minded, drive only for the one thing on which you have decided....

    —*SOLDIER OF DESTINY: A BIOGRAPHY OF GEORGE S. PATTON, Charles Peifer, Jr.*

Having a purpose is more important than having talent in creating and shaping your life. Patton's example proves it. You can "move mountains" with great resolve if you apply yourself persistently and consistently. That's why having a purpose, or a mission, is essential.

What are your goals, anyway? What are your aspirations? What's your dream? Do you even have a dream? Think of who you are today. Imagine yourself at your personal and professional best. Imagine feeling good about yourself in relation to your family and friends, neighbors, and co-workers or business associates.

What is your idea of success? A nurturing home life? A fabulous career? A prosperous business? Financial and time freedom? The happiest and best relationships with the people you love and care about? Strong bonds with those you need to support you in your quest for success? To make a difference in the lives of others, it is important to let your vision of who you are and what you want out of life guide you to your goals.

This chapter takes you on a journey that will help you define your purpose. Once you do, you will have taken a major step toward the future you choose. You will have acknowledged the possibility of being the person you would like to be. You'll be started on the path of living a life of accomplishing your dreams and goals. In addition to your commitment to self-responsible living, having a purpose is essential to start you on the *Staircase of Success*. As you move through the treasury of principles in Part II, you'll have an opportunity to learn how to order your values. You'll discover how to examine expectations, set the standards by which you'll play the game of life, and respect yourself and others more. You'll learn to communicate with people in more meaningful ways so you can develop the fulfilling and loving relationships you've always wanted. You'll gain a sense of contribution, of knowing you've made a difference in other people's lives.

You'll also learn (or be reminded) that *the most important human relationship you'll ever have is the one you have with yourself.* You'll have an opportunity to make changes in your life that will be in your best interest. Nonetheless, they will require self-discipline. You'll need the right mental attitude to sustain you on your new path.

No Excuse! shares how to nurture a sense of optimism and change negative thinking patterns into positive ones. You'll adopt cheerfulness, optimism, persistence, and integrity as your new personal by-laws if you haven't already done so. You'll have the chance to see how helpful these qualities can be in achieving your goals.

The Strategy that Wins Wars

In any military situation, the commanding officer relies on a course of action—a "general plan." This plan anticipates a favorable outcome and maps out a strategy of operations for all combined forces. The memoirs of Marshal Ferdinand Foch (Supreme Commander of Allied Armies in WWI) speak to the importance of the plan:

> ...*Even if one of these actions should come to a standstill or one group of these forces be particularly tried the commander of the whole must unflinchingly stand by his general plan, at the same time stimulating or sustaining the failing action, but never admitting that it can be wholly renounced or that its weakness can cause the relinquishment or even any change of that plan.*
>
> —*MILITARY MEN, Ward Just*

The general plan, or purpose, is the strategy that helps win wars. Wars aren't won without plans. It's one of those things that gives an advantage to the aggressor. It's also one of the reasons that even a peaceable nation needs to have a plan of defense.

On a smaller, more personal scale, consider the general plan as your personal strategy for reaching your dreams and goals. As you gain new insights and outlooks through *No Excuse!*, you'll be able to develop and adopt a plan of your own. It's important that you do. *Defining your own purpose in life is one of the most significant steps you can take in achieving success.*

Defining Your Purpose

Why do you think you are here on this earth? Your answer is your first step to being able to answer the question, "What is your purpose?" A child can legitimately answer, "To be loved." An adult could best answer, "To love."

Self-responsibility includes making choices about how you will use your energies. Who will you love? Who will you help? Which cause(s) will you support and fight for? When you reach the point where you are indeed working for who and what you believe in, you will more deeply understand what American author Joseph Campbell meant when he said, "Man is not in search of the meaning of life, but what it means to be alive."

Most of us want to feel what it means to be alive. When we are living a life guided by our self-defined purpose (rather than that defined by other people), we are likely to be better able to enjoy each passing day. Despite its challenges, we will probably be more grateful for life and eager to make the most of it. *Having a purpose helps self-responsible people be enthusiastic about life.*

Do you believe a grim demeanor is the sign of someone who is living self-responsibly? If your answer is "yes," you may want to reconsider. Yes, there are gloomy people who are very responsible. However, these are generally people fulfilling responsibilities imposed by others (e.g., boss, parents, spouse, or commanding officer). *Living with purpose is one of life's greatest joys.* If you have the courage to search your soul, you will find your purpose.

Many people live life as if Opportunity were Death knocking on the door. Those who ignore opportunities and fail to define and work toward their purpose usually fall into a slow spiritual stagnation. Pursuing purpose naturally leads to prudent risk-taking, warding off stagnation and boredom.

When you take charge of your decisions, and accept full responsibility for the outcomes, prudent risk-taking is easy. You can begin looking for a direction to move in. This helps you recognize your purpose. As your purpose evolves, it will guide your investment of energies and resources, and help you choose between attractive alternatives.

Self-responsible living brings an individual to a state of well-equipped readiness. You can compare it to a healthy, well-trained, willing soldier. When he is sent out on armed maneuvers, he is expected to make decisions regarding the use of the energies and resources at his disposal. Without a clearly defined purpose, he might wait, idly and anxiously, for someone else to take action. Or he might spend energy and ammunition on fruitless and dangerous displays of aimless action, shooting at shadows. In either case, a soldier handicapped by the lack of a clear purpose, no matter how self-responsible, is apt to be a danger to himself and his comrades. He will offer little or no aid to the cause.

How Purpose Pays Off

You are the ultimate decision maker in your own life only when you choose to be. Events and other people's purposes will direct you if you're not in charge of yourself.

It's pleasant to lie on a raft and float on a placid lake under a sunny sky. It's peaceful to let nature rule the day's events, without a care in the world. But some people never learn about the thrill of life with a rudder, a sail, an oar, or an engine. They repeatedly set themselves up in situations sure to lead to panic and the need to be rescued. They behave as if they are helpless, even when survival is at stake.

We all need to float at times to refresh and rejuvenate ourselves. However, the most vibrant people I know have equipped themselves for the challenges they are sure to meet. They look forward to the thrill of dealing with them head on.

Self-responsible living means knowing how to enjoy life and being prepared for the situations it presents. *No Excuse!* living isn't reactive. There's no room to make excuses that prevent you from taking charge of which direction to steer your ship. Your purpose helps you decide which direction to take so you can pursue your dreams and goals.

Lack of self-responsibility can cripple your life. You can never be alone! You always need someone to blame in case things go wrong. With self-responsible living, you can be alone or join forces with self-responsible partners. As you grow, you will come to recognize other self-responsible people. You're more likely to choose them for friends, partners, and supporters, and avoid associations with companions who refuse to be self-responsible.

As you apply *No Excuse!* your sense of self-responsibility will grow. You'll feel an almost indomitable strength at the heart of self-responsibility and purpose. It will prevail through obstacles which attempt to thwart its development. You can count on it. It's inside you. Feel it. Look back on your life. It's likely you'll find evidence of your strength.

The desire for self-responsibility and purpose exists, at some level, in every human heart. It can grow stronger every time we get encouragement. It can strengthen when we focus our energies on what we really want. Self-responsibility grows strong when we seek and take advantage of new opportunities to learn and grow. Purpose intensifies when new dreams and goals are developed and pursued on a regular basis.

Your Best Preparation for a Full Life

As I reviewed my life's experiences, it became obvious how the principles of self-responsibility and fulfillment of purpose were at work long before I recognized them. The goals I chose to pursue were rigorous and challenging. The odds were against me, but I focused and did whatever it took to achieve them.

From a growth and motivational perspective, the role and career changes I made were important because of the experience gained. You may agree that this is true for you too. One thing leads to another throughout life.

This is part of the reason for the transitions, certainly in my academic career. Have you noticed how your experiences are often linked to one another? Satisfaction with a job well done, however, eventually leads to dissatisfaction. Repeating a challenge you've overcome can get boring. When that happened to me, I looked for new horizons.

As you live more self-responsibly, you'll find more of a need to scrutinize and exercise integrity. Honestly focus on who you are and what you are capable of accomplishing.

To fulfill your purpose, select and focus on singular goals. Your scrutiny and integrity are essential as you shift to a combination of inward and outward focus. Your choice of goals needs to reflect and agree with your value system and your understanding of what you have to offer the world. *Knowing your purpose, while being true enough to yourself to work toward it, is the best way to prepare for a life full of worthwhile accomplishments.*

When you experience and recognize your success, working "on purpose" becomes more and more rewarding. It also becomes a habit. Here are some questions to consider as you reflect on the decisions you have made in your life:

- Has the opportunity to accomplish something meaningful ever come along and you ignored it?
- Did you evaluate timing and your priorities as you decided what activities to pursue?
- How alert have you been to indications that it is time to change directions in your life?

Most people give little or no thought to these questions. Many live day to day in a survival mode. They focus on maintenance activities like going to work, paying bills, and taking care of the house and yard. They concern themselves with keeping the children clothed, fed, and driven to their activities. These areas are often necessary, but exclusive focus on them can keep us from our purpose. We need to be aware of what else is going on and how we can best contribute.

Remember, *you get what you focus on.* If you are focusing only on doing minimal maintenance chores to get by and through each day, that's all you'll get: a life of gray mediocrity with little or no fulfillment. You would be living unconsciously pushed by circumstances rather than pulled by your dreams and goals. If you are one of these people, this book could help you shift to a conscious, purposeful, and self-responsible life. You'll be better able to achieve cherished, but often buried, dreams and goals.

Your Dreams and Goals

Right now, may I suggest that you take some quiet time to get in touch with your dreams and goals? Many are probably tucked away in your subconscious mind because you didn't believe you could accomplish them. Perhaps you didn't believe you deserved them. It's okay if you don't totally believe you can live the life you want. Just believe it a little bit for now.

Take some time now to list 20 or more dreams and goals, big and little. Assume time and money are not obstacles, and that you can become, do, and have anything you want. You may just want 20 minutes a day of uninterrupted time to read a book. Or you may want something as grand as a mansion or to give a million dollars to your favorite cause. It's whatever you want that matters. Go ahead, respect yourself enough to get a clean sheet of paper and write down your 20 most important, must-have dreams and goals. Believe you deserve them.

For many years I considered a career as a consultant and professional speaker. My business brought me into contact daily with people searching for ways to develop their talents. I was impressed, over and over again, at how willing people are to consider ways to develop themselves personally. These people helped me discover my newfound purpose.

"Ten-Percent" Living

William James, a professor of psychology at Harvard in the first half of the 20th Century, observed that the average person develops only ten percent of his latent mental ability.

Why do most people average out at only ten-percent living? Why are most people discouraged from exploring more of their potential? You'll often hear of musicians and entertainers born into a family with little experience or interest in those fields. Or you may find an athlete born into a family with no desire to encourage a youngster's participation in sports. These situations are quite common.

If your talents were not nurtured during your early years, you have this additional challenge to overcome. The first step for you is to acknowledge and accept this fact. You can then make a decision to seek support and guidance elsewhere, as you explore and develop your neglected talents. You may have years of stagnation to overcome before you uncover those desires that lie dormant inside you.

Then you may be someone whose innate talents are stored away or buried in safe places because of verbal abuse, usually in the form of ridicule. It is easier to ignore ridicule when you realize these unkind, unhappy people often resort to it in an attempt to bring others down to their level of incompetence. "Misery loves company" is the prevailing rule, whether they realize it or not. Every day I met people in my bookstore who wanted to discover the 90 percent of themselves where their unrealized talents, dreams, and goals lived.

Putting Purpose into Practice

For me, there's nothing as inspiring as meeting others striving for a full life. Customers inspired me. With each passing day, it became more apparent that self-responsibility was the key attribute for the success they sought. With increasing clarity I saw how critical *No Excuse!* living had been, and is, for me. As I introduced *No Excuse!*, it became apparent how valuable this concept was to people aspiring to a better life. I saw immediate and long-term positive results in their lives.

That simple phrase "No excuse!", from my West Point years, became the pivotal point of a practical approach to achieving success in all areas of life. Day after day, I saw the approach at work in the lives of people who accepted what I had to offer. I kept meeting people who were eager and willing to put it into practice in their own lives.

They quickly understood the idea of self-responsibility. They curtailed their old habitual retreats into excuse-making. They recognized that *fear always lies at the heart of excuse-making.* They uncovered their own fears and faced them and did what needed to be done to overcome them.

First, they learned to say "No excuse!" to themselves. In a stressful situation, as shadows of excuses began forming in their minds, the words "No excuse!" would come to rescue them. It was like the United States Cavalry taking the day, scattering the weak near-truths and falsehoods.

I saw how saying this simple phrase encouraged them to face the world. It became even more obvious when they exercised this new power as they encountered others. The excuses they once spoke were gone. Instead, they could honestly evaluate the reality of the situation. They grew personally through the process of facing and telling the truth. The results were honest, productive responses that served the best interests of everyone.

When the reality of a situation seems so overwhelming that you feel it can't be addressed, do you seek refuge in an excuse? You're only kidding yourself if you don't admit that excuse-making is rooted in fear. In fact, *making excuses leads to more fear.* Maybe someone will discover the truth. *Letting go of excuses diffuses situations. Where self-responsible living replaces excuse-making, purposeful, positive action replaces fear!* Here's a story that illustrates this truth.

Reaching for More than You've Ever Dreamed Possible

When I first began sharing *No Excuse!* with others, it became clear that most of them didn't recognize how their lack of self-responsibility negatively affected themselves and others. We looked back at their past behavior, and they learned to recognize how excuse-making had crept into their thinking. Their task was to identify every instance as it occurred, and persistently eliminate their excuse-making with *No Excuse!*

It was marvelous to see how the results came so quickly to those who used *No Excuse!* Again and again, self-confidence grew in the people who were willing to rid themselves of excuses and take responsibility for the results of their action or inaction.

As they continued to live *No Excuse!*, they reached for more and developed a higher purpose. The increased energy they experienced by living a *No Excuse!* life made it possible for them to see the options that existed in ways they had never imagined. With new courage and resolve, they began building a record of success.

Before I talk to the employees of a business or members of an organization, I get acquainted with its culture. This enables me to fine tune my presentation. My mouth fairly waters whenever I encounter a blamer, whiner, or complainer. I know I've got something that will help them break away from the endless cycle of unproductive behavior they've gotten themselves locked into.

I know that every blamer, whiner, or complainer impacted by *No Excuse!* becomes more effective on the job. He or she becomes a source of productive energy for the organization. It's exhilarating to help people open up and understand their excuse-making behavior. It's exciting to see how the simple message of *No Excuse!* works. I love to help people prepare to find their own way to the top of any mountain they choose to climb.

For you, the exhilaration and great pleasure right now is in *choosing* the mountain you wish to scale, in picking your purpose. *No Excuse!* will not fulfill its promise to you if it doesn't help you reconsider or discover your purpose. This can be done gradually. Your self-awareness can increase at an acceptable pace for personal growth, replacing old paradigms with new ones. It's valuable to evaluate your life as you live it. The more you discover about yourself and your purpose, the easier it will be for you to determine if you are on track in the areas that are important to you.

Nature helps us when the changing seasons remind us that time is passing. This helps us focus on the changing patterns of our own existence. The yearly calendar gives us boundaries we can use to complete one task and begin another.

For many, the new year means new beginnings. This explains New Year's resolutions, doesn't it? This is a time when we may choose to admit that there are areas of our lives we wish to change. This is an excellent time to develop or strengthen the belief that we are capable of making changes that will enrich our lives.

A Tale of Two Purposes

The intent of sharing the following two stories is to show you how having a purpose can be a powerful force in your life. In the first, a well-known movie character turned motivational speaker identifies and articulates purpose early in life. In the second, a child in a fable shares a secret of life with the ages.

THE BOY WHO WOULD PLAY FOOTBALL
AND INSPIRE A MOVIE

Once upon a time, a boy named Daniel "Rudy" Ruettiger had the dream of playing football for Notre Dame. He was the third of 14 children and grew up in the working class town of Joliet, Illinois. After high school, he worked at a power plant, joined the Navy, then returned to the plant.

When a friend was killed at the plant in an industrial accident, Rudy re-examined his life and began pursuing his dream. He wanted to play football at Notre Dame. All the while, he was being put down by friends and relatives. They would say, "Who do you think you are?"

His high school grades weren't good enough to get into Notre Dame, but he managed to get admitted to Holy Cross Junior College to prove himself. Despite suffering from a mild case of dyslexia, Rudy studied hard and earned good grades. He tried to get into Notre Dame three times and kept getting rejected. But he persisted until he was finally accepted. He also managed to beat the odds by winning a position on the scout team. Even though Rudy was only 5 feet, 6 inches tall, he was a giant in his thinking and doing!

Through his dogged determination, Rudy won the respect of his teammates and coaches. He had spirit; his persistence won the prize. Then his ultimate dream came true. He was sent onto the field to play the last few minutes of the last home game of his senior year. His final victory came when he tackled the Georgia Tech quarterback. The crowd roared, and his teammates carried him triumphantly off the field on their shoulders. Rudy was their hero.

Rudy received his bachelor's degree in 1976. Sixteen years went by, during which he accomplished little. Then in 1992, he began living another dream: involvement with the production of the movie *Rudy*, which became a box office hit!

Rudy now has a successful career in motivational speaking and corporate training, as well as a foundation for kids. He is an excellent example of the power of a dream and perseverance in achieving it. His mission is to help others grow so they can realize their full potential.

THE GIRL WHO WOULD BE HAPPY

As a young girl, Mona had been left orphaned and unprotected. She moved sadly through her days. One day, on a lonely walk through a meadow, she saw a butterfly struggling to release itself from a thorn bush. Mona carefully released the butterfly from its captivity. Her freeing touch caused the butterfly to turn into a beautiful fairy.

"In return for your kindness," the good fairy said, "I will grant you any wish." Mona thought for a moment and said softly, "I want to be happy!" The fairy leaned forward, whispered into the girl's ear, and flew off.

Mona developed into a beautiful woman and eventually grew to be old. She had left the sadness of her childhood in the field where she had met and aided the fairy. After that, Mona's years were marked by serene happiness. As the end of her life drew near, friends and admirers came to comfort her, and to say good-bye to this remarkable woman.

Mona's last gift to her friends was the story of her encounter with the fairy. She shared with them the words the fairy had whispered in her ear. As Mona spoke, her eyes shone with the joys of a lifetime of treasuring the fairy's message: "Everyone, no matter how secure they seem, no matter how old or young, rich or poor, has need of you."

Because she believed that, Mona had become a woman of purpose. *Happiness is a by-product of successfully working toward and fulfilling your purpose.* The expansiveness of Mona's purpose had given her a reason to live, and a long and happy life. Living with a purpose does that for us. Self-defined purpose does it best.

You Can Create Your Own Tale of a Purpose

Mona needed to know she was of value in an often inconsiderate world. However, her true value did not need to be proven at all. It already existed in her very being as a child of her Creator. First, she learned how to give and grow at the same time. Then she recognized the need in others and responded with a caring attitude.

Respect yourself enough to define your own purpose, and reshape it as needed as you move along. Each time you do, welcome the challenge as a life-giving, life-enhancing opportunity.

Welcome heroes and mentors into your life. You can stride along with them as you find your own pace. Look for generous ones who can see the fine qualities shining in you, just waiting to be brought out. You'll want to find a mentor who will affirm and support your desires for personal achievement, and who can help you believe in yourself. You'll want your mentor to assist you in finding your purpose. You'll need him or her to help you find the best path to follow in order to fulfill that purpose and re-alize your dreams and goals.

The Principles of Success

The ideas and concepts presented in this book have their origins in some great achievers, as well as from my own life experiences. When you apply *No Excuse!* to your own life, you will be living by *the* acknowl-edged principles of success, such as self-esteem, enthusiasm, attitude, forgiveness, goal-setting, and more. They will be both the roots and the fruits of your own on-purpose self-responsibility.

What will motivate you to be more successful? Is it external factors or your own internal drive? Both play important roles. Growth depends on external nourishment. However, your purpose will define the shape and direction your growth takes.

Your purpose is the essence of what's deep inside you to do on this earth, and reflects what you can achieve when you fully apply yourself. Given proper nourishment, you alone will determine the limits of what you can do. A healthy purpose will help you reach your full potential.

Motivation Is from the Inside Out

Does external motivation have a place in your life? Yes! You may want to sit quietly...reading, writing, and studying. However, if what you're studying is inspiring, it may motivate you to get up and take action. Also, if you have just experienced an exciting seminar, you could be moved to take what you've learned and put it into practice.

In the military, external motivation is a way of life. The consequences of not complying with regulations are swift and harsh, sometimes punishing. In corporate life, money is often the external motivator used to accomplish a task. This, coupled with the prestige of being listed high in the monthly sales ranking report, often encourages people to do things. Who would want to be last? The regulations and rankings didn't really drive me. They weren't my purpose. However, I had implicitly committed myself and my energies to them when I joined the companies that established them as their goals. But those purposes were what someone else chose, and your employment with a company implies you will help them achieve *their* dreams and goals.

Within most organizational structures, there are elements to stimulate both internal and external motivation. You can shine brightly in the organization as you learn to develop and benefit from their chosen motivators.

You may find, in situations you've chosen, there are external motivators that demand the impossible from you. They may even be directly opposed to your values and inclinations. You may or may not choose to continue with the organization, depending on how seriously their thinking differs from yours. You may choose to discuss the matter with someone in a higher position who oversees you, to reach a new agreement. You can create strong, internal motivators to help you achieve challenging goals. As you live self-responsibly, the strength to develop internal motivators will come. It'll help you overcome obstacles and may even empower you to move on.

In 1981 I attended the U.S. Army's Ranger School Training Course at Fort Benning, Georgia. This experience provided one of those challenges where survival depends solely on how much you believe in yourself and your abilities. As a result of the physical and emotional hardships, you discover just how powerful internal motivation can be. There are moments when *everything* depends on your own internal reasons for persevering.

I began my career at West Point with what I felt was the right mental attitude. I made it my mission to demonstrate excellence, confidence, and selflessness. They became my internal motivators. I was on the alert for opportunities to exercise these qualities, not for anyone else's approval, but for my own personal satisfaction.

On Ranger School graduation day, fewer than half of those who started with me made it through the course. There are quitters in every arena. The Ranger Training School experience, though, was a true testing ground for one's internal motivators. Many of the students did not have a strong enough desire to finish. They weren't motivated enough internally to withstand the rigors of the external motivators.

Desire is the key ingredient. If it's weak, it can lead to a person quitting before the completion of a worthy goal. Success or failure in the course was decided by each person's ability or inability to mold the external motivators to support their internal goals. *Ability can be developed when the desire is strong enough.*

There are many positive external motivators that can influence our performance and desire to excel. Incentives and awards are used successfully in many organizations. However, positive external motivators will only have short-term benefits if they don't support your life's dreams and goals as well as your personal definition of purpose. *You can have all the plaques and bonus points that exist, but they'll have little or no meaning to you if their achievement does not support who and what you are and want to be.*

Most of us know unhappy people who are perceived as being successful. Be assured, it's only a limited success. Their success is often not based on their purpose or value system. They may be solely reacting to external motivators. They may be blaming their unhappiness on others. They may be living a lie, being untrue to themselves and others.

My Ranger Training didn't culminate on graduation day. The greatest moment was a time of crisis when I had to balance intense internal and external motivators. It was much like preventing a team of horses from bolting!

What Happened When I Reached the End of My Rope?

In my mind I can see the movie reel of my Ranger Training days unwind. It's an indelible memory. You would understand that, if you are at all acquainted with the rigors of Ranger Training or something similar.

The code word for my moment of truth in Ranger Training was *Far-Side*. It had nothing to do with Gary Larson's comics. However, they did share a certain believability. It was a detached awareness that the experience of extreme circumstances offered, an opportunity to leap beyond what I believed was the outer limits of my endurance. This was similar to the humor of Larson's weird inversions of animal and human behavior. It depended on a momentary leap beyond possibility. The Ranger experience proved that dedication to high purpose can motivate anyone to achieve beyond what they had previously set as their outermost limits.

First, let's cover some background on the Rangers. The U.S. Army Rangers trace their lineage back to Rogers' Rangers. Major Robert Rogers formed nine companies of American colonists to defend British interests during the French and Indian Wars of the mid-18th century. Their battles were fought in what is now northern New York, New England, and the adjoining Canadian provinces.

Traditional European lines of march and attack had brought the "red coats" of the regular British forces to death and defeat. *Rogers' 19 Standing Orders*, such as, "If somebody's trailing you, make a circle, come back on your own tracks, and ambush the folks that aim to ambush you," helped make his raw American colonists into a real fighting force. They were capable of anticipating and responding to the particular demands of the enemy and the terrain they faced. Because of their success, Rogers' Rangers entered the annals of military history. To this day, *Rogers' 19 Standing Orders* are taught in military academies throughout the Western world.

Traditionally, Ranger groups were volunteers who were disbanded when wars ended. The history of U.S. Ranger groups originates from Rogers' men, to Morgan's Riflemen in the Revolutionary War. It was Darby's Rangers in World War II who spearheaded the amphibious assaults in North Africa and Sicily. They also performed with equal valor on the beaches of Normandy, and it was on bloody Omaha Beach that the Rangers got the motto that has stayed with them ever since. When the order was given for Darby's Rangers to break through the wall of defending machine guns, artillery, and trenches, the words they heard were: "Lead the way, Rangers!"

Today, the goal of every group of Rangers is to be a band of leaders, each self-sufficient to the highest degree. Every Ranger is dedicated to accomplishing the mission of the group, while adhering to the highest standards. A volunteer Ranger is required to undergo and survive some of the most mentally and physically demanding training in the world.

When I completed my Armor Officer Basic Training (tanks) and Motor Officer Course (maintenance), I qualified for Ranger School. I thought I knew what to expect. I knew deprivation of sleep and food would be built into the program. Beyond that, it was coupled with physical training and classroom work more strenuous than I ever could have imagined. Meeting the standard was an exhilarating experience. Each time I overcame an obstacle, I experienced personal satisfaction and enhanced self-esteem.

The Ranger Course, which is conducted by the Infantry School's Ranger Training Brigade, is the Army's premier leadership course. The soldiers who graduate from it are tough, competent, and confident. They can lead units into combat and surmount all obstacles necessary to accomplish their mission.

This is how Rangers are described in the course book:

> *The Ranger Course identifies and further develops leaders who are physically and mentally tough, self-disciplined, highly motivated and committed, who enforce high standards and are able to act quickly, and react effectively in stressful situations that approach (and possibly exceed) that found in combat.*
>
> *—INFANTRY, "Training Notes: The Ranger Course"*
> *May-June, 1991, p. 37*

Unfortunately, many of the soldiers who begin the course fail to complete it. I never for a moment felt this would happen to me, until the following incident occurred.

Those of us in my class who had successfully completed the Benning Phase of Ranger training, conducted at Fort Benning, Georgia, and the Mountain Phase, held in Georgia's Chattahoochee National Forest, were transported to Florida for the final phase. It consisted of days of waterborne training, night jumps, swamp infiltrations, and military operations on urban terrain. We arrived in late February of 1981 to experience the severest stretch of cold weather the people in Florida had encountered in many a winter.

I always felt good about my swimming ability. Through swimming, I was introduced to competitive sports. It was the first time I was recognized because of physical excellence, causing my peers to respect me. I don't think I was cocky about my capabilities, but admittedly, the waterborne aspect of Ranger training sounded somewhat comfortable. When I thought of what I had already been through and accomplished at West Point, and in the first phases of Ranger training, I believed the worst was behind me. I had no idea how my sense of purpose was going to be put to the test.

An expedient stream crossing called for a "Far-Side" lifeguard; and Rifenbary, the all-American swimmer, was given the duty. I hefted the ends of a sixty-foot and eight-foot rope to my shoulder. They would be the guide line and safety line for those following me. I entered the bone-chilling water and fought my way against a strong current to the reedy banks of the opposite shore. There I secured the sixty-foot rope to a tree. I then took the eight-foot rope and swam back to the middle of the crossing, where I was to remain treading water and be prepared to save a fellow student in the event he fell into the river. My orders directed me to be the lifeguard at the middle of the crossing. I rigidly stretched one arm to take the weight off the safety rope, as it threatened to leave my grasp and whip down the river like a snake. I used the other hand to grasp a reed for whatever support it could supply.

I had to do this until my companions made it from shore to shore. I remained in the water as they clung to the sixty-foot rope, traveling one-by-one, hand-over-hand, with full battle-packs hanging like shells of upended turtles.

I knew and felt the signs of hypothermia, but I used every mind trick I knew to convince myself that the symptoms didn't exist. My convulsive shaking attracted the attention of the Ranger instructor, who "encouraged" me with jeers and ridicule. The cramping in my limbs became so severe, I asked to be relieved. Finally, I was ordered to be hauled out of the water.

At that point, another instructor came to where I sat. I was still shaking uncontrollably.

"Wanna go home?" he sassed.

Another instructor joined in, "Wanna go home to *Mommy*?"

I thought the enlisted men at my side were like stone. Hear no evil, see no evil, speak no evil. I stayed silent. I knew what was at stake. *I had a decision to make.*

I knew that in the first phase, the Benning Phase, a medical drop had been used as an honorable way out of the course for most of those who had left. That was one way out. Then, of course, I could always voluntarily quit. That would be entered on the record as "lack of motivation." The harassment of the instructors kept on for ten minutes. One was at each ear, bending in low to shout insults and taunts.

I answered, finally, "No, I don't want to go home, sir." The order came: "Then get back into the water."

For the first time, I considered standing up and walking away. But something inside me stubbornly refused to let my tormentors decide whether or not I would be a Ranger.

I stood up and somehow found the strength to re-enter the water and to hold my post. I stayed until the blessed moment when the last classmate completed his crossing and pulled me out. A couple of men then wrapped me in blankets and prepared a fire to warm me before we began a 12-mile road march.

The triumph was that I didn't allow the privilege of fulfilling my purpose to be taken from me. I revisit the memory to recall my victory, despite the pain it vividly brings back.

I was deprived of food. I was deprived of sleep. I was also deprived of dignity. Imagine enduring the verbal assault of tormenting instructors. But I was not deprived of purpose! My purpose was to be a Ranger. If I was going to reconsider that decision, it wasn't going to be because someone might take pleasure in my failure.

I was not trying to meet the standards of those instructors. I was meeting my own standards when I re-entered the water. I was thinking to myself, "I may leave the Rangers tomorrow because of this experience, but the decision to leave will belong to me, not to my tormentors." And that's what got me through this experience. I have three traumatized toes to prove I braved that moment of decision. I also have a depth of understanding of what allows a human being to go beyond what he believes are his limits of endurance to achieve high purpose.

What Does It Mean to Be Alive?

Purpose gives meaning and value to our lives. It provides us with a reason to become the person we are meant to be. Most importantly, it offers us the opportunity to contribute to others. It is well known that senior citizens often live longer when they have a house pet or plant to care for. They have another reason to be alive. Those who retire from their professions without future plans or direction, sometimes have shorter life spans than those who do.

Purpose establishes, in your own heart and mind, that others need you and your talents. Countless studies have demonstrated the negative impact depression and a lack of self-esteem have on physical health. *Establishing a purpose can assist you in maintaining a healthier lifestyle.* Always conclude that you have something more to offer. You may want to communicate to others that you have a certain ability or talent. Then pursue the opportunities available to you to give what you would enjoy giving the most. For example, if you love spending time with children, you may want to seek an opportunity to work or volunteer at a local children's hospital.

Purpose enables us to enjoy more of life's pleasures. It's the greatest when our purpose becomes our pleasure. If my purpose is to motivate others to achieve success, then no other career is going to give me as much satisfaction as doing that. Therefore, it is not practical for me to spend a great deal of time fixing automobile engines. It's not where my talents lie; it's not what I've defined as a purpose; it's not what would give me optimal pleasure; and it's not what would enable me to make a difference.

What Is Your Main Purpose in Life?

It is important, both to you and others, to honestly admit to yourself what your main purpose in life really is or what you would like it to be. Here are six steps that can assist you in defining your purpose. You can also discover whether your work and outside activities are helping you fulfill your purpose. Get a blank sheet of paper and write down your answers.

I. What purposes are provided by your life's work?

II. What purpose does your employer expect you to fulfill? Or, if you are self-employed, what purpose do you expect yourself to fulfill through your business? *(Examples: represent the highest standards of the firm to the public; maintain the teamwork attitude of the workplace; justly conform to the firm's best financial interests.)*

III. What personal attributes will shape my purpose?

A. What do I do well? What skills do I have that reflect my talents?
B. What would I love to do? What would I do if I didn't need to earn money?
C. What do others appreciate about me?
D. What areas am I weak in? Are any of these skills necessary for accomplishing what I would love to do?
E. What do others not appreciate about me? Are any of these skills necessary for accomplishing what I would love to do?
F. What is my attitude like? Do people want to be around me?
G. What do I want out of life? What does it mean for me to be alive?

IV. What other activities are you involved in outside of your work where you are able to use your talents to do what you love to do?

V. If you have discovered that neither your work activities nor those outside work help you to fulfill your purpose, what could you do to move in this direction?

VI. What steps are you willing to take?

By answering these questions, you'll be better equipped to determine the true fundamentals for your purpose in life. What do you think it is? If you feel that you don't know, use your imagination. Pretend that you know and write down what your heart speaks. Get a clean sheet of paper and write down, "My purpose in life is…"

You've Done It

Good for you! Let yourself come away from this section feeling exuberant. Yes, the possibilities you once only imagined are now becoming real. The key to your success is defining your own purpose, which you've just had an opportunity to do! Your personal action plan may be beginning to unfold.

With the strength of self-responsibility as your support, and a well-defined purpose as your guide, your foundation for embarking on the *Staircase of Success* is not quite complete. Let's take a closer look at integrity, your cornerstone for success, both on a personal and professional level, and establish the guidelines of fair play.

Chapter 3
INTEGRITY
Your Cornerstone of Success

A nyone who is living self-responsibly and with purpose could now ask, "What does success mean to me?" Well, there's more to it than just defining your purpose.

With *No Excuse!* you'll recognize and appreciate the difference between success and purpose. Your purpose is defined by you, after careful evaluation of why you are here on this earth. The path to accomplishing your purpose is traveled by pursuing the goals you set for yourself; the journey is the success! Success means different things to different people. Success is also determined by *how* you go about getting what you want every day of your life. *Success comes by being consistently committed to your dreams and goals, and taking the actions which lead to fulfilling your purpose.*

For people practicing *No Excuse!* success is not found at the end of the rainbow. It's the way we behave as we journey through life that determines what our lives are all about. Success is the way we treat ourselves and others. Success is the love, self-esteem, and respect in general that we direct inwardly and outwardly as we work every day for a better tomorrow.

Some say successful people are those who get what they want. This is only partially correct; there's more to success than that. The task at hand is to determine what that "more" is. So roll up your sleeves while we work toward some answers.

Might Makes Right?

When a war "machine" rolls over its enemies, one of the joys of victory is the privilege of writing the first version that tells the story of its success. Posterity re-examines the victor only when the ghosts of the vanquished emerge from the fog of the past. They gather like shadows under triumphal arches, demanding a second hearing. It is the second writing of history that often echoes through the ages.

Homer told the story of the Greek victory over the Trojans. The world will always honor the defeated Trojans. Why? He draws a portrait of their integrity. Perhaps the greatest message of the *Iliad* is just this: *Victory alone does not define success.*

Integrity is necessary for us to find true success in victory or defeat. It's what's missing in so many people who are considered successful. However, as history reveals, the leader of the Allied Forces in the 1991 Persian Gulf War was a man of integrity.

Integrity Dictates True Success

No Excuse! weaves integrity into the strands of self-responsibility and purpose. It creates a tapestry of life that is beautiful and true.

Integrity is nurtured by living self-responsibly. In turn, your integrity keeps your purpose alive as you strive to become a decisive and action-oriented person. *It is virtually impossible to blame, whine, complain, and simultaneously have great integrity.*

When you lead a self-responsible life of purpose, you grow in wisdom. Look for integrity, in yourself and in the people you choose to work with, work for, and admire. It is mutual respect and integrity that come together to form the foundation for trust in your personal and professional relationships.

Funk & Wagnall's defines integrity as "uprightness of character; soundness; an undivided or unbroken state." *The degree to which you stand firm in your convictions and beliefs, and assume responsibility for what you say and do, determines your level of integrity.* Your integrity ultimately dictates how effective you are as a parent, salesperson, manager, leader, business owner, employee, social worker, spouse, teacher, or anything else. Your integrity dictates the measure of true success that you achieve.

The Key to Effective Leadership

One of the primary reasons for turmoil in any society is lack of personal integrity in political and economic leaders. We need leaders with integrity! It's essential to have self-responsible people in positions of power. They're the kind of leaders needed in government, business, families, and other organizations.

What interferes with good leadership? Ineffective leaders experience the same obstacles effective leaders encounter. Effective leaders learn how to handle obstacles by persisting and being creative. Ineffective leaders need to accept personal responsibility for their actions so they can be more effective. They are often fearful of not satisfying society's empty definitions of success, for example, a large house and a fancy car. This sometimes leads them to jeopardize their integrity. They may step on others to accomplish a goal or be dishonest in their dealings. Their fear may cause them to deny responsibility for the consequences of their behavior. They may know what they did was incorrect and want to avoid punishment or maybe even losing their job. Unfortunately, some people think it's easier to forfeit integrity, than to risk not moving up the corporate ladder. This can cause them to live in constant fear of being found out. Furthermore, the outcomes they create are weakened when they dodge responsibility or act based on their fear. It is likely they won't be pleased with their results.

Parents may be more concerned about being liked by their children, than in fulfilling their responsibility of providing consistent and effective discipline. Without discipline, how can children be expected to develop self-responsible habits and grow into adults with integrity? As a parent, how can you gain the respect of your child if you are not consistent with what you say and do?

The same is true for managers and leaders. Those who take certain actions because they want to please people, to be liked, are often weak, ineffective, and inconsistent. As a manager or leader, how can you gain the respect of your employees or followers if you are not consistent with what you say and do?

Integrity is key to effective leadership. Trust is a gift given by others to a person who displays integrity. A person of integrity may be thrust into a leadership role as a result of the respect and trust he elicits from others. One of the finest examples of this is the story of Rosa Parks. She demonstrated to the world the power of bravely and simply reflecting one's own basic beliefs. She went "against the tide" because she was a woman of great integrity, committed to principle.

Rosa Parks was an African American woman who lived in the then-segregated city of Montgomery, Alabama. It was December of 1955. She believed that a paying passenger had the right to sit on a public bus in any vacant seat. This had been denied to blacks, who were expected to sit in the back. She acted on her belief and sat in the front, whether or not other people agreed with her. She even faced angry threats. She boldly stood up to discrimination by her courageous action. She integrated her belief with her action and caught the attention of an entire nation. Her display of integrity contributed to the nation's increased awareness of racial injustices. As a result, she stimulated the movement toward greater justice and equality of treatment among races. Rosa Parks later co-founded the Rosa and Raymond Parks Institute for Self Development in Detroit, Michigan. Her last book is titled *Quiet Strength*.

Do You Stand Strong for What You Believe In?

How strong do you stand by your beliefs and convictions? When you are expected to act, or make a decision that is in conflict with your values and beliefs, what do you do? Do you waiver back and forth from one decision or behavior pattern to another? Do you stand firm with what you know to be right? If you don't stand for something, you may fall for anything.

Every time a person or group makes a decision that lacks integrity, they experience increased temptation to relinquish responsibility for that decision. It's human nature not to want to take responsibility for decisions or actions we know are morally wrong. These decisions do not reflect our belief system. Therefore, we don't want to own them. In these situations, it can be very easy for us to hold someone or something else responsible. If we choose to place blame elsewhere, and we don't experience the consequences of taking responsibility for our actions, we thwart our personal growth in that area.

On the other hand, when you make decisions that correlate with your values and beliefs, you are much more likely to be self-responsible and accept the outcomes. In addition, you are also more likely to correctly anticipate and deal with the results of your actions. Your integrity shows you have the wisdom to develop your values and beliefs and the strength to act on them. As a result, you are likely to have greater peace of mind.

My Personal Conviction

I recall an incident in the military where I was asked to sacrifice my integrity to feed the vanity of a higher ranking officer. He shocked me and the patrons of a local establishment by publicly belittling my superior officer. My personal conviction told me to publicly declare his remarks unacceptable. I knew I'd be risking his angry retribution. However, if I chose to say nothing, I knew I would be unworthy of being a leader. My personal convictions prevailed.

There were reprisals, as I knew there would be. I confronted them with all the fortitude I could muster. I responded to the ugly lies. I felt compelled to do these things even though it put my personal ambitions for promotion in jeopardy.

The reports of the superior officers who evaluated my performance demonstrated how committed I was to excellence and earning advancement and recognition. Here is an example of one of the six reports, all of which were equally complimentary:

> *The most dedicated junior officer I have ever supervised, loyal to subordinate and superior alike....*
> *He is the type of officer a commander wants—he accomplishes every mission in a superior manner.... Never in six years of service have I met*

a more motivated officer. Respected by subordinates and superiors alike, this officer develops excellent communication with the soldiers— they know he cares about them and the mission.

I quote this commendation not to brag, but to show you how important it is to have integrity and establish excellent relationships with the people with whom you associate. To preserve my own integrity, I had no choice but to respond to the officer who, without justification, verbally assaulted the integrity of my superior officer.

My decision to be loyal to my own values negatively impacted a professional relationship with the offending officer. However, the relationship with myself was my key priority. I knew I could not be the officer and person I wanted to be, if I did not heed the call to a higher duty when I heard it. *It is unlikely you will become the person you want to be if the decisions you make conflict with your values.* Remember, integrity is the driving force and essence of true success.

Success Can Be Learned

The catalyst for true success is learning. It leads to knowledge. Knowledge leads to understanding. Understanding leads to wisdom.

No Excuse! is an approach for achieving success. Its principles, when you make them a part of your life, will lead the way to honorable behavior and outcomes. The steps of the *THESAURUS Factor* exclude all unscrupulous thoughts and actions. When you are given a choice between taking or rejecting an action that is against your value system, *No Excuse!* will give you the understanding to make a wise decision. It'll help you be happy, with no regrets and a clear conscience.

Every successful person experiences times of challenging decision-making. The path of success is paved by one decision after another, and some of them may be tough. Sometimes it may not be easy to make the right decision. As you incorporate the steps of the *THESAURUS Factor* into your everyday life, you'll be able to call on them as a standard for decision-making. I believe you will find the *THESAURUS Factor* a valuable resource for leading a successful life of integrity, happiness, and fulfillment.

Imagine there's a nominee for public office with an incident of questionable judgment in his past. Do you believe he could have made wiser choices if he had used sound decision-making principles based on his value system? There are times when conscientious objection leads men and women to willingly endure sacrifice, even while they disagree with a law. This is different than breaking a law because it's convenient and then hoping no one notices. The latter leads to fear and unhappiness.

The road to happiness is mapped out in the *THESAURUS Factor*. It's a guide that helps you protect your integrity as you work effectively toward your goals, so you can fulfill your purpose. As a *No Excuse!* person, you'll have a new opportunity to become a mature, decisive achiever, if you aren't one already. You can be free from the habits of blaming, complaining, and whining. They're losing habits. No Excuse! guides you to a life of honesty and integrity, and away from the temptations caused by unscrupulous greed. You'll learn how to develop habits of respect for yourself and others, which can support your efforts to achieve your dreams and goals.

You Are the Commander-In-Chief of Your Own Life

Generals develop a plan to guide their soldiers in battle. *No Excuse!* teaches you how to be an excellent commander-in-chief of your own life. With the basic training of *No Excuse!*, you can strategize and set goals as effectively as the greatest generals. You can then carefully choose your role models, mentors, and associates. Of course, accepting responsibility for your decisions is part of a *No Excuse!* life.

No Excuse! living encourages you to be the creatively focused engineer of your own life. You can use the *Staircase of Success* to examine your actions and powerfully design your own life. There is no need to drift, as some people do, like a ship without a rudder, at the mercy of life's winds and currents. Your better judgment will win out over the grip of inner passions and needs. With *No Excuse!* self-awareness, you will learn to see what's happening in your life. You'll discover what you're doing to yourself that's not in your own best interest and be encouraged to take action to correct it.

I meet truly happy people every day, and I know their secret. Happiness results from *No Excuse!* living. These people do three things:

- They accept responsibility for their own lives.
- They design a purpose for themselves.
- They establish standards for themselves that they won't violate;
  they maintain integrity.

Sound simple? I hope so, because it is. Sound easy? I hope not, because it isn't always easy, especially at first. It's like learning to pedal the wheel of the tricycle while steering it at the same time. And like anything else, like any new habit you develop, it gets easier with practice.

How to Make Your Life More Meaningful

As Robert Louis Stevenson said, "To become what we are, and to become what we are capable of being, is the only end of life." This simple but powerful statement explains the basic premise of *No Excuse! You make your life meaningful by knowing who you are. You make your life worthwhile by fulfilling your potential with integrity. Success is found in that combination.*

The only way to get to know and understand who you really are is to be somewhat introspective. Some people are so focused outward on other people and things, that they may fail to look inward and realize the power they have to take action in their own lives. They're always fearful and on guard. They try to protect themselves by finding someone or something else to blame if things go wrong. They spend their lives trying to look good, be right, and cover themselves. But always remember this: When the going gets tough, the weak blame!

It's impossible for you to fulfill your potential if your life is only a repetition of earlier successes. Those successes are dead ends when they become nostalgic memories that you dwell on. You're safe alright. However, you can end up regretting you didn't move on. High school heroes can be found in every community. Some people with potential live on the memories of the glory they achieved in their youth. Unfortunately, they are often afraid of failure. They are often in the comfort zone, or familiar zone, commonly called a rut. They never seem to apply their model of previous success to new endeavors. Use reruns of past successes to gain confidence to pursue your next adventure. You did it once, you can do it again.

No Excuse! helps people break free from faulty thinking patterns which have trapped them much of their lives. Again and again, *No Excuse!* helps people eliminate the habit of blaming others. The energy previously used to avoid self-responsibility can then be transformed into a determined strength. It's almost miraculous to watch as people reach their self-defined goals.

Purpose begins to grow in a self-responsible person freed of the burden of blame. Their accomplishments may be small at first, but they can celebrate each achieved goal. They can continue to move toward fulfillment of their purpose. People of purpose speak a common language; they are happy about their accomplishments. They can better appreciate the good things life has to offer.

No Excuse! works like yeast. Your life has bounds that hold and shape who you are, like a bread bowl. You can choose to change many of your bounds and create a bigger bowl. Life also brings in new raw material every day. It gives you experiences to process and develop. These are the ingredients, the stuff of which life is made. Your approach to living is like the yeast that gives growth to the materials brought to the bowl each day.

No Excuse! will work for you as long as you wholeheartedly adopt it and persist to make it a daily habit. As you study the lives of successful people, you'll see how they used the *No Excuse!* principles to achieve their goals.

Does Giving Have Anything to Do with Success?

Surely the increased capacity for giving, that comes with success, is its crowning glory. It is wonderful to be able to give freely, whether it is to charity or to assist people in other ways. True success always involves giving. Sure, you can give inherited money. However, this money wasn't the result of your own success, but someone else's. Before you can get to the point where you can give whatever you choose to contribute, you usually need to be a giver of your talents, skills, and caring. After I began implementing *No Excuse!*, it became so rewarding I felt compelled to share it to help others enrich their lives. It was the best gift I could give and the best use of my time and talents.

As I looked back on my life, I realized I was happiest giving to others. My greatest joy came by helping friends and associates discover and use their own unique talents to work together to accomplish common goals. That's called teamwork.

At first glance it may appear to be solitary work, rather than teamwork. However, if you look closely, you'll see that the task of empowering others to motivate themselves is an interdependent process. Success for me is knowing that *No Excuse!* is helping others, as well as me, to live a purposeful life of contribution.

Everyone's application of *No Excuse!* will differ somewhat due to personal and situational factors. Your life will provide the container and the ingredients. You will devise the recipe for the success that only you can define for yourself.

No Excuse! is effective because you are in charge of your own decisions. You can examine the results of your decisions with new clarity gained from self-responsibility, purpose, and integrity. You can determine whether you meet your own standards of success in all areas of your life.

True success is connected to giving without expecting to receive something in return. When you have a "taker" attitude and are solely concerned with what you get, if you are working, you're always only and endlessly just making a living. To design a great life, you need to be more concerned with what you're giving. Your giving allows you to also receive. This is a cause and effect world. You may not receive from the same source to which you gave. It is important to give graciously and receive with genuine appreciation and acceptance.

Is your life a balance of giving and receiving? Do you agree that a life well-lived will have both? Can you truthfully answer yes to the following questions, honestly and with pleasure? "Did I give today?" and "Did I receive today?" With *No Excuse!* living you can.

No Excuse! means paying attention to the people in your life. When you take responsibility for your decisions and actions, it is likely you'll become more open to receiving. People will gladly give you time, money, objects, compliments, friendships, teachings, and counselings. When you no longer need to blame, whine, and complain, or moan and groan, you can really enjoy and appreciate the experience of giving and receiving. As you begin to nourish others with your appreciation of their gifts, you'll notice their ability and willingness to give increases. You're likely to have more strength to stand up to people with negative attitudes. In addition, you'll most likely be better able to find a number of true friends who will support your dreams and goals.

No Excuse! is for those who are interested in moving on. It's for people willing to live with integrity. It takes courage to be honest about whether you have a giver or a taker attitude. It takes strength to humbly accept how important you really are in the lives of others. And nowhere is this fact more likely to be true than in the course of your daily associations with family and friends. Being important to these people implies the necessity of being responsible in your actions toward them.

Building an Army of Allies

A *No Excuse!* life has a purposeful, self-responsible person at its center. A *No Excuse!* person builds a successful life by reaching out with integrity. A *No Excuse!* person bonds and develops strong, healthy relationships.

The military has a hierarchical structure with a chain of command that needs to be fulfilled. But every great general has known that alone is not enough to foster cooperation, loyalty, and productivity. It depends on the bond between him and his troops. A strong bond inspires them to do their best. Inspiration is not linear. A small push on the edges of your limits can lead to great victory.

Your relationships with your family and friends, however, do have linear aspects. They are directly affected by the quantity of time we invest in them. Children are ill-served by parents who relinquish their authority.

Groups of friends and associates often need leaders too. Family and friends are so important to *No Excuse!* living that a whole chapter in Part II is devoted to them. Ultimately, the quality of your relationships with them determines your true success in life.

As a society, we are in a time when the definition of family is shifting. Generally speaking, children seem to grow best in families. However, for many of them the traditional family does not exist. In order to compensate, we may need to work more diligently to bring loving care to our relationships.

The same is true of friendships. How many of us have the luxury of daily contact with all of our lifelong friends? Many of us need to nurture some important friendships long-distance. We live in a mobile society; there may be quite a distance between us and our lifelong friends. Therefore, *we have a responsibility to ourselves to make new friends.* We can never have too many friends.

How well do you choose and court (develop a relationship with) people you'd like to have in your life? How well do you treat them once they're a part of it? *No Excuse!* can help you succeed here. By using *No Excuse!* in your work, you can attract new relationships. You can eliminate the clutter of excuses from your life. You can develop special relationships you'll treasure as you travel on your path of success.

Do You Fear Success?

Many people find that once they learn to stop making excuses for their failures and mistakes, they have a different challenge—making excuses for their successes! After you've learned to eliminate self-imposed defeatist behaviors, your next step is to allow yourself to enjoy your success. You deserve it!

Success can be uncomfortable, even scary, at first, because it also brings increased responsibility. Therefore, increased integrity is required. Some people use excuses to explain why they never accomplish much in life. When they finally achieve some success, the excuse-making habit may still be so strong that they begin making excuses for their achievements. For example, they may say that it was just luck when they worked long hours to achieve their goal. When someone makes excuses for their success, they'll feel like a person with losing behavior, even though they exhibit winning behavior.

You'll feel pleased about your success when you eliminate excuses. Give yourself credit for what you've accomplished. Also, give credit to anyone who helped you along the way. Accept compliments graciously from people who appreciate your efforts. Your positive feelings will help you be a more supportive family member, friend, and businessperson. Set your own goals and achieve them with integrity, and both you and others will benefit. Enjoy your success, and invite family and friends to celebrate with you. You'll be free to wholeheartedly enjoy *their* accomplishments too.

You Are Your Own Business

You are your own business; running your life is your business! How you treat yourself affects everything, including your financial picture. Taking excellent care of *you* is essential.

You are taking excellent care of the business of life when you surprise a friend with the affirmation "I admire you"; when you affirm a young person's achievements when they aren't expecting attention; when you openly appreciate a golf partner's contribution by saying, "You're on your way to becoming a great golfer"; when you say to someone, "Thank you for being here!" These things will pay off. Your own achievements will be magnified. You'll find yourself surrounded by people who are also committed to live purposeful, self-responsible lives of integrity. *A spirit of generosity goes hand in hand with prosperous growth.*

In my mind I return again to the moment when *No Excuse!* was born—at the grand opening of my success store. The thought that I was in business for myself jolted me into a new awareness: "I'm also in business by myself." It seemed to mean that it was all up to me, and in some ways it was.

Being in business for yourself does mean it's up to you! No one else can set the tone of the life you'll lead. If you believe your life is controlled by other people, you might want to ask yourself, "Why?" and "What can I do about it?" If you want to regain control of your life and you choose not to take action, you are making an excuse; you have lost integrity with yourself.

Start with a clean sheet of paper, and list the names of three people you feel control an area of your life. Beside each name, state at least one undesirable aspect of the power you believe they have. Now, devise a plan. Prepare for a conversation in which you negotiate with that person in order to remedy, or at least modify, the situation that bothers you. Then push all excuses out of the way and go for it! *When you use integrity to change or eliminate an undesirable situation, you gain experience in living a more powerful life.* You're starting to take charge!

Having Successful Relationships

No Excuse! is a way to develop relationships of a higher order—

relationships of mutual respect and support. As relationships grow and change, people sometimes grow apart. Letting go of a grown child, for instance, is the healthy culmination of a career of parenting.

Couples who breakup hopefully have learned something from their relationship. This could be helpful if they choose to build another relationship with someone else. But if they don't learn anything from their previous relationship, they are likely to repeat the same ineffective behaviors with someone new. It's important both partners realize and have gratitude for all the good shared and the lessons learned before entering their next relationship. These romantic courting relationships can serve as a training ground for anyone who seeks to select a mate for a solid marriage.

It takes courage to lead a life of integrity, and to acknowledge the people who have supported you along the way. *No Excuse!* doesn't mean "No thanks!" *No Excuse!* helps you to be a thankful person who lights the path to the future with a glow of gratitude for the present and the past.

The first step of the *THESAURUS Factor* is designed to enable you to let go of the pain of the past. This allows you to travel into your future without the weight of unforgiving ills on your heart, on your back, or on your conscious or subconscious mind. To climb the *No Excuse! Staircase,* begin by laying down the burdens of the past.

You may have *allowed* people to hurt you in the past. I say allowed because no one can hurt you without your permission! View an incident in a negative way and it will influence you negatively. It's simply a choice. And while it's nearly impossible to live in this world without experiencing pain, some of us are more wounded than others. Outward appearances may lead you to believe that the wounds aren't there when, in reality, they may be many and deep. You become your own worst enemy when your excuses keep them open. You hurt yourself even more when you use more excuses to infect the wounds. Remember, *no one can hurt you without your permission.* Look closer at where your wounds and infections are and start healing them.

The Hero-of-the-Month Club

Now might be the time for you to start a Hero-of-the-Month club. You can learn from heroes, use them as examples, and fill your mind with their winning ideas and ways. When I ask audiences to name some heroes, I always get a fascinating variety of people of integrity who have influenced our society and how we see ourselves. For example:

- Charles Lindbergh—the gift of daring to bring the people of the world closer together.

- Winston Churchill—the gifts of perseverance, courage, and integrity even at the risk of possible defeat.
- Mr. Rogers—the gifts of caring, sharing, loving, and helping our future leadership (children).
- Amelia Earhart—the gifts of guts and determination to explore new realms and break old barriers.
- Martin Luther King, Jr.—the gifts of non-violent protest for social change, and freedom for everyone.
- Mother Teresa—the gifts of selflessness, faith, and dedication to those less fortunate.

No matter what heroes are suggested, I always see by their example that the *first step* for attaining *No Excuse!* success is by *respecting our own desires.* You can respect your desires like these people and other heroes have done. Most people's idea of success includes acquiring something. Your idea of success may be money, cars, homes, or other material things. Hopefully, your success includes personal growth, helping people, championing a cause, and progressively achieving a worthwhile dream or goal. You're probably aware of the basic steps you need to take to get what you want. But remember, "success is a journey, not a destination."

General Ulysses S. Grant knew that he would only achieve complete success when Lee surrendered. He knew many battles, large and small, won and lost, would come before full success was his. This understanding set Grant apart from McClellan, whose reluctance to engage the enemy in preliminary encounters caused Lincoln to replace him with Grant as head of the Union Forces. Grant's success as a general didn't begin with Lee's surrender. It began the moment he sat down and began defining his first encounter with the opposing forces.

Your success as a person in charge of your own life begins the moment you plan a strategy to meet and overcome the forces that oppose you. If McClellan had realized his inertia was only an excuse, he might not have disgraced himself. Grant, however, used *No Excuse!* principles only in his military career. If he had also used them during his Presidency, he would not have earned disdain for his term in office.

How Can You More Easily Adjust to New Environments?
Grant missed the structure of the military and did not learn to operate from his own principles within the political arena. Some people feel anxious when they leave one environment and enter another. A child going to

school for the first time is leaving a place of known boundaries and comforts for an unknown environment. The boundaries of the new structure will be different. The child will need to develop skills necessary to interact more interdependently as he transitions. These periods require focus and energy until the new environment becomes more familiar.

The same is true during any time of transition in our lives. We may have experienced success within a certain structure, like school. When we leave that structure, we may find a part of us still wants to return to that comfortable arena. So it's critically important to our future that we internalize the principles of success. When they are a part of us, they can guide us in any new environment.

No Excuse! provides principles we can use as we move from structure to structure in our daily lives. But the *Staircase* of the *THESAURUS Factor* guides us to success beyond structures. It can ultimately lead to *the truest success there is—satisfaction with a life you've defined for yourself.* This happens only when you've outgrown both immature definitions and those dictated by someone else or society. It only happens when you have the courage to find out who you really are and who you can be if you are willing to utilize your potential. It happens with sustained *No Excuse!* living.

The Rewards of *No Excuse!* Living

The rewards of *No Excuse!* living can be immediate and tremendous. They can draw you closer to the goal of the wisdom extolled by philosophers down through the ages—"Know thyself."

Know what you love to do, what your talents are, and what you desire. Allow yourself room to grow as a person. What do you love about yourself? What do others love about you? What would you love to do with your life? Have enough integrity to be honest with yourself.

People often find themselves working in occupations they don't love or for which they have little aptitude. They end up toiling away with little reward for their labors, except some regular monetary compensation. Such a life is merely one of existence or survival. It's the same old activities over and over. *No Excuse!* helps you get beyond that to where you can experience greater success.

Your life's work is to grow and become the best you can be while making a bigger difference in the world, not only in your personal life but in your career as well. *No Excuse!* is practical. It is important to create a balanced, productive life. *When your work turns into drudgery, it means you are ready for a new challenge.* Be self-responsible enough to admit it.

If you are unhappy with your work, be honest with yourself. You may want to start looking for other opportunities. This doesn't mean you look for someone else to blame for the lack of satisfaction you are experiencing. Start looking for new ways to be in integrity with your own inner desires and with the people around you. It means sharing an optimism that will create a positive environment for yourself and everyone around you. You are already successful, to some extent, when you've done that much. The rest will come as you continue to grow and become the best you can be.

Nothing Ventured, Nothing Gained

Ralph Waldo Emerson said, "It's one of the greatest compensations in life that no man can help another without thereby helping himself." *One of the most valuable gifts any of us can offer others is our willingness to assist their efforts in being self-responsible.* Helping others is a joy, rather than a burden, when you are sincere.

When self-responsibility is at work, people begin moving out of their comfort zone of routine responses. This means taking prudent risks and letting go of irresponsible impulsiveness and cowardly reluctance. It also means living your life with integrity.

Truly successful people take a chance when the time is right. They know they will turn even failure into an advantage by learning from it. In all the decisions you face every day, how well do you weigh the consequences of your choices? How well do you weigh the consequences of your inaction? You can choose to pay the price of success, or you will pay the price of failure by default!

Too many people avoid moving ahead in life because they fear they won't get the results they want and will regret taking the risk. But they miss the excitement of a rich and full life experience. If you want to be truly alive, prepare to take risks by living a *No Excuse!* life.

Now that you've decided to open your mind to *No Excuse!*, keep persisting and maintain your integrity even when you feel challenged. Step right up to the *Staircase* of the *THESAURUS Factor,* confident your efforts will be rewarded. The outcome may be different than what you expect. Nonetheless it will be beneficial. You've had an opportunity to explore the excuses you may have made to keep some or all of your life safely in the comfort zone. Like most of us who get too complacent, you may be good at making excuses for staying there. Remember Ben Franklin's words, "He who is good at making excuses is seldom good at anything else."

Fleeing the Flea Syndrome

There is *No Excuse!* for you not to achieve success in your life. I do mean *you*. I do mean *your* life. I wish I could be standing there before you, to take you by the shoulders if necessary, look you in the eye and say, "Yes, you!"

I'd tell you what a wonderful life lies ahead for you. What joy you'll have when you take more responsibility for your own life. You'll be able to convert energy you've been wasting on excuses you may have used in an attempt to guard yourself against criticism and failure. You'll be able to direct this energy into personal growth and the fulfillment of your dreams and goals.

Fleas are trained by keeping them in a covered container. They can jump amazingly long distances; that's how they get to new food supplies. But keep them in a lidded container long enough, and you can remove the lid without them jumping out! As the fleas hit the lid repeatedly, they become conditioned. They believe they can only jump as high as the lid, whether or not it's in place.

Limits affect people as well. We often live within the narrow limits we have set for ourselves. Have you been fooled into believing in false limits? It's time to let them go! Are you like a conditioned flea? Or are you willing to take a chance and jump out of the jar?

Elephants are conditioned, too, when, as babies, they are chained to a stake strong enough to keep them from getting loose. It tries and tries to break free but, of course, it can't. After a while, it becomes conditioned to believe it will never be able to break away. As the elephant reaches adulthood, it can be tied to its stake by only a small rope. It could actually break the rope, or pull the stake out. But it doesn't even try because it's been conditioned.

Are you conditioned to break away or stay right where you are? The only way you are going to make a difference is by taking a chance. You risk failure but you also risk success!

Most people don't need to see a psychiatrist or go into all kinds of intricate details on how to break bad habits and condition themselves to be happy and successful. They just need to recognize what's going on and change it. By reading positive books and listening to positive CDs, you can learn a great deal. You can turn idle time into personal growth time by reading. You can turn your car into a "university on wheels" by inserting a CD and pressing "play." These are success habits that can help you condition yourself to change your life.

In Part II of this book, we're going to cover the principles of success. You'll discover what it's like to deal with failure, and the impact it has on your life. You're going to learn about the *THESAURUS Factor,* and the *No*

Excuse! lifestyle that can ignite your potential to help you jump out of that jar. You're going to learn principles that can help you break the chain from the stake and move on.

It is likely that you know the general direction you need to take to lead you through the life lessons that await you starting with the next chapter. I believe you'll find it to be a fantastic voyage through a treasury of timeless principles. Think of them as best friends, always there for you, exerting a positive influence on your life, helping you stay the course.

Chapter 4
PRELUDE TO
THE THESAURUS FACTOR
Your Staircase of Success

P icture that our paths have crossed. Imagine we are standing side by side at the entrance to a palatial mansion, awed by the grandeur before us. We are particularly inspired by the magnificent staircase that seems to stretch endlessly to light-filled upper reaches. We are dazzled by the beautiful, spacious chambers that seem to promise fulfillment of our hearts' desires and abound in all directions.

It's a pleasure to welcome you. In our brief time together, you will have an opportunity to learn the secrets of the kingdom ruled from this special place.

The *Staircase* may appear awesome to you—insurmountable. But have confidence. Let go of the idea that it needs to be a struggle. Believe you can make it to the top. Enjoy all the steps along the way, and revisit them as often as you wish.

The joy of *No Excuse!* living is not just for those who have reached the top. No! Success and happiness is found right now in the journey. Life is sweet for those who live life fully every day. Seize the moment and move ahead.

Take One Step at a Time

The *Staircase of Success* is magnificent. In fact, each step is actually a stage: a stage for playing out the best life has to offer; a stage for dancing to your life's music; a stage that welcomes "another opening, another show." It could be a new show blazing onto the scene like a comet. Or it could be a revival, bringing back a beloved work for a fresh interpretation.

Each step of the *THESAURUS Factor* along the *Staircase of Success* can be adapted to your needs whenever you visit it. And one step is just as important as another since you can enter the mansion only by way of the *Staircase.*

As you climb the *Staircase* and use its principles, you'll become more self-responsible. You'll experience more peace of mind. With this new state of mind, you'll come to accept and enjoy periodic solitude or quiet time, a hallmark of a maturing person's search for fullness of life.

Each step contains opportunities for wisdom, limited only by your openness and willingness to practice what is offered. Once you have reached, acquainted yourself with, and practiced each step, a new freedom to "dance" begins. Your dance is personal and determined by your own wants and needs.

If you need to invest a long time on the first step, great! Give yourself time to understand and use the ideas. Relax as you take a stand on *Totally Forgive,* the first step. Don't force yourself to sprint to the next step, *Have Self-Esteem.* Wait until you feel satisfied that you have gotten what you need for the moment before you move on.

As you climb the *Staircase,* determine your own pace. There's a time for marching for a common cause. There's a time for choosing a partner for a waltz under the stars. Then there are times when temporarily skipping a step is the thing to do. With *No Excuse!* living, you'll know when those times have come. Listen to your heart.

People who haven't found what inspires *them* may tend to get caught up in the excitement of other people's dreams. Often they never develop a dream of their own. If that happens to you, you can use the skills you've acquired by living a *No Excuse!* life. They can lead you to totally self-responsible behavior. Take a deep breath and search inside for your own routine and pace, and you'll discover the desires of your heart. You *can* make your dreams come true.

Is Success Just an Uphill Battle?

Since you're on your own path of success, it doesn't matter whether you're going up or down the *Staircase.* You can move along it in either direction if you really want to become all you can be. The mastery of each step is a growing process and is interdependent with the others. The *Staircase* is where people learn which step they need to jump to, or carefully step up or down to. Which step you dwell on depends on your needs and what skills you want to develop.

Your moves along the *Staircase* will be something like those of a xylophone player. He knows the instrument so well that his mallet instinctively touches the right bars, as he moves from low notes to high notes, and back again. His creativity and experience guide him to the perfect tone, the sound that will fill the moment. He may be creating sounds based on the music he hears in his head. Sometimes it's Mozart, sometimes it's a new piece. He's in charge. He strikes the bars that will give him the notes he needs to create a beautiful harmony.

The search for overlapping combinations gives life to music and music to life. Like the musician, you are likely to find your greatest satisfaction along the *Staircase* as you take charge and make your own music. When you have the wit and wisdom to risk leaping about to create new tunes in your life, you can really grow. Since every journey begins with the first step, be kind to yourself if you falter when you hit some sour notes. Gently pick yourself up, dust yourself off, and keep going! With practice you'll become more proficient.

The *Staircase* Has a Spirit All Its Own

When the idea of the *THESAURUS Factor* was initially developed, it became clear that climbing isn't always perceived in a positive way. What's your perception of climbing? Negative or positive?

Let's consider the image of a climber. *Webster's Dictionary* says a climber is "one who goes upward with gradual or continuous progress." Within the context of the *No Excuse!* philosophy, a climber is someone who seeks to develop personally and professionally in all areas of life. The goal is, of course, to live the life you choose.

Why do some people believe it's wrong to strive for a better life? Why do some people criticize and shy away from someone trying to achieve something he or she doesn't have or wasn't born with? Quite often, selfishness causes this negative reaction or judgment. Many people feel no one even has the right to dream! How sad...

Some people don't want anyone to have what they don't have themselves. They often feel powerless to change the circumstances they blame for their own unhappiness. They prefer to belittle anyone they believe naively attempts to scale the unscalable mountain. They are the people who scoff, complain, whine, moan, and groan. They often have lazy habits and may have a jealous attitude.

Then there are people with selfish attitudes who believe that only those born into the so-called good life are worthy of it. They believe only those born with much, deserve prosperity. Snide remarks give these supposedly superior individuals away. Those who snicker and sneer at others usually have either selfish or jealous attitudes.

When climbing the *Staircase* of the *THESAURUS Factor*, it is best to do it with a spirit of generosity and democracy. It is important to believe everyone has the right and responsibility to make the most of themselves. People who are committed to the principles of our founding fathers are most likely the ones who will help keep our country strong and powerful. These visionary men established a society that gives growing room to and nurtures what Thomas Jefferson called a natural aristocracy—a meritocracy. People get rewarded for what they do, as in a free enterprise economy.

When we rise to the occasion and fully contribute our skills and talents, society prospers as we do! That was the idea in Jefferson's time, and it still offers mankind the best promise for the future.

In the military, success depends on each individual acting responsibly in the best interest of the company. This is similar to the principles of *No Excuse!* Ultimately, a sense of responsibility to be ambitious and generous evolves, oftentimes even with the enemy. This combination turns military triumphs into true victories when the war is over. Peace, harmony, and new mutual understanding can then occur.

Temper ambition with generosity if you want to reap the full benefits of your efforts. Success built on sharing and helping others results in multiplied benefits.

Part of the reason *No Excuse!* living leads you to success is that it helps you eliminate any anxiety you may have had about other people's good fortune. This anxiety could have robbed you of precious energy, as well as caused friction. Eliminating the anxiety gives you more energy to climb your mountain. You'll have peace of mind knowing you did your best. You'll be glad for the company of your fellow climbers. You'll look back only to encourage them to keep up their effort. You'll climb with a lot more assurance than someone who puts others down. Anxious folks are insecure and may use their energy in a negative way by trying to step on the person behind them.

Many people are unsupportive, or neutral at best, toward achievers. They often put down ambitious dreamers who go for it. You may have even felt that way yourself at some point. To be more successful, we need to eliminate this prejudice, especially as it applies to ourselves. Recognize the negative attitude you may have toward your own personal desires to be more successful, happy, and fulfilled. Sometimes we can sabotage our own efforts because of a negative attitude. We may not even realize it's holding us back!

Take a good look at where you stand on this issue. If you used to look askance at ambitious people, are you ready to accept the fact that you're one of them? Get ready to climb the *Staircase of Success* by joyfully supporting yourself and others who are adventurous achievers. It's an exciting journey, and you're going to grow a lot as you go. Hopefully you'll be inspired to achieve greatness by choosing to make a bigger difference in the lives of others. *You can do it!* There's *No Excuse!* anymore.

Chapter 5
TOTALLY FORGIVE
First Step of the THESAURUS Factor

Ho w would you feel about a potion so powerful it could free you from the wrongs of the past? How would you feel about using a powerful idea that could help you move on?

What is it? Forgiveness. What does forgiveness have to do with success? It's amazing. It is associated with your energy. Forgiving frees you from the negative grip of the past. Think of forgiveness as giving it up—letting go of resentment and anger. It's simple. If you don't forgive, you're going to waste a lot of time and energy on the past.

Forgiveness provides a fountain of energy. It releases negative energy from the past and unlocks positive energy in the present to help you move into the future. When you forgive, you have more energy to contribute to life. It's part of ultimate wisdom. *Forgiveness is love.*

"As you sow, so shall you reap." This biblical phrase is just as important today as it was thousands of years ago. Forgive others and *you* are more likely to be forgiven.

When a military campaign is over, there's a need for forgiveness; the victor for the vanquished, and vice-versa. The length of any peace depends, largely, on how well each side forgives the other.

We've all had occasions where forgiveness was necessary, either on our part or someone else's. *Are you aware that real prosperity is more likely to occur when we are at peace with our past?* When you know the truth, you'll realize there is power in forgiveness. Also, forgiveness may be needed before it is possible to have the necessary cooperation from others that can lead to success.

How Do You Deal with Failure?

Forgiveness can enable you to have abundant, productive mental and physical energy (vitality) in exchange for disappointment, rage, and feelings of failure. If you feel you've been denied, simply forgive yourself for any ill feelings you may have. Also forgive others for what you believe they have done. With forgiveness, you can often eliminate the troublesome feelings usually associated with a loss.

If people are unforgiving about deprivation and injustice, they may allow those situations to ruin their lives. Successful people forgive and rise above such challenges to become all they can be. Don't let your life be ruled by loss and regret. Forgive yourself and others when things don't work out the way you want them to.

We've all failed at something; it's just a part of life. Forgive yourself for it and move on. *Successful people view failure as a learning experience.* In fact, we may literally fail our way to success. Failure is an opportunity to grow. It could also be a wake-up call telling us that we need to make a change.

Earl Nightingale said, "Luck occurs when preparedness meets opportunity." Luck can also be defined as Labor Under Correct Knowledge. When you first begin your quest for success, some people may say you're crazy. After you're successful, they may say you're lucky.

Don't believe in luck. You can be on the *Staircase of Success*, but if you're sitting still, doing nothing, nothing will happen. The more you do to contribute toward the outcomes you want, the "luckier" you're likely to get. Be prepared for opportunities as they arise and take action on them.

It can be difficult to accept failure, but it's essential if you want to move ahead. If you fail at something, don't quit. Love yourself anyway. Failure is just an event, an opportunity to learn something. It'll help you be stronger for the next challenge. Face it, deal with it, learn from it, and move on.

Plato said, "The measure of a man is how he bears up under misfortune." For instance, consider that the average age of a millionaire is fifty-seven, with most of them having failed five times before they made it! It's incredible. The greater the obstacles overcome, the greater the victory. Many can do well under ideal circumstances, but it's when the going gets tough that the tough get going to become the best they can be.

We All Need a Mentor or Two

When you look at the adversity in your life, you can look at the example of the young man and say, *"No matter what happens there's always someone out there who can inspire me to become all I can be."* This is mentorship. Is one of your chief wants in life to have someone who will give you unconditional support and inspire you to become all you can be? It's true for a lot of people. Is it true for you? Do you have a mentor in your life? We all need someone to help us to empower ourselves to do something we really want to do, yet wouldn't do without some support. If you are willing to look, and humble enough to recognize your need, you'll find a few people available who could be your mentors.

Looking to others for inspiration can be uplifting and help us move out of our comfort zone. It's important to have someone we can follow as an example of how to be and do. Then, as we continue to personally develop and understand ourselves better, we can become more and more of who we really are. Everyone needs a mentor. In fact, some people have a mentor for each area of their life. And while forgiveness deals with failure, it also relates indirectly to mentorship. We may need someone who can teach us to forgive. Mentors could include your parents, teachers, or someone else you respect and admire. An excellent mentor has the knowledge you need and is interested in you and your success.

Why Is It Important that I Forgive Myself?

Forgiveness of self is essential. We've all failed. It's how we deal with failure that matters. We need to forgive ourselves if we want to move on. We can cause ourselves a lot of grief by saying things like: "If only I were thinner, smarter, or more educated." "If only I had done this or that." May I suggest that you just accept where you are and let go of your self-destructive thinking? Otherwise, it's like carrying around excess baggage. Have you ever been at an airport, carrying your own bags and unable to find a skycap? Soon your arms may start to ache. All your energy is directed toward moving those bags, and you're hurting more and more.

If you don't leave the past behind, you can't go forward. You can't get to second base with one foot on first.

There's a difference between forgiving and forgetting. You can forgive, but you may never forget. That's okay, because forgiving makes your memory powerless. You may always remember who or what you forgave, but the memory won't influence you negatively. You can remember lots of hurts and pain, but your memories won't affect you after you let them go.

If you don't forgive yourself it affects your energy. Take the energy you have used by not forgiving yourself, and put it to good use to move on. Renowned college football coach Lou Holtz said, "The good Lord put eyes in the front of your head so you can look and move forward, not focus on the past."

Letting go of the past and taking action are the primary keys to growth and success. Also understand that codependency and recovery issues are very important as well. Codependency means one is dependent on or is controlled by another person who is controlled by compulsive behavior, chronic illness, alcoholism, or drug abuse. Recovery is generally used when discussing alcoholism, as well as other addictions.

Recovery could also be used in a more general sense to describe when one is coming back from a challenging situation. Among other things this could include mourning the loss of a loved one, recuperating from an illness, coming out of a depression, losing a business through financial challenges, or losing a job.

We can learn to understand why we behave the way we do, what may be holding us back, and how we can change our behavior. Understanding can lead to forgiveness. There are some excellent books, support groups, and organizations available if you want to explore this further.

You need to take that first step. You need to get out of that comfort zone to grow, challenge yourself, and change your behavior. When you finally face the fact that the comfort zone (sometimes known as a rut) may actually be more of a familiar zone, it may no longer be comfortable; you're just familiar with it. It's simply a known quantity.

Forgive yourself for any injustices you may have put on others. They're over and done with. You probably did the best you could with the awareness you had at the time. In fact, you may want to write down all the things you forgive yourself for, then crumple the paper and throw it away. Once you forgive yourself, you have no reason to blame yourself for anything. You are being self-responsible and are then free to learn and grow.

I'm Hurting—*Why Do I Need to Forgive Others?*

Forgiveness of others may be more challenging. How many people do you feel you have allowed to influence you in a hurtful way? How many times have you felt that someone did you an injustice? To move on, you need to forgive them—not for them, but for yourself.

My father's passing away is a good example. It could have been a wonderful excuse. I could have used his death as an excuse when things went awry. I could have said, "If Dad had been here I'd be better off; I'd be more educated; I'd be a better person." The truth is, while he was here, he contributed everything he possibly could to my life. For me to use his absence as an excuse would have bottled up my energy and prevented me from going forward.

If you use what people did or didn't do in the past as an excuse for not moving on, you'll never achieve the success you want. If you focus on people you believe hurt you, it's difficult to focus on the future.

Remember, no one can hurt (victimize) you unless you let them! You must give them permission. No one has that power over you, unless you think they do. A lot of feeling hurt is self-pity. And when you throw a pity party, guess who shows up? No one! Saying someone hurt you is not being self-responsible. It's an excuse. Blame can be like quicksand. You could easily sink deeper and deeper into the quicksand of blame.

When asked who hurt them the most, the majority of people point to their parents. The number two response was siblings, while number three was children.

Forgiveness of others is essential for your well-being. We've all felt hurt. It's just an excuse to say, "If only I had better parents"; "If only I had a better boss"; and, "If only I had this or that when I was young."

This does not mean forgiving others is always easy. It may be a challenge, and it could take time. It is a process. Be patient with yourself. *Forgive for you, not the other person. It helps you heal.* Think about it. If you stay focused on what someone did or didn't do in the past that affected you, you can lose a lot of precious energy that could be directed toward your dreams and goals. You want to look forward and take action, rather than allow yourself to stay stuck where you are. You may need to loosen up; then let go of the control you've allowed someone else to have over you—so you can move on.

Do You Have an Easy-Going, Forgiving, or Uptight, Unforgiving Attitude?

Are you still carrying around thoughts and feelings that weigh you down? Are you still harboring hatreds and resentments toward others? It all takes energy. What happened cannot be changed, but you can forgive. Forgive for you. It's a very liberating, healing experience. Whether the other person accepts your forgiveness or not makes no difference at all. That's their responsibility. In fact, you may not even choose, or be able, to tell them. How would you feel if that person passed away before you forgave them? Even if they do, you can forgive them in your heart and let it go.

Think of the turmoil you were in before you forgave. Remember the relief you felt when you let go of a life-spoiling burden? It didn't really matter whether you needed to give or receive forgiveness, did it? The feelings were remarkably the same.

What about not forgiving? When we need to give or receive forgiveness and don't, we tend to avoid that person psychologically, emotionally, and physically. We restrict our own freedom. We cut off our options and limit our growth.

Who are we to judge others? As Dale Carnegie wrote in *How to Win Friends and Influence People,* "Never criticize, condemn, or complain." We could add to that, *never compare yourself to anyone else* either. Comparison is just a trap; someone is almost always doing better than you, and someone is almost always doing worse.

Jesus put it well in Luke when he said, "Don't worry about the speck of sawdust in your brother's eye until you take the plank out of your own." Who are we to understand others and decide if their behavior is appropriate? We need to first look inside ourselves and understand what we are about and correct our own behavior. You grow by correcting your own behavior, not by putting others down.

Live by The Golden Rule. Or go one step further, if necessary, and follow The Platinum Rule: "Do unto others as they would like to be done unto." Not everyone prefers the same treatment as you. Love the people that hate you. When you give to others, when you show them you care, it will come back to you! It may not come back from the same person(s). It may not be tomorrow or next week. It may be three, five, or ten years from now. Just let it go. Get out of your comfort zone and be confident that you'll get yours.

Ralph Waldo Emerson said, "What you are speaks so loudly, I can't hear what you're saying." What we are is who we are. It's important to recognize that we communicate who we are through our attitudes and actions, and they are often imperfect. Therefore, forgiveness of self and others is essential—on a daily basis, if necessary. Have an easygoing attitude; forgive and let go.

Ben Franklin said that "People who do things make mistakes, but they never make the biggest mistake of all, and that is doing nothing." What did we learn from our mistakes? That's what counts. How did we use the experience to better understand ourselves and others? Did we use it to avoid making the same mistake again? Did we forgive ourselves and move on?

Forgiveness is such a powerful gesture. Here's a story about a remarkable little boy. It'll remind you how empowering it is to have the right tools to face life's challenges.

Say Goodbye to Regrets and Recriminations

When we don't forgive someone, we give them power over us. We give them the power to influence us in a hurtful way, even though the event may be long over. Ironically, they may not even be aware that we have been influenced by them. They may have had good intentions, but we didn't perceive it that way. Most people are well intended in their actions. Their motive is probably self-directed to avoid pain or gain pleasure. It would seem we were denying *them* something when we refuse to forgive them. However, the reality is that when we are unforgiving, we deny ourselves freedom! We bog ourselves down with negative feelings until we forgive and let those feelings go.

Forgiving ourselves for not acting in our own best interests, or for saying or doing something we regret, is like forgiving another! Say to yourself, "I forgive you (insert your name here) for (insert the event here). I let it go." This is an act of self-love. When you do this, you are recognizing your desire to act differently in the future.

To acknowledge something is to admit it exists. Acknowledging a reality strips it of pretense, strips it of any lingering excuses that might otherwise cloud it. Acknowledging anything gives you a clean slate to work from. You can then recognize the problem for what it is and get to work on the solution. After all, *a problem is just an opportunity for a solution!*

Failure is just an event, not a person! Can you believe that? Can you forgive yourself and others for failing, and then move on to success? Reflect on and learn from your past. However, protect your vitality by knowing that *you control your future.*

Why not make an effort to forgive someone right now? Think of someone you feel has harmed you and forgive them. Envision looking them straight in the eye and saying "I forgive you (insert their name here) for (insert the event here)." You'll experience a sense of relief and feel your face soften, as you give a gift to yourself that only you can give. Do this again and again.

Making a forgiveness list is helpful. Write, "I forgive you (insert their name here) for (insert the event here)." Do this for everyone you need to forgive. One by one, give up the hurt and welcome in the peace as you resolve to forgive and move on. You may choose to tell them; you may not. What's in your heart counts more than whether they know you forgave them. Even if you don't tell them, they are likely to feel the difference in your attitude toward them. Remember, forgiveness is a process, and like anything worthwhile, it will take some time. Remember to congratulate yourself each time you successfully forgive someone.

Now, can you forgive yourself? Make a forgiveness list for yourself. Can you return to an earlier time and see yourself in a past moment? Was there a time when you did not behave as you wish you had? Perhaps it was when you failed to defend a principle or value. Maybe it was a moment of aggressiveness when you overwhelmed a vulnerable person. Forgive yourself for that failing, and you'll begin to live free of its burden. Forgive yourself for personal behaviors you don't like; maybe it's a habit you'd like to change. *Forgiveness based on honest acknowledgement frees you from regret and recrimination.*

Forgiveness Heals All Wounds
Once you understand the principles of *No Excuse!* living, they seem so

obvious, don't they? If forgiveness is practiced knowing the results are guaranteed, why isn't everyone more forgiving?

Why don't many people know that forgiveness is such a powerful tool? First of all, what we are taught about forgiveness is often misinterpreted. Take, for example, the biblical story commonly known as "The Prodigal Son." Who is the real hero of that story? Why is he frequently overlooked? The father, of course, is the hero. But the drama is stolen first by the son who goes off with his fortune and returns full of regret. It is also stolen by his brother, who hasn't yet experienced the need to ask for forgiveness or learned to grant it.

Forgiveness is a powerful healer. It can resolve difficult, painful, and complex human interactions. Forgiveness is the kind of closure human beings long for.

Do you know what a burden it is to have something undone hanging over your head? Did you ever have something expected of you that you deliberately forgot about, or didn't get around to? Did you get that sinking feeling of failure every time you thought about it?

Whether or not you are consciously thinking about issues that beg forgiveness, they negatively affect you. Get them out into the open. Say to yourself, "So you never did go back to college and finish." "So you walked out of that job when you didn't have another one waiting." "So you made promises you weren't sure you wanted to keep." Look into the eyes of that younger, less experienced, less wise you from the past and speak kindly.

Where does the power of forgiveness come from? There are two main areas: (1) Ending a wallow in guilt that may really be just an excuse to keep on doing something you are ashamed of, or (2) finally looking at a human error for what it is—a passing event that doesn't need to determine your whole future if you don't let it. Both of these actions require facing the truth and dealing with it, letting go of the past, and moving on.

When you forgive someone, it's just as freeing. *By forgiving another, you stop seeing yourself as a victim.* You may have allowed yourself to be a victim, but you can stop the endless replay of your victimization (in your mind) by forgiving.

Make Daily Deposits in Both Your Own and Others' Emotional Bank Accounts

Stephen Covey, author of *The 7 Habits of Highly Effective People,* talks about how we all have an emotional bank account. And like a financial bank account, we make deposits and withdrawals. Sometimes we may withdraw more than we deposit.

Are you depositing daily into the people in your life, or are you just withdrawing from them? Are you building up your emotional bank account or depleting it? When you treat someone with kindness, respect, courtesy, or proper instruction, you add to *your* emotional wealth. You have invested more of what you might need in the future. You have something you can count on. What you gave out will come back through the same or other source(s).

How do you make emotional withdrawals? Simply by being unkind, disrespectful, and discourteous toward others. When all you do is make emotional withdrawals from others, you are likely to lose their support. Without money, you can't pay your bills. When you have no love in your emotional bank account, it's difficult to count on other people to support your dreams and desired outcomes. Chances are you won't be able to depend on others to help you go forward if all you do is take from them emotionally.

Unforgiveness Is an Incomplete

Have you ever left anything undone? When you think about it, unforgiveness is actually an incompletion of some event in your life. Were you ever given a task you didn't finish because of other priorities? You thought something else was more important or you didn't want to do it, so you just didn't complete it. It was necessary to do, yet you always did something else instead. Did that bother you? Did it seem to control you? You knew you needed to get to it, but you never did. It sapped energy from you, didn't it? Eventually, when you finally completed it, the negative feelings left. What a relief.

Forgiveness works the same way. If you don't forgive, you're letting an incomplete interfere with your progress. Knowing this can help you have the strength and determination to forgive. You're letting it have an influence on you by your own inaction. In a sense, you're giving it permission to influence you.

If you have a document due to someone, and you don't deliver it on time, you may nag yourself about it. You take energy from yourself because you're thinking about it. You may dwell on it. Unforgiveness works the same way.

How do you forgive? Take the "for" away from forgive and you have "give." That's how you forgive. It's as simple as that! In reality though, it can be a real challenge to forgive. *The basic element in forgiveness is giving of yourself—to other people as well as to yourself.*

"As you sow, so shall you reap." Your world is a mirror of you. How you treat others is how they'll treat you, in most cases. Give kindness and you'll receive kindness. Give love and you'll receive love. You can usually get the response you want from others by treating them as you believe they want to be treated.

Forgive yourself for what you could have accomplished today but didn't. But don't use this as an excuse not to achieve what you want tomorrow. Forgive others for what they did or didn't do to you (or for you), or it'll be difficult to move forward. Don't fall into the trap of using that as an excuse either.

Like anything else, you can become excellent at forgiveness by practicing it, by living it. When you do, you'll start to feel better and have more energy. By letting go of any grudges, resentments, and hatreds, you are freeing up your precious energy, which you may have wasted before on blaming or complaining. By forgiving, you are becoming more self-responsible because you are doing it for yourself! You are doing it to help *you* to excel and receive the outcomes you want. As a result, you'll be able to help others more too.

Forgiveness of the Environment

Once you have learned to forgive yourself and others, begin focusing on your environment and your surroundings. Your environment is all the events and circumstances you experience. It is inevitable that there will be environmental factors that can't be controlled by you or anyone else. They will require your forgiveness if you are going to get on with the business of life.

Have you ever been in a traffic jam? It was no different than yesterday's jam, but you took a different route and thought you had escaped it. Did you get down on yourself for the choice *you* made? Forgive yourself and move on.

Did your car ever break down? Did you ever swear at it? Did you ever mentally beat yourself up over it? Forgive the car; don't blame it. It's doing the best it can, considering the attention it has been given! You may need to forgive yourself for not practicing preventive maintenance.

Did you ever notice how people blame the economy or the government for the way things are in their personal lives? It's easy to use what society is doing as an excuse. It's really easy. Then we don't feel the need to take action. We can simply rationalize by saying, "It's all *their* fault."

How about the weather? Did you ever use the weather as an excuse for not doing something? How does the weather affect most things? Not much at all! Yet you hear excuses all the time when some people let the environment dictate whether they will continue their planned activity. Have you ever fallen into that trap?

Will you let the weather or the activities of the state or society dictate that you can't be successful? It's easy to blame the economy. It's easy to blame the government. It's easy to blame someone or something else for having a negative impact or influence on where you want to go.

Forgiving your environment is essential before you can take charge. Do it rather than blaming something external. It's easy to blame something on the outside, even when you know in your heart that it's your internal fortitude that counts. It's an inside job. Your life is your responsibility. How you deal with it is critical. Whether you deny or accept the situations, the challenges, and the people with whom you associate, how you work with them largely determines your level of success.

When we forgive, we bring new respect to every person and circumstance we encounter. We can start fresh. There's no need to endlessly sort through the debris of the past. It would only hinder our chances to meet and handle future challenges. Where will your new respect come from? It will come from being a powerful forgiver.

The Professor Who Asked for Forgiveness

Many years ago, a professor at the University of Edinburgh was listening to his students as they presented oral readings. One young man rose to begin his recitation, but the professor abruptly stopped him. "You're holding the book in the wrong hand," he criticized. "Take your book in the right hand and be seated."

Responding to the strong rebuke, the young man held up his right arm. He had no right hand! The other students were deathly quiet and began to squirm in their seats. For a moment the professor was dumbfounded. Then he made his way to the student, put his arm around him, and with tears in his eyes said, "I regret what I said. I never knew. Please, will you forgive me?"

Sometimes, like the professor, it takes humility to ask for forgiveness. It takes knowing that no one is always correct. We need to forgive ourselves and sometimes request the forgiveness of others to move on. Otherwise we may replay the scenario over and over in our mind and regret our behavior for a long time.

Have You Ever Felt Victimized?

If you're feeling victimized (hurt) by someone or something, it is an indicator that forgiveness is needed. Most of us have felt victimized. But you need to realize that, in most cases, no one can be a victim unless they permit it.

Once again, keep this within the context of your use of energy. Where are you directing your thoughts? Where are you directing your feelings? Are they going toward the past or the future?

Certainly, it is important to understand the past. That's part of forgiveness. First, you need to recognize who or what you thought influenced you in a hurtful way. Only then can the healing process begin. In the beginning, part of that healing process is often feeling victimized. This is an important process to work through. As you forgive, you need to take responsibility for yourself and let go of the idea that you're a victim. Lack of forgiveness adversely affects your behavior and, as a result, your relationships suffer.

What Happens When We Don't Forgive?

Three main types of behavior patterns can develop as a result of lack of forgiveness. You may have seen these patterns of expression in your dealings with people, or even in yourself. The three behavioral types are: self-pitying, irresponsibly justifying, and abusing.

First you'll want to gain an understanding of each type of behavior to identify it in yourself and others. Then you can consider what the payoff is for you or others to behave in these ways. In other words, there are some perceived benefits, or the behavior wouldn't continue. For example, the payoff could be that the behavior causes the person to get more attention than they would have gotten otherwise. To change the behavior, it is important to be ready to let go of the payoff.

Self-Pitying

When someone regularly assumes the role of a victim, he or she is often in a state of self-pity. Have you ever been around someone who constantly feels sorry for himself? Have you ever felt sorry for yourself? Have you ever been around someone who "just can't believe" something has happened? They think they can't move on because of what happened! Have you ever felt that way?

This can be a natural first response to a challenging situation. Most of us have felt helpless at times—full of self-pity. You can see it reflected in behavior. People who are self-pitying get stuck. They don't get beyond this reaction to take charge of their lives and overcome their challenges.

How do you express yourself to other people? Do you often feel sorry for yourself? Or do you acknowledge the past, make an effort to grow, and move beyond it? It's easy to see this behavior in ourselves.

Irresponsibly Justifying

A person who irresponsibly justifies frequently acts irresponsible and then justifies his actions by making excuses. You can see it in his behavior. He's the one who doesn't fill-up the gas tank when it's on "E." He may have a dozen or more excuses. He's the one who leaves the garbage cans in the driveway, rather than pick them up and put them away with the lids on. Then he complains when they roll into the street and a car runs over them, even though he didn't fulfill his responsibility of putting them away.

People who irresponsibly justify simply feel justified because they believe people have hurt them or that they have failed. They feel like victims because of what has occurred. They believe they can always justify their actions. They believe they don't need to be as considerate of other people. After all, they perceive others don't have as many problems as *they* do. In reality, many other people may have more or worse situations than they do.

People who irresponsibly justify believe they don't need to be caring and giving to other people because they've been hurt. They may be full of resentment and hatred. They believe their actions toward others are justified because of what they believe life has done to them. Have you ever known someone like that? They are hurting because of not forgiving past hurts.

Most of us have felt like people who irresponsibly justify at times, justifying our actions because we have felt hurt in the past. Most of us have been at a point where we chose to focus on the past so we didn't have to make a decision in the present.

Abusing

Then you have people who act in an abusing way. They are in constant denial. They feel victimized and believe they need to have an abusive, mean attitude toward everyone; which is reflected in their thoughts, words, and actions. Most of us have felt like this at times, at least to some degree. These thought patterns also cause us to criticize ourselves. In fact, self-criticism is where it begins.

Can you see how this behavior is not being self-responsible? People with abusive attitudes don't forgive themselves or others. It is not realistic to behave like this and expect to move ahead in life. It just holds you back and keeps you stuck.

How Do You Make Decisions?

Decision-making is a fundamental cornerstone of success. Indecisiveness is devastating to your success. The ability to make decisions is essential to moving on. Do you accept responsibility for your decisions? Do you "pass the buck" if the results aren't what you wanted? Do you say, "Oh no, it's not my fault"? Instead, do as people with winning habits do. Make a decision, and then do what it takes to make it work out.

When you make a decision regarding forgiveness, follow it through with action. When you make a decision to become self-responsible, follow it through. When you make a decision to define your purpose and be successful, follow it through. Make that decision. Take action. Keep making deposits—decisions that help you move ahead—into your emotional bank account. Then, as you take action on each decision, feel your self-esteem improving. It's crucial to moving on.

Why Did I Forgive My Father?

I became a stronger person when my father died. Even though I was worried and frightened by the pitying expressions of sympathy that surrounded me, I vowed I'd make it. And I did!

I suffered for many years with the burden of not having forgiven my father for dying. Irrational? Yes, of course. However, the heartache we may experience because of our attitude toward events we have no control over is as real as any other heartache. Our suffering continues, even though we may try to hide it. It's likely to stop once we've accepted the fact that the situation occurred, and we've forgiven all parties involved, including ourselves. We can let go of our sadness and go on to live a joyful life. Lack of acceptance, i.e., continued denial and unforgiveness, kills our joy and peace of mind.

The moment came when I could acknowledge the extent of my loss. I finally felt able to look in memory into my dad's eyes. He was the man who was everything I longed to be. He was gone even though I was still eager to spend every possible moment with him.

Finally, I spoke from my heart, "I forgive you. I forgive you for not being here. I forgive you for dying." I did it for me. I did it to let go of the past, enjoy the present, and move on to the future.

What Could be Keeping You from Moving On?

Could it be that you are letting regrets prevent you from finding your way to forgiveness? Could it be the harm done when someone (intentionally or unintentionally) or something interfered with your efforts to make correct decisions? Nonetheless, you felt you had to bear the responsibility for those decisions with dignity.

Have you been caught up in a corporate, organizational, or political structure where that has happened? Were you never given the opportunity to take responsibility for and correct your mistakes? Were you never recognized for your triumphs and achievements?

Have you answered "yes" to any of those questions above? Who hasn't had some lost opportunities? Who hasn't felt hurt by people or circumstances? Most of us have. It seems to be a part of the human experience.

So, why do some people get bogged down and begin to drown in oceans of regret, blame, and self-pity? More depression results from unresolved blame than ever comes from natural causes. The more unresolved regret, blame, and self-pity you hold onto, the more burdened you'll feel. *Nothing else will hold you back as much as these negative emotions.* Holding on to your excess baggage will make it impossible for you to dance along the *Staircase of Success* and move on to live the life you want.

Are You Stuck?

Imagine yourself on a five-mile march in heavy combat boots, pulling one foot at a time from the muck and mire of regret, blame, and self-pity. Imagine getting one foot free, only to have to place it back down again, just inches forward, into that oozy swamp that seems to go on forever.

If you have the habit of regret, blame, and self-pity, you'll find that, as more events occur where you feel victimized, you'll feel more and more despondent. It's like a downward spiral. Ultimately, your regret, blame, and self-pity can add up to despair.

There is a way out! The answer to the quagmire of despair is right in front of you. It's simple. It's called forgiveness.

If it's regret that's got you bogged down, forgive yourself. Face up to the injustices you've done to yourself and others. Be courageous enough to list them on paper. You may want to share one or more of these things with a mentor or close friend, provided the relationship is strong and they have total, unconditional acceptance of you. When possible share that, given a second chance, you would do it differently (if that's true for you).

Almost everyone has faced these issues. No one with regrets ever reaches the joy and fullness of life without letting these regrets go and forgiving themselves.

Why Is It Important to Reflect?

Whenever you feel yourself wanting to glance over words in this book and hurry to the next page or section; whenever you find yourself saying, "I know that; that's nothing new; that's not what I wanted to read about," ask yourself, "Why am I so anxious to get through it?" Could it be you feel uncomfortable because the message is hitting home? Could it be stinging a bit? When you find a message that strikes a chord with you, close the book, keeping your finger in it to hold your place. Reflect a bit on the message. Give yourself time to reach a new level of understanding and acceptance in this area.

Have you been courageous enough to take responsibility for behavior you regret? Have you admitted to someone that you made a mistake? Have you been able to share all your feelings about the event? Have you forgiven yourself? It is an ultimate act of responsibility to accept what can't be changed and to move on. *Admitting your regrets doesn't mean they don't exist anymore. It means you will no longer be giving them the power to negatively influence your life or to affect your chances of helping others have a better life.* Go on; do it.

What have you done for yourself lately in this area of growth? Have regrets crept in undetected, their only symptom being that life seems heavy? Are your days beginning to be something to slog through without your really being aware of them? Do you feel burdened, as if the world is on your shoulders? Perhaps it's time to look for the "worm of discontent," and send it on its way with forgiveness.

How About Forgetting and Forgiving?

You'll never hear me say, "Forget what needs to be forgiven." Forgetting isn't really helpful when genuine forgiveness is at work. In fact, forgetting is frequently a way to avoid forgiving.

To forgive, you need to remember! That's one of the reasons forgiving can be challenging. Memories involving the need for forgiveness often include the misery or regret of the pain of reliving the painful incident. It's often easier to put the memory in the back of your mind, but that's only temporary. It'll fester until it rears its ugly head again. It's our responsibility to remember our incorrect actions if we want to avoid repeating what we regret.

Perhaps you have experienced the freedom that comes from forgiveness. Perhaps the torment has ended, and you have peace of mind because you forgave yourself or someone else.

When true forgiveness takes hold, you'll forget about unimportant things. They are discarded like old, worn out clothes. They no longer clutter your life and are easily left behind as you press on.

Teamwork Makes the Dream Work

This is the key. You rarely hear about forgiveness as a prerequisite of success. Yet it's the first step in moving forward with your life. Why is it important to give to other people? Doesn't society often define success as getting on top as fast as you can? Why consider the feelings of other people? Why take into consideration the teamwork, the team-building aspect of success?

It's simple. You can't become successful alone! Build your success on forgiveness and you're likely to attract a number of people to assist you. People, in most cases, will feel safer with you and more accepted by you when you have a forgiving nature. This doesn't mean you are acting like a doormat. You can still be assertive and forgiving at the same time. No matter how assertive you are, people will still need to be forgiven for improper behavior.

The decisions you make about forgiveness are crucial, yet most people simply don't realize it's related to success. When you practice forgiveness, it can make a big difference in your life.

Your dreams can come true. Set your mind and heart to something you love, and you can achieve it. Even if you don't receive the exact outcome you want, you'll be better off for striving. Forgiveness can be a wonderful aspect of achieving your dreams and goals. You can give yourself peace of mind with forgiveness. Some people may avoid forgiving because it hurts; it opens up some feelings. Be forgiving anyway. It's essential to your success, happiness, and fulfillment.

What happens when you incorporate forgiveness into your life? You begin to be more self-responsible. Think about it. When you're not blaming and complaining, you're taking charge. It can be a challenge because you are more vulnerable as you open up to more people. But *vulnerability is an important part of relationships. It helps you reveal the real you and is the essence of true and lasting friendships.* Sometimes this is an unexpected result of forgiveness.

When you begin acknowledging areas where you still need to grow, you'll be on the correct path, and something exciting can happen. You'll probably notice that everyone else needs more development in certain areas too, and that it can be fun to work and grow together, helping each other. Just say it's okay. It's okay to make mistakes. You're human. It comes with the territory!

As you employ forgiveness, you'll gain more control over your life. You'll feel less stressed and more optimistic about the future.

Chapter 6
HAVE SELF-ESTEEM
Second Step of the Thesaurus Factor

As defined by The McGrane Center for Personal Transformation, whose ideas I've integrated into the *No Excuse!* philosophy, "Self-esteem is the respect you *feel* for yourself." It is absolutely essential for success. You cannot respect others, either, until you first respect yourself. "You can only give to others what you have, nothing more!

"Self-esteem is at the core of all you think, say, do, and feel." It affects the seven key areas of life: Spiritual, Mental, Physical, Family, Social, Financial, and Career. Your self-esteem is always changing, and always in process; it is intangible and recognizable by your behavior. As a result, you may feel a lot of self-respect one minute, not much the next.

"Self-esteem is not a result of your income, reputation, occupation, race, the clothes you wear, your religion, educational level, ethnic background, possessions, sex, home, car, or zip code. It does not depend on your objectives or your net worth. Noted psychiatrist and author Carl Jung said, 'Simple things are always the most difficult. In actual life, it requires the greatest discipline to be simple, and the *acceptance of self* is the essence of the problems of a whole outlook upon life.'"

Many people base their lives on spiritual beliefs. The religions of the world offer such core beliefs as: "All life is sacred," (Hinduism); "Gaining a complete knowledge of the inner self," (Buddhism); "Love thy neighbor as thyself," (Judaism/Christianity). Unfortunately, in the past the Western Judeo/Christian culture did not encourage us to love ourselves. It was often considered egotistical and unacceptable. Yet we need to first love ourselves before we can love others!

Self-esteem, then, is at the core of moving toward spiritual excellence. You can only respect others when you feel respect for yourself. You will learn, grow, have peace of mind, be generous, manage, lead, accept differences and responsibility, have Total Unconditional Acceptance (T.U.A.), love, sell, teach, parent, and behave in general, based on your self-esteem. Once again, you can only give away what you possess.

Have you ever believed you had what would bring you happiness? Did you ever feel satisfied while feeling something was missing? That's called being unfulfilled. Remember, no one has perfect behavior; we are all learning. We all make mistakes, yet we all have talents and skills. We all need other people; no one is an island unto themselves. Self-esteem enables us to communicate, work together, and achieve. People with self-esteem are more likely to be happy.

Value judging is the only thing that will injure or destroy your self-esteem. When you value judge, you're comparing your value to that of others. About 90 percent of value judging is done on the subconscious level; you don't even realize you are doing it. However, you *feel* it! Some examples of value judging include: labeling, name calling, sarcasm, controlling, manipulating, put-downs, comparing, criticism, and putting people on a pedestal.

We were all born with self-esteem. It's our birthright! As babies, we were open, curious, loving, spontaneous, and accepting. We didn't have the skill to nurture and build our self-esteem. Since we were dependent on others for our survival, we learned self-image behavior. We discovered that we were accepted and included by what we did or had. Parents, siblings, relatives, teachers, friends, television, and society all taught us self-image behavior. Society taught us that feelings were *not* as important as knowledge, and acquiring and having material things. Once your self-esteem is replaced by self-image behavior, you never reclaim it until you have somebody who unconditionally supports you, someone like a mentor, who is genuinely interested in you and can help you reclaim your self-esteem and make it a skill. You may live your life by self-image behavior if you wish, but be prepared to always be value judging and comparing. That's a sad way to live.

It is true that some people use the word self-image when what they really mean is self-esteem. These people are well-intended. However, like the rest of us, they were probably taught self-image languaging. As the old cliché goes, "Say what you mean and mean what you say." It's so very important to our relationships, success, and happiness.

How Important Is Self-Esteem?

How can you achieve success if you don't respect yourself? Why would you want to? You'll always doubt what you can achieve if you don't respect yourself. So why do some people lack self-respect?

When you define success for yourself, develop a purpose, and begin to forgive, you'll start to *feel* better about who you are. *Success results in bringing out the best in you. Its essence is inside you.* It is an inside experience way before it manifests itself in an outcome which may be visible to others. *Your self-esteem affects all your thoughts and actions.* Without it you are lost; you can never be truly successful. Self-esteem is, in fact, a life and death issue!

How you feel about yourself will help determine the direction you take. How and what you think will largely determine what you become. And as much as we're talking about principles, the secret to success is, in fact, how and what you think and feel. Employ the correct principles, and feel respect for yourself and who and what you are, and you'll be a success.

In his classic, *As a Man Thinketh*, James Allen writes:

A man's mind may be likened to a garden. Just as a gardener cultivates his plot, keeping it free from weeds, and growing the flowers and fruits which he requires, so may a man tend the garden of his mind, weeding out all the wrong, useless, and impure thoughts, and cultivating toward perfection the flowers and fruits of correct, useful, and pure thoughts. By pursuing this process, a man sooner or later discovers that he is the master gardener of his soul, the director of his life. He also reveals, within himself, the laws of thought. He understands, with ever-increasing accuracy, how thought forces and mind elements operate in the shaping of his character, circumstances, and destiny.

What Are You Cultivating?

Like a garden, a *No Excuse!* life requires growth in many directions. You'll learn how to develop deeper roots. You'll be better able to draw inspiration from other people and events as you strengthen your purpose and resolve.

Your growth will be determined by how eager you are to learn new things and take on new opportunities, challenges, and experiences. You'll likely be better able to deal with whatever comes your way. You will learn how to grow and prosper, even through challenging times. I believe you will find that self-esteem is essential to accomplishing these things.

Would you like to have more self-esteem, that is, feel more respect for yourself? Does your language and thinking support your self-esteem? The following sections will help you determine that.

How Do You Create an Affirming Self-Esteem Lifestyle?

What would it be like for you to be free of devaluing yourself? Do you ever wonder what it would take to really enjoy yourself, others, and daily life? People have been asking these questions since the beginning of time. Is getting to the root of these issues important to you?

Many say, "Give me success and I'll figure out how to live with it later." Living a self-esteem lifestyle begins by knowing how you feel and the outcomes you want.

If you always do what you've always done, you'll always get what you've always gotten. Most adults tend to determine their wants intellectually, without consulting their physical or emotional feelings. Just because you were hugged, loved, well-educated, have traveled the world, and have wealth and power, doesn't guarantee you'll feel good about yourself. You need to consciously choose self-esteem. Start by getting in touch with your feelings, both physical and emotional. Then you will begin to recognize the outcomes you really want.

Does Your Language Support Your Self-Esteem?

Words create feelings! Self-esteem is *a feeling*. What language do you use in your self-talk? Examine this, because what you say to yourself will create feelings.

As you go to seminars, read books, listen to CDs, and watch DVDs, you may see and hear many words being identified as self-esteem. Let's consider the following words and definitions:

Thinking A mental process using the logical or left side of the brain.
Feeling An emotional state of consciousness using the right side of the brain.
Egotism Self-centeredness. Constant excessive reference to oneself. Conceit. "Unsatisfied hunger for self-esteem." (Robert H. Schuller)
Self-Concept What you think about your developed and undeveloped areas (skills).
Self-Confidence A belief or trust in yourself. It is a skill developed over time.
Self-Image An imitation or representation of a person. It is what one would like to project to the world. You might even think of image as an acronym for "I Measure and Gauge Everyone"! (In other words, image is based on value judging and comparison.)
Self-Esteem The respect you *feel* for yourself. It is *a feeling*. Be aware of what you say to yourself and how it affects your behavior. Research shows one second of negative thinking takes ten seconds before you can entertain a new thought or feeling.

What's Involved in Self-Esteem?

Much like plants, human beings depend on nourishment for endurance. However, unlike plants, we can become aware of who we are, envision what we want to be, and then make it happen.

Who do you think you are? Now there's a question most often asked with an edge. And it's usually asked by someone shocked at another's presumption. Let's play with that idea.

Bill McGrane II, founder of The McGrane Center for Personal Transformation and author of *Brighten Your Day with Self-Esteem,* said:

> *Self-esteem is the core of a person's physical, mental, and spiritual well-being. You can instantly observe a person's self-esteem by the way they treat you. The entire focus is on a very difficult word for many people: love. First, have love for yourself; then, and only then, can you love anyone else. In other words, you can give only what you have and no more.... Self-Esteem is the respect you feel for yourself.*

Babies begin understanding their place in the world by gradually discovering who they are. It is sometimes an alarming discovery and often leads to a loud cry to be held. The baby needs to feel safe, contained, and part of a bigger being.

As time goes on, experience usually teaches the child that it can creep, crawl, walk, run, and tumble. In most cases, it eventually realizes it can independently explore all that lies within reach.

How many times have you held a child who was squirming to get out of your arms? His head and body twisted and turned to keep in sight the delight that had his attention. He envisioned having what he saw and was filled with desire to satisfy that want. Every time a child's desires are understood and respected, not merely fulfilled, a leap in self-esteem occurs.

Self-esteem begins at birth. We are all born with pure potential. As children we were uninhibited and unafraid until we were taught to be otherwise. All the things we could be or do will never be realized in our lifetime. Therefore, making choices will always be a necessary part of life.

Who Affects Children's Self-Esteem?

When you were born all you had was *you!* Babies are like a clean sheet of paper. How parents (including other caregivers who assume the parental role) treat their children has a big impact on how the children feel about themselves. Parents have an opportunity to help their children grow up to be adults with self-esteem. To do this, it is crucial that parents develop their own self-esteem. Parents cannot teach children self-esteem behavior if they don't practice it themselves. Admittedly, there are other factors affecting children's self-esteem. Teachers, friends, acquaintances, and other societal influences (e.g., TV) all have an impact. However, parents, to a much greater extent, serve as role models. How parents treat their children affects their self-esteem.

Children take chances based on how they were parented. Parents need to teach their children to recognize and develop their ability to make choices. This will help the child realize his greatest potential, satisfaction, and fulfillment. The ultimate goal is that the children will feel respect for themselves, that is, have self-esteem.

Fear of Failure and Rejection Holds People Back

Fear of failure is fear of yourself (doing something), while fear of rejection is fear of others (not accepting you). Experiencing some fear is natural, but because of your new understanding, your fear no longer has to be an obstacle to your success. No matter what happens, if you're honest and sincere, you are less likely to fear failure. If you live your life in a way you feel is important, a way that goes along with your values and beliefs, you're not likely to fear rejection either. When your self-esteem is intact, the more likely you are to eliminate those fears.

With self-esteem, you're likely to take greater risks. With self-esteem, you're less likely to fear failure and rejection. When you know who you are, respect yourself, and know where you're going, you won't be concerned about what others may think or say about you and what you say and do.

An important part of success is overcoming resistance. An airplane needs to overcome air resistance to fly. A boat needs to overcome the resistance of water and wind to move ahead. Winners overcome various resistances to succeed.

To be a successful leader, you need to overcome the resistance of yourself and other people. Salespeople cannot be effective unless they learn to overcome resistance to rejection. With self-esteem, you are not likely to be affected by rejection. It all boils down to self-respect and belief in yourself.

How you perceive and what you believe about yourself helps structure what you achieve. It all depends on your self-esteem.

The more you know yourself the more likely you are to allow yourself to become more vulnerable. You will tend to open up more to other people. You are more comfortable with yourself. Are you sure you want to let people see who you really are? It's okay not to be sure at first. Can you openly and honestly present yourself to others with the attitude, "Here I come, faults and all," while still working to develop your skills? Initially, this idea can cause a great internal conflict until you are peaceful with yourself and who you are. Are you willing to stop faking people out with an image and be the real you instead? It takes courage and you can do it.

Once you reach an understanding about yourself and recognize who you are, it gets easier to open up and let others recognize who you are. The rejection we perceive from others often starts with us and the rejection we give ourselves. We can cause ourselves a lot of pain when we reject ourselves. In other words, once you accept yourself, you open the door for others to accept you more easily.

Fear of failure. Fear of rejection. How many people do you know who are living their lives based on everyone else's expectations? How many people pleasers do you know? Are you one of them? Have you ever operated by trying to please other people? Have you ever thought people wouldn't like you, or may even reject you, if you didn't please them? Did you ever stop to think that your perception of what pleases someone may be incorrect? Well, *people pleasing doesn't work.* When you do what is truly correct for you, without harming others, it will be correct for them also. They may not realize it at first, but they will eventually. Stick with your convictions. You're the only one who truly knows how you feel.

How can you achieve success in your life if you live it based on what others expect from you? Do you find yourself getting angry and wondering, "When will it be my turn"? Maintain self-esteem and you'll never have that attitude. With self-esteem, if you choose to please someone it will be because you feel happy doing so, not out of fear of rejection or obligation.

The key is, don't let the outside world or society try to manipulate you into doing things that aren't on your agenda. You'll probably feel used and abused if you do. It's your life, and you'll be more respected by yourself and others when you take charge and say no to people when necessary.

What Do You Think You're Worth?

Keep things in perspective. You are a valuable and worthwhile person; you were born that way. You most likely wouldn't be where you are already if you didn't have some special qualities, skills, talents, and gifts. Again, ask yourself, "What do I love about myself?" "What makes me the person I am?" It's so important to recognize those things about yourself and to also instill this sense of self-appreciation in your children.

Our children are inundated every day by what society thinks they *should* be, have, wear, and do. If they're not wearing certain sneakers and clothes, are they considered worthless and odd? If they're not listening to a particular type of music, are they thought of as unacceptable? Blind conformity is a sign of poor self-esteem.

Consider the idea of self-worth. If society considers acquiring money makes you worthy, are you worthless if you're not doing that? *How you feel about who you are and how important you think you are determines how much you let what others say influence you.* When you know you are worthy because you were born that way, your confidence can't be shaken when faced with society's false external value system for determining worthiness. After all, we were all created equally worthy in the eyes of God. He didn't make any junk! We were born to succeed, while society often conditions us to fail.

Self-esteem is vital. You will never achieve true success if you don't feel respect for yourself. Remember that *success and happiness come along the way, not just at the end of the road.* By then the journey is over. Happiness is for today, not just tomorrow! After all, tomorrow may never come. Live each day in the moment, because all you really have is now and it's gone. Tomorrow is guaranteed to no one. Sir Edmund of Canterbury said, "Work as though you can live forever. Live as though you were going to die tomorrow."

How Do Criticism and Love in Childhood Affect Fear of Failure?

Two conflicts can occur in children. *The first is the conflict between corrective discipline and criticism.* Children are born with pure potential. Often, however, their parenting (discipline is a major factor) determines how much they fear risk, failure, and rejection.

When children are constantly exposed to criticism, they often develop fear of failure which, as you'll recall, is a fear of self. They develop the fear of trying something new. They fear they won't be able to do it. As a result, they are likely to feel disappointed, possibly angry, and fearful of criticism. When children are criticized all the time, they cannot grow and develop self-esteem.

Criticism is a clever symptom of insecurity. How many youngsters could have excelled in sports, arts, music, or academics, if they hadn't felt defeated by a parent's expectations of perfection? How many children have been discouraged by a parent's laughter at their so-called unrealistic idea? How many parents have put down their children when they tried to achieve something that was important to them? Was this behavior caused by the parent's general lack of success and vision for both themselves and their children? Or, did the parents try to live vicariously through their children, hoping or expecting them to achieve something at which the parents failed?

"Take care" is an innocent cliché parents and other adults often use. Yet these two words may have done more harm than you might believe. While well-intended, these words can set up an over-cautiousness that leads to fear. When someone is facing an obstacle, challenge, or setback, it might be better to say, "Take a chance." After all, life is an opportunity. Without taking a chance, nothing much happens.

Remember the children's book, *The Little Engine That Could,* by Watty Piper? If you constantly tell that little engine that it can't get over the mountain to deliver the candy and toys to the girls and boys, it probably never will. Parents are usually their children's most influential role models, and therefore they can be their greatest mentors. Children are likely to believe what they hear from their parents more than anyone else. What do you want your children to believe about themselves?

When you yell, criticize a child with anger, or attack their personhood, why would they ever have any need to try something new? Why would they want to take the risk?

Suppose your child came into a room, bumped a lamp and broke it, and you said, "You stupid idiot, you broke the lamp. Go up to your room, I don't want to see your face anymore." That's criticism, which many of us have experienced.

Corrective discipline would address the *behavior,* rather than attack the child. Remember that discipline means a disciple of, a way to behave; a way to speak; a way to sing. To criticize means to find fault with the person! Discipline the behavior rather than attack the child.

When using corrective discipline, either with yourself or others, deal with the behavior only and make suggestions to correct for errors and goofs. *A person is not their behavior.* You and others can always correct for errors. No one needs to fail at living.

Corrective discipline might go like this: First, identify what is really going on inside of you? How do you feel? Are you remembering things you heard as a child, or are you able to be objective and deal only with the behavior?

Second, own your feelings by describing them with "I statements." For example: "Jamie, I'm unhappy (sad, angry, uncomfortable) that the lamp was broken." Now say exactly why you feel this way. "The lamp was from your grandmother and had sentimental value to me. I realize it can be replaced; however, I need to deal with my feelings about this particular lamp. You may be able to identify how I feel because of how you would feel if a car ran over your bike."

Third, affirm the child and give them the opportunity to describe their feelings. "Jamie, I know you didn't mean to break the lamp. How do you feel about what happened?" Allow the child to release the feelings that are going on inside, whether they're appropriate, extreme, or nonchalant. Do your best to practice unconditional love at this moment, with no judgment.

Once the child completes describing her feelings, proceed to the last step.

The final step is to go for the solution. What is done is done; it cannot be undone. What are the consequences and responsibility of the behavior? Ask the child, "Jamie, what responsibility do you feel you need to accept for the broken lamp?" Listen for the response, as it will let you know the child's *ability to respond;* that is, you will know immediately how responsible the child is at this particular time.

You may need to say, "Jamie, may I suggest you accept responsibility for your behavior by replacing the lamp? We can go to the store and choose one. You can pay for it with your allowance, your savings, or the money you make doing odd jobs. We can come up with a payment plan once we know the cost of the new lamp. I realize you may not like this outcome; however, it is important you learn to accept responsibility for your behavior. We all make mistakes; and it is up to us, individually, to correct our own errors."

Although idealistic, this response respects the child and maintains her self-esteem. This acknowledges her mistake and separates who she is from her behavior. Corrective discipline may require more thought and time on your part. It takes time to describe feelings, ask questions, and listen to yourself and the child. In the long run, you and your child's self-esteem will be enhanced. You will also be teaching the child how to accept responsibility and discover appropriate behavior for all the situations he or she will encounter in life.

Most people fear failure at some time, regardless of their childhood experiences; it's only human. Therefore, your self-esteem may need repair from criticism. Your self-esteem determines how much you let fear of failure control your thinking and performance. This is true in both your business and personal life.

The second conflict that occurs in children is the one between conditional and unconditional love. Conditional love is given only if something is expected from the beloved. Unconditional love is the pure giving of love, without expecting anything in return.

When children are exposed to conditional love, they frequently develop the fear of rejection. They feel their parents won't love them unless they perform as expected. They don't feel loved just for being themselves. The child feels rejected and his self-esteem gets injured.

I believe everybody wants to be loved and accepted. Some people will do almost anything to get it. They don't realize that if they need to do something to be loved, that's conditional love. To receive it requires the constant effort of performance. They get caught up in a treadmill of doing, only to earn fleeting and unfulfilling conditional love. They end up in the vicious cycle of pleasing people to get conditional love and approval. When we have self-esteem, however, we can handle the rejection of others who may not have our best interests at heart. By confidently handling their rejection, we can acquire the respect of even those who dislike us; we can also find out who our real friends are by how they love us. Fairweather friends love us only conditionally. Real friends love us unconditionally. As is true for most people, you may not have many real friends. When you implement *No Excuse!* principles, you are likely to develop more real friendships.

Here's a little story that illustrates unconditional love…

Occasionally, I would be asked to appear as a success consultant on the early morning news for a local television station. One morning after I got out of the shower, I found the note "I love you, Dad," written across the steamed-up mirror. Without my knowing it, my daughter, Nicole, came quietly into the bathroom while I was in the shower and left the note.

That's an example of unconditional love; she didn't expect anything in return. She made my day! It was the most important thing that happened all day. No matter how things went on the job, it didn't matter. I had been loved unconditionally that morning, and it was all I needed.

It is necessary for children, troops, and the people we lead or influence to understand the limits of acceptable behavior and to be self-disciplined. Their willingness to live a *No Excuse!* life will depend on their self-esteem and the respect they have for themselves and others.

Troops who know their commander has a sincere interest in them are more likely to be inspired to achieve victory. Members of an organization who know their leader cares are likely to perform far better than when there is little or no regard shown for them.

Children need to know they are unconditionally loved and respected by their parents, regardless of their achievements or failures. No matter what our age, it makes a difference to be loved unconditionally. It's one of the reasons being a parent who is loved unconditionally by the children can be such a deep human experience.

Young children give us unconditional love. Why would we give *them* anything less? If you have any doubts about the value of developing intact self-esteem (which includes unconditional love for yourself), and working to maintain it, remember that you can't give what you don't have. You need to have self-esteem and unconditional love for yourself first before you can nurture anyone else's self-esteem and give them unconditional love.

Be sure to smile more often—unconditionally. It can help brighten a per-

NO EXCUSE! I'M DOING IT—JAY RIFENBARY

son's day, as well as your own! Smile without expecting one in return, and you'll probably get a smile back anyway. A smile is universal and lets others know you're friendly.

Unconditional love is not the norm. But when you give it to other people, it is likely they'll feel better, and so will you. Remember, what you give out to others comes back to you, if not from them, then another. In other words, "What goes around comes around"!

Self-Esteem Is Your Birthright

One of the greatest gifts a parent can give to nurture children is to encourage them to have a wholesome respect for and belief in themselves. Parents can model and teach the skills that lead children to better understand their own uniqueness and capabilities.

Of course, not all parents are even aware of their own talents and potential. All too often our parents are ill-equipped to be parents. With all the wonderful things our parents pass on to us, especially the gift of life, they may hand us some less desirable things as well.

Everyone who aspires to be fully mature needs to sort through the lessons learned at home. This is not an indictment of our parents for their imperfect behavior. Be thankful for the valuable lessons they gave us. And other than learning what not to do, we need to lay aside teachings and experiences that have hindered us.

We spoke earlier of the importance of forgiveness. Here's a real opportunity to forgive. Search your memory for instances when you felt injured in your childhood (mentally, emotionally, and physically), not with the thought of an eye for an eye (retaliation), but with the intent to forgive. Accept that you may have to work through some painful anger to get to forgiveness. You can do it if you keep your eye on the prize. By forgiving, you can reclaim the self-esteem that you had when you were born.

When you follow The Golden Rule you'll be better prepared to forgive yourself for damaging another's self-esteem or injuring them in some other way. In the new awareness of your own restored self-esteem, you're more likely to resist attacking others. You'll reject putting down others as unrewarding and unworthy behavior, which the old you may have used in an attempt to repair your self-esteem. You have had the opportunity to learn that this technique is ineffective.

Parents have a responsibility to guide their children and fulfilling it can be risky. Some parents never try; that's called abandonment. Parents can live in the same home as their children and still abandon them in many important ways. Some parents are mentally childish themselves, and know only limited and often spiteful ways to deal with others, including their own children. Some parents have been so unskillfully parented themselves, that they have developed only ineffective patterns which govern their parenting abilities. These patterns can be passed on from generation to generation if no one realizes what harm is being done. With awareness, the pattern can be broken and replaced with skillful behavior.

No matter where poor parenting stems from, the fruits are often all too much the same. Fear of failure and rejection can plague the child's growth in such an environment. *To the extent a child is given love and nurturing, along with corrective discipline, his fears will probably be minimal and most likely won't interfere with his personal growth and development.* The more a child is denied unconditional love and respect, the more his self-esteem may be damaged, and the more his belief in his potential may be negatively influenced.

Who Is That Person in the Mirror?

On average, 75 to 80 percent of our self-talk is likely to be negative! Fortunately, with practice, this can be changed. When you wake up in the morning, are you thinking positively about yourself and the day ahead? Do you look in the mirror and say, "I'm excited and happy; this is a great day to be alive"? Do it tomorrow morning and see how you feel. Repeat it several times if necessary.

What you see in others is a mirror of you. You can only see qualities in others that you had, have, or are developing in yourself. Your reflection will undoubtedly be your direction. How you perceive and feel about yourself, in many cases, determines the path you take.

Self-esteem is vital. To even begin succeeding, you need to respect yourself enough to believe (even a little bit) that you can do it and that you deserve success. Henry Ford said, "If you think you can or you think you can't, you're right."

Tomorrow is promised to no one. Be happy now. As Lincoln said, "A man is about as happy as he makes up his mind to be."

With self-esteem, you are more likely to make each day count. This is your life; it's not a dress rehearsal! Your life on this earth is like a movie. It has a beginning and an end. What would you do if you had a year to live? Are you doing it? If not, why not? What's preventing you from living the life you want? A lack of self-esteem?

Our attitude toward the world around us depends on our personal history, our qualities, our beliefs, and how we feel about ourselves. If we have a selfish attitude, we are likely to be suspicious of others. If we have a generous attitude, we are likely to be more trusting. If we are honest with ourselves, we are unlikely to anticipate deceit in others. If we behave fairly, we probably won't expect to be cheated by others. In a sense, looking at the people you've most closely surrounded yourself with is like looking at yourself in a mirror. You'll probably find that as you personally develop, you'll attract more personally developed people into your life. Furthermore, you may no longer be able to relate to some friends who have chosen not to grow with you. This often happens when we choose to move on and have the self-esteem to know that it's okay!

Replace Can't with Won't

Our early childhood experiences teach us to expect certain things from ourselves and the world. Take the Omar Bradley story, for instance. The nature of his childhood experiences helped foster his self-esteem, which greatly impacted his later life.

Sometimes what we were taught as children was incorrect. Later, after we leave home, we are more exposed to the world where negative expectations may predominate. This thinking can cast a gloom on life. Our behavior patterns, if based on our negative thinking, tend to produce the negative results we expected. On the other hand, if we were to expect positive outcomes, our behavior patterns could adjust accordingly to produce positive results. In other words, life is a self-fulfilling prophecy.

You may have entered adulthood with preconceptions that are, in fact, misconceptions. However, you can liberate yourself from these. "So how do I do that?" you ask. "How do I sort out misconception from reality?" Reading excellent books about personal and professional growth can help you tremendously. Listening to CDs of people whose thinking is clear and on-target can boost your understanding. Associating with people living in integrity with their purpose and committed to growing and serving can really help.

Every time you want to say can't, discipline yourself to hold that thought. Can't means it isn't possible. You give away your power and abandon your responsibility when you say can't. Instead, say won't, and see what happens. Suddenly, you're in control. Can't is usually just an excuse, a cover-up for poor self-esteem. Can't usually means you're afraid to face someone with the truth that you don't want to do something.

Saying "I can't ski," for instance, may mean many things. Maybe you've never seen snow, never had skis on, or never had anyone show you how. Perhaps you skied a few times and didn't do well. You let yourself feel discouraged and quit before you succeeded.

Saying "I won't ski," (or, "I choose not to ski,") takes self-esteem and an understanding of the issue. You won't vacation where it's cold and snowy, or you won't budget for skiing lessons. You may have explored skiing as recreation and did not find it satisfying enough to invest more time and money into it. Or maybe you found something else you'd rather do.

When you say "I won't," or, "I choose not to," you're being honest and clear, both with yourself and the person you're talking to. You are showing that you respect yourself and realize the decision is yours. It doesn't matter what that person may think. You weaken yourself by saying can't and empower yourself by saying won't!

Release the need to inappropriately please people; it's a dead-end street! By saying "yes" to get them to like you, you forfeit what you truly want. It may work for the moment, but shortly thereafter you begin regretting or resenting it. Have the courage to say "no." You'll feel a lot better about yourself and give your self-esteem a boost.

Personal growth begins when we start challenging the language we use to describe who we are and what we are capable of doing. It's wiser *choosing* not to do something, instead of projecting ourselves as unable. We feel more in control and our self-esteem is maintained.

What does it mean to ski? Who can't slide down a hill on two boards? "But that isn't skiing," you say. Even though you may not think it is, someone else may! If you look at it that way, you can indeed ski…to some extent anyway. If you still choose not to, that's OK. It's your decision; you're in control.

What do you think excited audiences when Peter Pan exclaimed, "I'm flying," while zooming around a Broadway stage suspended by a wire? They exclaimed with Peter because he was flying. When you're doing something, you're doing it! Forget the can't. It's only an excuse! So this was a kind of flying made possible by extraordinary means. Most worthwhile things are done with help.

Honesty and integrity are at work when we are brave enough to replace "can't" with "won't" or "I choose not to"! This empowers us to develop the habit of being honest with ourselves and others.

You may be reluctant to let go of the "can't" because it often came from a safe part of childhood. "Won't," on the other hand, may seem risky. When parents or adults say "you can't do that" to a child, the message often has to do with safety. "You can't cross the street alone," for instance, comes with a heavy-duty warning. It really means you aren't allowed, rather than you're unable. On the other hand, when a child uses "I won't," it often brings a scolding. Therefore, a child may learn to say "I can't," when "I won't" is really what he means. "I can't" seems safer.

For every positive statement a child hears, he or she, on average, hears fourteen negative ones. They are often statements like: "Don't do that"; "You can't do that"; "You're no good for nothing"; "Sit down and shut-up"; "You'll never amount to anything." By the time the child is eighteen, on average, he's heard something negative over 148,000 times! No wonder his self-esteem gets damaged.

When we begin to believe the "can'ts" that fill our thoughts and language, our self-esteem takes a hit. How you feel about yourself largely determines what you will attempt, let alone achieve. All the great motivators have told us this. If you believe you have a chance to get what you want out of life, you have a reason to work for it. If you still don't believe you have a chance, keep growing and repair your self-esteem. You'll find you'll have more energy, more enthusiasm, and more desire to achieve your goals.

Stop and Smell the Roses

Stop and smell the roses. Say "Thank you" to yourself every once in a while. Appreciate who you are and what you do. Appreciate the wonderful things—the little joys in life.

Did you ever have a child graduate from preschool? It may seem insignificant, but it's a day when most children are very happy with themselves. It's a real self-esteem booster. It may seem inconsequential in the overall scheme of things, but it's very important to the child and often the parents. Enjoy these little successes along with your child.

How about a boy's or girl's climb up the ranks of their Boy or Girl Scout organization or their development of musical talent? It may seem so simple, yet it can make such a difference in the child's self-esteem. These things can be an important part of a child's life as he or she becomes an adult. They have created a foundation of success that they can repeat in other areas. Your interest in your child's development here is crucial. It's part of *No Excuse!* living.

Forget about work for a while. Forget about everything that's going on out there. Take a look inside and realize that some of the joys in life you experience are much more important than your daily routine. When we can remember and appreciate these things and take delight in them, we are stopping to *smell the roses;* we're creating more joy in our lives.

We're not talking about anything new here. This is just to refresh and renew you. It isn't anything revolutionary. It's just a way to inspire and help you motivate yourself to experience the fullness of life. It's a way to help you put things into perspective. Tomorrow after you go to work and come home, or whatever it is you do every day, you can say, "Yes. I'm glad to be alive."

Forgiveness is important. Belief in who you are is important. Self-esteem is important. It is also important to instill these things in your spouse, children, other loved ones, and the people around you, even at work and other places.

In the work environment, we may often get the message that these things don't matter. Instead, the emphasis is often on: "You've got to make that quarterly report; you've got to make that bottom-line; you've got to make sure you get this and that done." It will probably get done. But if you destroy yourself in the process of getting there, what do you have? You may develop poor health and a broken family who wouldn't take any more of your neglect and abuse.

If you live your life based on what everybody else expects from you, what do you have left? You may find yourself a thin, broken-spirited shell, deeply frustrated that you didn't do what *you* wanted to do with your life. This is part of the midlife crisis. You may have accomplished a lot with your career but didn't take the time to enjoy anything. How can you be happy unless you enjoy the journey?

When you're constantly responding to the barrage of demands and ex-pectations placed on you, your self-esteem suffers. If you watch the TV news and read the newspapers, it's easy to get the idea that things are not right, they're not going well, and the whole world's falling apart. You can see how this affects everyone around you, including your family. You can really bum yourself out!

How can you better deal with all this negativity around you? How do you enhance your self-esteem? One way is to take time to "stop and smell the roses." Take time to engage in a sport, hobby, or recreation. Reward yourself along the way. Remember, "All work and no play makes Jack a dull boy." It's OK, and maybe even essential, to do without these things for a period of time when you are focusing on a business goal, for exam-ple. This may be a necessary part of delayed gratification. Then, in the future, you may integrate some sport, hobby, or recreational activities back into your life.

The *Do-Right* Philosophy

In his book, *Fighting Spirit,* Coach Lou Holtz presented a wonderful way to enhance self-esteem. It's called the *Do-Right* Philosophy. It can help you to maintain a sense of integrity within yourself.

First of all, *do the right thing.* What does that mean? It means *be honest and sincere* in everything do you. How could this not make you feel good about who you are? It's when you jeopardize your integrity and are dishonest, that you open the door for excuses to take over. When we are not true to ourselves, when we're not honest, when we don't maintain a sense of integrity within ourselves, it's very easy to relinquish responsibility. It's very easy not to be in control of where we want to take our lives. When you maintain that sense of doing the right thing, of being honest and sincere no matter what, you'll feel good about who you are. It's so simple, it's almost insulting. But it's so hopeful that such a simple thing can have such a major influence on your feelings of well-being.

When faced with a choice, are you decisive or indecisive? Rosa Parks is a perfect example. She said, "I've had it. I'm not sitting in the back of the bus anymore!" She displayed a sense of self-esteem and value, and acted with integrity.

She said "No more," and stood firm on what she believed in, no matter what the consequences. She made a decision and lived by it.

Are you willing to take responsibility for your decisions, no matter what the consequences?

Have you ever been in a situation personally, or in your career, where you could have jeopardized your integrity? Did you ever compromise your values and morals just to suit the whims of other people, or even to keep your job (or so you thought)? It can be challenging because often you need to make a decision. Do you maintain the status quo, or do you stand up for what you believe in? Are you going to do the right thing? Are you willing to tolerate that tug of war in your conscience?

Parenting is much the same way. Many are concerned over whether or not their kids like them, instead of employing correct, effective parenting skills. Think about it. If one day you say this, and the next day you say that, how can you be an effective parent?

Integrity means being decisive, being strong. It means standing up for what you believe in. When you do, you are congruent with yourself and your values. You are no longer struggling. You'll have more respect for yourself. No one is here to pass judgment or dictate what values you should have. Only you and your heart can determine that.

Secondly, *be committed to excellence.* No matter what you do, do the very best you can. Don't you feel good whenever you go all out for a goal, no matter what the outcome? If you don't pull out all the stops in your pursuit of a goal, you open the door for excuses, which lowers the degree of success you could have achieved.

Be committed to excellence in whatever you do. When you do the very best you can, you'll feel good about who you are. You'll enhance your self-esteem.

Third, *live by The Golden Rule.* No matter what faith you are or what belief you may have, treat others the way you want to be treated. Most of us want to be treated with respect, kindness, love, and sincerity. When you treat others how you want to be treated, it'll come back to you. How could you not feel good about who you are? Once again, your self-esteem will be enhanced.

If you find that *The Golden Rule* isn't working as well as you'd like with a particular person or group, use *The Platinum Rule.* Maybe their model of desirable behavior doesn't match yours. For example, a friend of mine's former administrative assistant had an illness that caused her to feel poorly in the morning. So my friend's cheery "Good morning" only irritated her since she maintained that mornings weren't good for her. She preferred "Hi" instead. This is an instance where treating someone like you would like to be treated may be ineffective. In other words, meet people at their need. If you get caught up in yourself and forget about other people's needs, it's easy to blame and complain. Do you see how everything interacts? Do you see how even forgiveness enters the picture?

Do you see how being self-responsible determines success and how purpose interacts with this? It's all part of the puzzle. *As you think and behave, so shall you become.* It's so vital to understand this. Why does it work? You'll see the whole picture better as we move along.

There are three primary questions, according to Holtz, that go along with the *Do-Right* Philosophy. **The first question he asks is,** *"Can I trust you?* Think about that. You may have asked that of your boss. Although you don't come right out and say it, still, in the back of your mind, you may question it. You may feel you have a right to question until he consistently proves he is trustworthy. Or, you may be more trusting, and trust him unless he proves he is untrustworthy.

When you go to buy a car, do you ask yourself if you can trust the salesperson? You see, to one degree or another we are likely to ask that of one another. Clients ask that of consultants. Customers ask that of a business. Parents ask that of children, and children ask that of parents. Managers ask that of salespeople, and salespeople ask that of managers. And the list goes on and on. Approaching people suspiciously is ineffective. However, it is best to be discerning.

This is why maintaining a sense of integrity is so important. What happens when someone breaks that trust? Do you feel the same about that person? Do you feel the same about that business? No way. Then what can you do? You can take a step back on the *Staircase* to *Totally Forgive!* That's why honesty and a sense of integrity are so important. Do people trust you? Always remember that honest, effective leadership paves the way for trust.

The second question is, "*Are you committed to excellence?* Wouldn't you ask that of an automobile manufacturer? Are they providing a vehicle that lives up to its advertising? Of course, you expect that. The customers and people you serve expect that from you too. In many cases, when excellence is taught at home or school, children expect it from parents, and parents expect it from children.

The Secret of Living Is Giving

The third and final question Lou Holtz posed was, *Do you care about me?* Do you care about me as a person? People don't care how much you know until they know how much you care.

Do you wholeheartedly assist, help, and support others? What you give to other people is key. True success comes through giving, which leads to a happy, fulfilled life. If you want to be successful, just help enough other people succeed. Be committed to giving of yourself to others in everything you do. You'll feel good about yourself, and you will succeed.

Do You Care About People?

As an example, let's say you go into a computer store looking to purchase a new computer. Some of us are knowledgeable about computers; some of us are not. Let's say you know very little about computers. Two salespeople are in the store.

The first salesperson comes up to you and says, "Hi, how are you? I've got a 128 MB 100 megahertz Sync DRAM TSM, with a 40 GB hard drive, with an Intel Pentium IV 700 megahertz processor with 256KB integrated full speed L2 Cache…" You may be standing there, scratching your head thinking, "I don't know what you're talking about." The salesperson says, "Do you want the computer?"

The second salesperson comes up to you and says, "Before I tell you about the features of our line, let me ask you a few questions: What specifically are your needs? What kinds of things do you want to do with it? Are you interested in desktop publishing?"

All you said was, "I want to be able to balance my checking account at home, and my kids want to play games. I don't think we need anything real high-tech."

Who would you want to deal with, the one who "knows it all" or the one who cares about your needs? The goal of both salespeople is to sell a computer. I believe you'll want to deal with the one who first cares about you and can meet your needs, even if he doesn't know all the details and consults with someone else to learn more.

Do you care about me? What a difference that makes! If you want to make a sale, show your clients you care. If you want to be a better parent, show your kids you care. If you want to be a better manager, show your employees you care. If you want to have better relationships at work, show your co-workers and boss you care. I believe you'll find that if you're going to build a team and loyalties from your people, caring about them can make a major difference in your operation. This is true for families too.

Do the right thing. Be committed to excellence. Treat others as you, or they, want to be treated. And remember the three primary questions people are likely to ask of you: 1) Can I trust you?; 2) Are you committed to excellence?; and, 3) Do you care about me? As simple as it sounds, using the *Do-Right* Philosophy will dramatically enhance your self-esteem.

Let People Know Who You Really Are—*Just Be Yourself*

Hugh Prather said, "Some people are going to like me, some people aren't. So I might as well be me because then I know that the people who like me, like *me*." Why not be yourself? Then you'll really know how others respond to *you*. You can then be confident that they are, in fact, responding to who you are and not an imitation.

No one does everything perfectly, so we can all stand to grow. We were all born with self-esteem, but it could have gotten beat up along the way. Read personal growth books, listen to personal development CDs, and attend seminars that help you grow. Put yourself on a continuing education program so you develop to where people really know who you are—so people can like the real you.

In the past, you may have hidden your real self from others, and even from yourself. This is called masking. Before you leave this earth, make sure you let people know who you really are. Let your unique talents, gifts, and skills shine through. Going to a funeral always reminds us that we're only temporary; we're just penciled in. Life is too short, so go ahead, be yourself and move on.

Make the most of yourself, because that's all there can be of you. Let go of the bonds of self-image and let people know the real you. It is gratifying to know your relationships are based on genuineness. It feels wonderful when you know that the people who like you like the *real* you; be yourself and you'll be much happier.

Unless you reach an understanding about yourself, and until you start to recognize who you are, you are unable to really open up to other people and share your real self. When you let other people in, so they can recognize you for who you are, you are also accepting yourself. If you refuse to do this, you'll get lost in the artificial image you are trying to project. Once you accept yourself unconditionally and let others know you, you've taken a major step toward achieving the outcomes you really want.

Be sure you learn more of what you are all about through your personal development program of books, CDs, and seminars. You are on a mission of self-discovery! After you know more of what you have to give, you can pass it on to others. Your self-discovery continues as you grow into the person you were meant to be. Share your unique talents, gifts, and skills with the people at home, at work, and with the world. What you have to give is important and can make such a difference. Guess who benefits the most from your growth and sharing? You do! After all, how can you achieve true success and make your dreams come true if you don't use what you were born with and developed along the way? Yes, be yourself, but also be willing to grow and become the best *you* you can be.

Self-esteem is one of the fundamental steps along the *Staircase of Success*. Forgiveness and self-esteem get you started on your success journey. With a foundation of purpose, self-responsibility, and integrity, the base of your *Staircase* is built on a solid footing.

Believing in who you are, knowing what you're about, and feeling respect for yourself are so important. To be happy and fulfilled, you want to make sure you are living your life based on what *you* expect from yourself. You don't need to let fear control you.

Say No Excuse!—*Smile and Forgive with Self-Esteem*

Once you have self-esteem, wonderful things can begin to happen. You'll want to share it with other people. You're likely to become more self-responsible. And remember, you, too, can adopt the goal of throwing out excuses. Your attitude can be that there's simply *No Excuse!* anymore. Your goal this week or this month could be to, one by one, eliminate the excuses from your life. Just do it!

When I came home from West Point one time, I decided to throw out my old excuses. Since I was accustomed to saying "No excuse, sir!", I used it on my mother. She said "Do this" or "Why don't you do that?" and I said "No excuse!" She said, "What?" It was not only productive, but fun!

Say "No excuse!" to the people you work with and they'll probably be very surprised and think, "You mean you're not going to blame anyone? You're not going to blame anything? You're not going to make an excuse for why you didn't do something?" They may not say those things out loud, but it is likely they will be thinking them.

You'll find it's catching. People will almost inevitably look at you differently. Go in smiling where you didn't smile before. When you go into work with self-esteem, it can spread to others who are interested in making a change in their lives. When you go in to work looking for something in life other than what everyone else expects, you have a better chance of finding that there's a person of worth inside you. Once you do, you'll probably want to share that with other people. How do you do that? It's reflected in your attitude and enthusiasm, the third step on the *Staircase*.

When you forgive and let go of the past, you have no reason to harbor ill feelings for other people. When you begin to live a self-esteem lifestyle, you can let go of self-doubt.

How Good Are You at Giving and Receiving Compliments?

How do you feel and respond when someone pays you a compliment? Do you say "Thank you"? Or do you say, "No big deal," or "You didn't have to say that." How you respond to another's gratitude and sincerity is an indication of whether you have self-esteem. Do you feel respect for yourself and believe you are worthy enough to receive that person's generosity? Do you realize that it is a gift they are giving you? When you negate their gift, you are doubting their judgment and rejecting their compliment. Just say "Thank you!"

Have you ever had anyone, particularly a friend, offer to buy you lunch, but you refused to let them? Do you realize how that might feel to them? Aren't you rejecting their offer? The kindest thing to do is to just say "Thank you!" Be a gracious receiver. Perhaps at a later date you can offer to buy them lunch, if you want to. Then you'll realize how good it feels when they say "Thank you" to you.

What's inside you is the only thing that can come out. You can only give what you have. If you don't have a generous attitude, you may have trouble accepting generosity. Are you open to receiving? Do you have self-esteem? Be positive. Smile often. Not only can you brighten someone else's day, but yours as well.

When you get to work tomorrow, smile at someone who never smiles. They may not smile back; it really doesn't matter. The point is, *you're* going to feel better. When you smile, you're giving a gift to the other person. You are giving them a compliment. Your smile says, "I'm happy to see you."

Remember, success comes by giving, and whatever you give away will come back to you. When you operate with self-esteem, you'll feel better about yourself and be better able to give. You'll discover that giving is fun and rewarding.

Do you feel good when you give to your place of worship or a favorite charity? How do you feel when you help an elderly person cross the street? Don't you feel good when you help someone less fortunate than you? Giving is a sign of a successful person. Giving is a sign of self-esteem.

Chapter 7
ELEVATE YOUR ATTITUDE
AND ENTHUSIASM
Third Step of the Thesaurus Factor

William James said, "It is one's attitude at the beginning of a difficult undertaking which, more than anything else, will determine its successful outcome." You can alter your life and affect the lives of those around you simply by changing your attitude. So prepare yourself to develop and maintain an elevated attitude and enthusiasm.

The dictionary defines *attitude* as "a state of mind expressing a certain opinion. A position of the body that indicates a certain expression or opinion. Posture. A feeling or emotion toward a fact or state." It defines *enthusiasm* as "strong excitement or feeling. Something inspiring, zeal, terror, warmth, or eagerness."

Elevate Your Attitude and Enthusiasm is an express step on the *Staircase.* Think about it. How you express yourself helps to determine the ideas and feelings people have about you. It also influences how fast you move toward your desired outcomes. Learn how to express, rather than impress!

When you like and respect yourself more, and appreciate the possibilities that exist for you, guess what happens? A natural tendency to shine kicks in; you're on your way to becoming a leader. An elevated attitude and enthusiasm are marks of a leader, and *esprit de corps* (enthusiastic comradeship) is the mark of a group led by that person.

Of course, having "an attitude" (a 'tude—arrogance or nastiness) is another thing altogether. A person with an attitude cuts off communication. Ultimately, it's the mark of a loner. A true leader skillfully maintains morale in the group and has confidence in his ability to lead his people.

An elevated attitude begins when you understand what you want, and start to resolve the conflicts in your life. In our hectic society, many people are often fragmented and unfocused in their thoughts and behaviors. They may be in the survival mode, not looking at the bigger picture of what they really want. An elevated attitude helps us to have the desire and energy to remain focused on what we want to accomplish. As we continue to focus, take action, and start to get the results we want, we become a role model to others. Our elevated attitude and enthusiasm can inspire others to also take action in their lives. In other words, it can be contagious.

Where Does Elevated Attitude and Enthusiasm Begin?

When you're self-responsible, define your life's purpose, stop making excuses, and don't blame anybody or anything, your life will be different. As you forgive and direct the energy previously wasted on resentment and anger to where you know it can make a difference, you'll feel better about yourself. You're likely to want to share this revelation with others. And that's where your attitude and enthusiasm come in, as you share these ideas with others.

Earl Nightingale said, "Attitude is the magic word." And it's so true. It can provide magical results both at work and at home. *It's your attitude and not your aptitude that determines your altitude in life.* It tells you and others where you are. For example, it communicates whether you have a forward-thinking mentality and are living a purposeful, passionate life. Or do you just have a poor-soul mentality, existing in gray mediocrity? Your attitude helps determine how other people respond to you.

Are You Smiling?

When you wake up in the morning, are you happy? Do you say, "Good God, it's morning!" or "Good morning, God"? Do you look at your spouse next to you in bed and say, "I love you"? Does he or she smile and say, "I love you, too, Honey."

Is your glass half-empty or half-full? Your attitude is one of the first indicators that tells others what kind of person you are. As Dr. Robert Schuller says, "Happy is the person who is motivated to be a beautiful human being."

Why don't some people smile? Do they think it's silly or unsophisticated? Are they afraid to let people know they like them or at least that they're a friendly person? Are they always focusing on the negative and, therefore, always frowning. Smile! When you do, others will usually smile back.

Some morning on the way to work see how many people look happy as they wait for the traffic light to change. You probably won't find one! In fact, you might notice some pretty grumpy-looking faces. We're not suggesting drivers should be jumping up and down and waving to everyone! All we're saying is that a cheerful expression would help brighten their day and that of others. Relax your facial muscles and think pleasant thoughts. Let go of your frown! A lot of people don't realize they look angry and, because of that, people may be afraid to approach them. Wear a relaxed and happy countenance. It attracts people.

Almost everyone gets discouraged. Your attitude can help you overcome it. Your attitude largely determines the first impression you give to others, and your smile can make a difference in their lives. When you get a person with a negative attitude to smile, their attitude becomes a little more positive. It's amazing to see what happens to our attitude when we choose to smile instead of frown. Our attitude can spread like wildfire.

If, rather than being pleasant, you project a negative attitude toward the people you're speaking to, it is unlikely they will want to be around you, unless they are negative too. You may literally repel them to the point where they only associate with you when they feel they have to.

The word *communication* comes from the Latin word *communicatus*, which means *to share*. A smile shares joy. A smile says, "I'm happy to see you." It's a form of communication. The intent of this book is to share techniques that can make a difference in your ability to overcome obstacles and reach new levels of personal growth, success, happiness, and fulfillment. I believe applying them in your life, and sharing them with others, will help you take giant leaps forward.

Be positive with other people. Be positive with yourself. Much of your self-talk may be negative. It is important to change that; talk positively to yourself if you expect to be more successful. If we aren't careful, we can fall into the trap of negativity and discouragement because of various challenges. Circumstances can affect our attitude only if we let them. Face your challenges with a smile. Most of them are temporary; remember—this, too, shall pass.

How Does Perception Affect Your Attitude?

The key to your attitude is your perception. How do you perceive the situation? Will it matter five years or even five minutes from now? How important is it, really? Are the people's feelings more important in the long run than the situation itself? How do you perceive life? Is it your perception that life is meant to be perfect with no challenges? If so, you are setting yourself up for many disappointments.

Remember the last time you went on vacation? What did you focus on before you left? The cost? The kids being with you because no babysitter was available? The drive to the airport? Dealing with airport parking, tickets, bags, and everything else? You may have put yourself in such a huff that, before you even got on the plane, the vacation seemed ruined!

How do you look at things? Do you focus on the work of getting there or the pleasure of walking on the beach awaiting you? If you feel what you have to do before you get on the plane is a big hassle, you'll discourage yourself. But if you focus on relaxing on the beach, or whatever else you enjoy, it'll be easier for you to handle all the challenges with a positive attitude. It'll seem worth it. Focus on the desired outcome rather than the details. They'll all get done a lot easier when you focus on what you want.

Do You Tend to Have a Positive or Negative Attitude?

Do you look at the positive aspects of work? Do you have positive feelings about your home and family? Do you focus on the negative or positive aspects of your life? The self-responsibility way is to admit that *you* put yourself where you are, so you might as well make the best of it. Of course, you also have the power to change certain aspects of your situation: get another job; move to a different location; start your own business; or whatever else you may decide to do. You are not stuck! That alone is a positive aspect; you have the power to choose.

Attitude Versus Aptitude—*Which Is More Important?*

What's your attitude up to? Is it helping you or hindering you? About 90 percent of the results you get in life stem from your attitude, while about 10 percent come from your aptitude. For example, let's say you are in a position to hire someone. If that person goes through the interview with his head down, whining and complaining about benefits, you're not going to hire him no matter what his aptitude is. On the other hand, when a person is enthusiastic and positive about who they are and what they can do for you, you'll be more likely to want to hire them. Then you can train them. That's easy when they have a positive attitude.

How Do You Measure Attitude?

You can measure your attitude by the way other people react to you. When you're positive, people are more likely to respond positively to you. If you're negative, and a real headache to be around, forget it. Other people are likely to react the same way and avoid you whenever possible; most people don't want to be around negativity. They have enough of their own challenges; they need to be uplifted rather than "negged out." Of course, you may attract other negative people to join you in the muck and mire of your attitude. But they will only contribute to your negativity and lack of success. It's like a downward spiral.

The more you know yourself, the better you can understand and work on your own unskillful behavior. The more you accept yourself and others, the more positive you'll be. When you look at life as an opportunity rather than a burden, struggle, or headache, you'll have a more positive attitude and greater enthusiasm. This takes time and effort, but it's well worth the effort. As a bonus, you'll be able to attract more positive people.

Is There Opportunity in Failure?

How you perceive situations, and how you let society and the outside world influence you, affects your attitude and enthusiasm. Do you perceive a recession as a negative or an opportunity to shine, be innovative, and use different approaches? Every potential failure also has potential opportunity. Have you ever noticed that? You might think you experienced the worst failure of your life. Then, by golly, it turned out to be your greatest lesson, which helped to propel you to even greater success.

Woodrow Wilson said: "I would rather fail at a cause I know would ultimately succeed, than succeed at a cause that would ultimately fail." In other words, it's better to attempt something great and fail than attempt an unworthy project and succeed. The great projects will never die, even if you failed in your contribution. On the other hand, unworthy projects will eventually fail, even if you've succeeded in your contribution.

What Difference Does Attitude Make at Work?

Attitudes have a tremendous influence at work. What happens when the boss comes in with his head down, angry, slamming his office door? His attitude can be assessed by observing his body language and emotional state. Would you be as motivated to be productive and efficient, manage your time well, and communicate with the people around you if your boss is negative? Unless you have an elevated attitude and enthusiasm, you are likely to be de-motivated. It's your choice whether or not you let someone else's attitude affect or determine your own. If the people in the hierarchy don't care, why would you? Would your own attitude sustain you?

When the people in the hierarchy smile, the atmosphere is different. Enthusiasm can have a powerfully positive effect on people. A smile seems to make everything more worthwhile. It's amazing. It's fascinating to see what effect your facial expressions can have on yourself and others. Experiment with smiling, frowning, and neutral expressions, and see how others react. You may be surprised. You may find that people will smile back when you smile first. When you frown or exhibit a neutral expression, people may not acknowledge you. They may even avoid you.

What About Your Attitude at Home and Other Places?

Elevate your attitude and be enthusiastic, both at work and at home. As we progress along the *Staircase,* you'll see how vital, how important home is. *No Excuse!* isn't just for work. These steps and this entire program are for everyday life. Everyone carries their attitude and enthusiasm (or lack of it) with them wherever they go, whether it's at home, work, church, stores, school, or recreation.

The same success principles that apply at work also apply at home and everywhere else you go. If you're honest and have integrity at work, what would cause you to be any different at home? If you forgive at work, wouldn't you forgive at home? If you believe in yourself and want to instill belief in other people at work, would you be equally inclined to do that for your family at home? Some people treat virtual strangers with more respect and caring than their own families. This can be devastating to their family relationships and lead to a lot of avoidable grief. Some people take their families for granted. Be wholehearted in your enthusiasm and attitude, and uplift everyone you can wherever you are.

There is no difference. Success is for work, family, and other parts of your life. Your attitude and enthusiasm are a major part of your first impression. They're also vital parts of the first *expression* you give to other people. When you elevate your attitude and enthusiasm, they'll produce "magic" for you.

The Best Pitcher in the World

Children can teach adults about attitude and enthusiasm. One day, a gentleman was walking past a playground when he noticed a young boy with a baseball and bat. As the man got closer, he overheard the boy saying, "I'm going to be the best hitter in the whole world." The boy had been throwing the ball into the air, trying to hit it. He threw the ball up, swung the bat, and missed. He did it again.

The boy continued; he wouldn't give up. He picked up that bat, threw the ball up in the air and said again, "I'm going to be the best hitter in the whole wide world." He swung the bat and missed. It was interesting to see the man's fascinated observation as the boy persisted. For the third time, the young boy said, "I'm going to be the best hitter in the whole world." He threw the ball up in the air, swung, and missed.

At that point, the boy noticed the man looking at him. The boy then turned around and said to the man, "Hey mister, did you see that? Three balls up in the air, three strikes, no hits; I'm going to be the best *pitcher* in the whole wide world!"

It all depends how you look at things. As the young boy did, we can all learn to look at things differently, to have a more positive attitude and greater enthusiasm. There's always a positive in every negative situation. The man *perceived* the boy was failing at his effort. The boy chose to view the situation in a positive light. Your attitude and enthusiasm can help you find it. Remember, there is usually someone who has a worse situation than you. You might be doubtful and ask, "Where is that person that has it worse than I do?" Remember that *life has too much potential for joy to waste time on everything that seems to be wrong with it.* There's so much to be gained by having a positive attitude and being enthusiastic with other people.

The Power of Positive Thinking

It takes a combination of courage and hope to elevate your attitude and enthusiasm. It's called *chutzpa!* As Eleanor Roosevelt, a woman of elevated attitude and enthusiasm said, "No one can make you feel inferior without your consent." She recognized the threat we are to ourselves when we succumb to someone else's opinion of us. Eleanor knew the courage it takes to insist on our own worth and to take action to fulfill our potential.

Think of George Washington at Valley Forge as he walked alone on cold winter nights, between the tents of his sleeping soldiers. He believed the new nation had a right and responsibility to exist. It was truly Washington's elevated attitude and enthusiasm that helped keep the spark of hope alive in his men. It helped them endure the bitter winter and persevere without quitting.

The true test of a military commander is his troops' morale. According to the dictionary, *morale* is "the state of the spirit of a person or group as exhibited by confidence, cheerfulness, discipline, and willingness to perform assigned tasks." Performance improves when the morale is high. When morale is low, energy is spent on negative thinking, weakening the will to win. This also holds true in civilian life.

Attitude and Enthusiasm Affect Our Success

Whenever possible, associate with people with positive attitudes and enthusiasm. This will help you to maintain a great attitude and stay enthusiastic.

Did you know that attitude and enthusiasm follow the laws of physics? One of Newton's Laws states that an object at rest tends to remain at rest unless acted upon by another force. Also, an object in motion tends to remain in motion unless acted upon by another force. This is true for people's attitudes; they'll stay negative unless influenced by a positive attitude. Attitude and enthusiasm can be the force needed to get beyond negativity to the outcomes we want.

What About Dealing with People Who Have Negative Attitudes?

Although you may not want to hang around people with negative attitudes, they *do* need your encouragement. How can you successfully deal with them? The key is to change your perception of them and their behavior. Their intentions may be good; look for the joy, the positive, and the benefits. Realize they may be hurting inside. Most people are, to one degree or another. They may just need some attention; someone who cares about them. Look at things in a different light, and you can feel kinder toward them. *How you perceive what you believe will help structure what you achieve.*

Here's an example of changing perceptions. You may see a "Beware of Dog" sign on someone's fence. Your perception may be that a dog probably lives there. Imagine taking that sign and putting it on your boss's office door. Now you probably have a different perception of what that means. You may think there's a dog in there, but more likely something else. Your perception depends on how you interpret the information you receive.

For example, suppose you change the frame around a picture. The picture may appear different to you. The new frame may enhance the picture. It may cause the picture to look larger or smaller. When you put a different frame around a certain situation, you'll find it tends to change your belief about it. You're looking at the situation a little differently. For example, you can view a person's unskillful behavior with either an angry attitude or a caring attitude, giving them the benefit of the doubt. When you re-frame, imagine no harm was intended by the people you may have thought intended to harm you. Their intentions may have been fine, even though their behavior was unskillful.

A Sense of Meaning Elevates Your Attitude and Enthusiasm

A great book that demonstrates the importance of attitude is *Man's Search for Meaning* by Viktor Frankl. If you've never read it, you might want to, especially if you're ever feeling down and out. He talks about the horror of the Nazi concentration camps, what he went through, and how he survived.

Frankl basically said that *life is 10 percent what you're given and 90 percent how you react to it.* He said he never lost his sense of self. He shared that they could physically abuse him, torture him, and take all the basic necessities away from him, but they could not destroy what he was about. No matter what they did to him, he maintained his attitude.

Frankl said people who survived the camps (about 5 percent) had a reason to live. Frankl wanted to see his wife again and get his first book published. He had a reason to live; he had a purpose. Those who gave up hope and lost the reason to live didn't make it.

Life's the same way for us too. Those who have developed a purpose, a mission beyond just getting by (survival), are more likely to become successful, happy, and fulfilled.

Frankl's book is deeply inspiring. It can be a powerful experience to read about someone overcoming hardships. Can you imagine yourself in that situation? Can you relate their difficulties to your own challenges? If so, you can then bring yourself to a new level of understanding, realizing that you, too, have a chance to make a difference in this world. Know in your heart that you have an opportunity to take what life has to offer and use your skills and talents to benefit other people. What a wonderful sense of significance you can have.

Man's Search for Meaning; what a great title! What is the meaning of life? If you still don't know the answer, rest assured, you are not alone. Many of us are still searching. You'll know the answer when you find it. For me, life is an opportunity to grow, while helping others grow, through teaching *No Excuse!*

Many believe the meaning of life is to love. This can be achieved through caring about others, doing what you love to do, and sharing your talents and skills with others. William James said, "The most important thing in life is to live your life for something more important than your life." *How you think structures what you become and whether you use your talents and skills. Thinking is the essence of success. Your attitude and enthusiasm are core parts of your thinking; they affect your success, happiness, and fulfillment every day.*

The Success-Happiness-Fulfillment Relationship

Based on the teachings of Dr. Viktor Frankl, I have developed a pie-diagram to show how success, happiness, and fulfillment relate.

When we're successful and fulfilled, we're happy. When you define and work toward what being successful really means to you (deep, down inside), without any outside influence or trying to please someone else, you feel fulfilled as you go along. The result of going toward your vision is called happiness; it is a by-product.

When we're successful but unfilled, we're unhappy. For example, say you achieve great success in your career, but you did it for the wrong reasons. Perhaps you defined success based on someone else's expectations, like maybe what your parents wanted you to become. You didn't do what you really wanted to do because you thought they wouldn't approve of it and maybe even reject you. After you realized the situation, perhaps during a midlife or other crisis, you suddenly understood why you weren't happy, even though you had achieved what *they* expected. This unhappiness can lead to other undesirable behaviors in efforts to compensate for not achieving what *your* idea of success is.

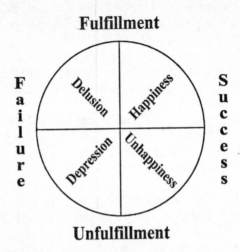

When we're unsuccessful and unfulfilled, we tend to get depressed. Nothing we do seems to work or give us any satisfaction. Perhaps you never defined success for yourself, and you have no idea what you want out of life. If you have no purpose, there's nothing you are going toward. You have, in effect, failed by definition and default. If you don't know what you want to accomplish, it's impossible for you to become fulfilled. If this keeps up, long term depression can turn into despair.

Finally, we have delusion. When we feel fulfilled by what we do, without having or recognizing our true purpose, we are only deluding ourselves. An example of this could be a situation where you love your job, but you don't earn enough money to properly provide for your family. You are fulfilled by your work, but certainly not successful. You've failed your family. This individual is basically acting selfishly, and all kinds of problems could develop.

Are You an Optimist or a Pessimist?

Have you ever heard the story of the little twin brothers, Harry and Larry? Harry was a pessimist and Larry was an optimist. The little pessimist was always complaining and very negative. The little optimist viewed everything through rose-colored glasses. It was their birthday, and their father decided to test their attitudes. He bought every kind of toy imaginable for the pessimist: a new bike, a basketball, a rifle, and dozens of things that could give any little boy pleasure. For the optimist, a pile of horse manure was his only gift.

As soon as Harry, the pessimist, saw all of his beautiful gifts, he began to complain, "If I ride this bike on the street, I might wreck it and hurt myself. I know if I take this basketball outside, someone will probably steal it. This rifle is dangerous. I'll probably end up shooting somebody's window out." Harry went on and on with his deep negativity. He turned his birthday into gloom and doom. The little pessimist saw life in a negative light and found fault.

Then it was the little optimist's turn. When Larry saw the pile of horse manure with his name on it, he got excited. He began to run through the house looking in all the rooms, in the garage, and in the backyard. When his father caught him by the arm and asked, "Son, what are you looking for?" Larry replied, "Dad, with all the horse manure you gave me, I just know there's gotta be a pony around here somewhere!" The little optimist was an example of a person with an elevated attitude and enthusiasm. Optimists look for the good in people and situations.

What's Realistic?

Some people believe they're recognizing reality when they think negatively. But when your idea of reality allows *only* for the negatives, your sense of reality is seriously flawed. Furthermore, positive outcomes are possible from negative situations when you look at them as opportunities. There's a silver lining behind every cloud, and you can't have a rainbow without rain. *Realistic—for you—is whatever you believe.*

As an example, in the business world, patterns of *hiring* and *firing* have evolved. The reduction of staff may be called re-structuring, down-sizing, right-sizing, or eliminating departments. Such events, coupled with an employee's desire to make changes, means the average working person could experience three to four *career changes* or more over a lifetime. Be prepared to negotiate these rapids of change.

Firing isn't as negative as it first appears. Can you picture yourself fired up for all the good things that can come when you are free to make new choices? Whether the decision to move on has been yours or not, it can turn out to be the best thing that ever happened to you. It can give you time to learn more about who you are and what you want. The people who make well-thought-out decisions about what comes next in their lives can reap great benefits from adversity. They may find the career, whether it's a job or a business, of their dreams. These people have an elevated attitude and enthusiasm. They face challenges with a sense of adventure. What they believe *becomes* realistic for them. They recognize and use adversity as an opportunity to move on.

Can You Find the Sunny Spot on a Rainy Day?

Think of all the things people choose to be down about. Think of the weather. How many times do you hear people say, "I can't take this weather anymore." It doesn't matter whether it's sunshine or rain. Whatever the weather, if the same pattern goes on for awhile, you'll probably hear someone complain. When you hear those words, ask yourself, "Do I have a problem with my attitude? Am I allowing rainy weekends to negatively influence my attitude? What can I do about it? Ah ha! Maybe I'll spread that fertilizer on the lawn so the good earth can soak it up and really make my lawn green."

Ask yourself, "What one outrageously fun thing could I do to help cope with another rainy weekend?" Why not reserve a suite with a hot tub and invite some friends to grab their swimsuits and drop by? They may be feeling the same way about the weather as you do. You'll provide the spark people depend on from their leaders. You could make the jacuzzi a think tank to brainstorm a business challenge or lift somebody's spirits. Maybe you could develop a plan to support a worthy cause, or just relax and share funny stories and jokes.

The point is, unconventional settings can stimulate creative thinking. When you elevate your attitude and enthusiasm, people around you are more likely to do the same, and creative thinking can flourish. You can help others turn their negativity about the weather into a positive.

A word of warning. Elevating your attitude and enthusiasm does not mean endless rah-rahing. You want to be genuine, and show a lot of respect for where other people are in their lives. Give people space to experience their challenges, acknowledge their situation, and gently uplift them with your encouragement.

Just as there is day and night, there are fruitful and fallow times in life, especially in the creative area. A time of tremendous growth is often followed by a period of introspection that can almost appear as dormancy. This is a time to regroup, refresh and renew, consider new objectives, or prepare and strategize for your next challenge. During these times, when the fires of expectation are low, repairs can be made to the furnace. An elevated attitude and enthusiasm really shine through. They protect and shelter your hopes and dreams. As a leader, you help protect and shelter the faith and trust of those around you.

How Attachment Affects Your Attitude and Enthusiasm

When you are attached to a person, thing, idea, outcome, or event, you are holding on to your belief of how things "should" be. You may be unaware of other options or concerned about the unknown. Being attached is unhealthy, and it shows you are inflexible, fearful, and anxious. It's like you're hanging on for dear life, so to speak, and if things don't go your way, it'll be a tragedy! In other words, you don't have the faith to believe things will turn out in your best interest. This is a sign of insecurity and lack of confidence.

Attachments often occur in relationships. For example, say you finally find the person you want to marry. You may hang on to them desperately, hoping they won't leave. You may believe your overly attentive behavior is love. However, you may be smothering the person and depriving them of some much needed private time and the opportunity to stretch and be who they are. Attachment may seem endearing at first, but it can become old and stifle the relationship. It can lead to manipulation and other tactics that could drive the person away. This is the exact opposite of the desired outcome of a healthy, balanced relationship!

You can't force a successful relationship by being attached to it. Part of your responsibility is to let go of attachments by letting that person decide if, and to what degree, they want to participate in the relationship. If they choose to participate, great! If they don't want it and you try to force it, you'll probably drive them away. Grow through the experience. Their not wanting a relationship may be the best thing that could happen. But may not seem true until later.

If you think being attached to someone makes you happy, you'll probably be in for a rude awakening. Nobody can make you happy; it's a personal choice that's up to you. You can't get all of your emotional needs met by someone else either. Imagine being around a person with an unhappy, negative, taking attitude, who is trying to get all his emotional needs met by you! What an energy drain. Happiness is an attitude you can carry around with you wherever you go. It comes from inside.

One way to let go of an attachment to an outcome is to ask yourself, "What is the worst thing that could possibly happen?" Then just accept it! Once you've done that, you'll be grateful for practically any result you get, as long as it's not the worst case scenario.

Another example of being attached might be when you apply for a promotion. You may think that, without a doubt, the new job is the one for you. Being attached can be like a mental latching on. You may appear desperate and anxious. What do you do? Of course you want the job; it pays more. You'd have a bigger office and other perks. Who wouldn't want that? To protect yourself, you could adopt the attitude that "I *prefer* to be promoted to that job; however, I am not *attached* to it. I am flexible. I'm confident that if I don't get the promotion, another opportunity as good or better will come along." By not being attached, you're also less likely to feel disappointed if you don't get the job.

To maintain an elevated attitude and enthusiasm, we need to *let go of attachments and state preferences instead.* Apply this approach to any area of your life where you may be holding on. Your new flexibility will help you adjust to the ebb and flow of life, which often has elements that are outside your control. You could look at it like this—*What happens to you happens for you!*

What Is the True Mark of a Leader?

I have always been inspired by excellent leaders, beginning with my parents. They both had strong personalities, and set and worked for personal, family, business, and community goals. There were also adults in my extended family, teachers, and friends with similar qualities.

I enjoyed something of a leadership role, early on, with my military peers. I first realized that during the summer between my sophomore and junior years at West Point; I had an ability to influence and help others to be motivated. Every cadet has several options from which to choose a summer training session. I chose Cadet Troop Leadership Training and was sent to Schweinfurt, Germany, to serve as a tank platoon leader. Still a cadet, I would experience the responsibilities of a 2nd Lieutenant. Pretty heady stuff, I thought.

I was ready to use some of the skills I was learning at West Point, so I jumped right in. I sincerely cared for the troops under my command and they knew it. My self-confidence was bolstered by their positive response to my leadership. My ability to lead boiled down to communicating positive expectations that we could accomplish whatever goal we set. I consciously conveyed my belief in them and saw them grow. The power of elevated attitude and enthusiasm worked.

At the end of that summer, the troops and I parted company, and I went back for my last two years at the Academy. I was elated that I was capable of being what I had set out to be: a leader who could inspire others to rise to challenges. The officers and soldiers with whom I spent the summer, openly expressed their admiration of my abilities and the path I had chosen. This experience is, to this day, a powerful reminder of the link between leadership, attitude, and enthusiasm. I believe excellent leadership is only possible with an elevated attitude and enthusiasm.

As a young soldier, I was happy about being given the opportunity to grow as a leader. For all the positives I remember, I also remember certain negatives. I wouldn't compare them to the difficulties of Valley Forge, but they were tests of my ability to elevate my attitude and enthusiasm and stay positively motivated. Not everyone around me had the same attitude. Most people are negative at times, but some are habitually negative. I'd rather be surrounded by habitually positive people. Encouraging people around you to change their attitudes can be challenging, but it is the mark of a leader. To the degree I was able to do that, I became a better leader that summer.

Get Rejuvenated by Elevating Your Attitude and Enthusiasm!

Attitude and enthusiasm are like static electricity. They can rub off and cling to someone else. Attitude is your first indicator for success, while enthusiasm helps you sustain it.

If you're a salesperson, do you have a positive or negative attitude when you call on someone? If it's negative, it's highly unlikely you're going to close the deal. When you get home, is your attitude positive or negative? If it's negative, you're less likely to get much done. Also, you'll feel miserable while doing your work.

If you ever feel your attitude and enthusiasm slipping, it's time to go back to this step to refresh your positive energies. Your elevated attitude and enthusiasm can produce seemingly magical results at home, work, play, or wherever you go. They do make a difference.

Get some of this special magic going in your life. Elevate your attitude and enthusiasm and you'll open up to the exceptional things that go on around you every day. Open your eyes to the remarkable opportunities that are out there for people with elevated attitudes and enthusiasms.

Elevate your attitude and enthusiasm and you'll be well on your way to becoming happier, more successful, and be empowered to make a greater difference.

Chapter 8
SUSTAIN SELF-CONTROL
Fourth Step of the THESAURUS Factor

Self-responsibility is the essence of self-control. The key word is SELF. Being in control of anything depends mostly on how well you are able to control yourself. Webster's defines self-control as "restraint exercised over one's own impulses, emotions, or desires."

What happens when someone loses control? It changes the atmosphere immediately. In dangerous situations, it spells disaster for anyone who lacks self-control, especially a leader. Even situations that don't start out as dangerous can become so.

Self-control is the testing ground for how effective you are in employing the other principles of the *THESAURUS Factor*. Your self-esteem and how well you know yourself largely determines your degree of professionalism in your career and maturity, as well as how you deal with others in general. These attributes are related to your self-control. If you have a negative attitude, you will probably not have nearly the degree of professionalism and self-control in thought, word, and deed as you would if you had a positive attitude.

Dwelling on the past, blaming, complaining, and whining makes it difficult to maintain self-control. Professionalism and determination to take charge of your destiny slips away. It's a choice, not a chance!

Self-control is a gauge of where you are at all times. How you handle yourself, day in and day out, is a measure of your self-control. Self-discipline, a part of self-control, is your first test for all the steps along the *Staircase. Webster's* defines self-discipline as "...controlling oneself or one's desires, actions, habits, etc."

If you perceive yourself as weak, and you lack self-control and self-discipline, you are also likely to let circumstances influence you negatively. If you think you are weak, you may lose control when you're bombarded by things that test your professionalism, maturity, self-control, and knowledge of who you are.

When you perceive yourself as strong, have control of yourself and exercise discipline, you can rise to the occasion. Circumstances won't matter. Did anyone ever say to you, "Well, under the circumstances..."? That's really just an excuse! Did you ever say that to someone? Weren't you just blaming the situation; using it as an excuse?

There have been brilliant military officers who have damaged their careers and lost the respect of their peers, superiors, and subordinates. They didn't maintain self-control at a social event or while on duty. This may have occurred because they were frustrated by someone else's failure to meet their expectations, or they may have been under the influence of alcohol. Regardless of how exceptionally they may have performed at their job, it no longer mattered to those observing their behavior when they "lost it." *Self-control becomes jeopardized when you let your emotions control your behavior.* Loss of self-control can damage your career and put everything you've worked for at risk.

When a crisis occurs at work, how do you react? Do you get emotional or angry and lose your cool? Do you go absolutely bonkers and look for someone to blame? Or do you look to see why the crisis occurred in the first place? Do you maintain a sense of professionalism, contain your emotions, and then respond to the crisis? Take care of the situation, solve the crisis if you can, and move on. After that, you can concern yourself with who's responsible or why the crisis occurred to begin with. In other words, wait until the dust settles! By the way, this is also true for handling crises at home.

For life to be well lived we need to exercise self-control. Yet there are so many talented, attractive, and accomplished people who get near the top (the highest position of rank or achievement) without developing self-control. That's just it. They only get *near* the top. Because they lack self-control, they often blow their chances for true success. Their out-of-control emotional reactions get them into trouble. If they make it to the top and they lose self-control, they will lose the respect of their peers and the people they oversee. They may also lose their position.

Self-control is very much a measure of where you are within yourself. How much do you believe in you? How much are you in touch with how you feel about yourself? If you don't have an excellent relationship with yourself, how can you have one with anyone else? How's your self-esteem? The respect you feel for yourself largely determines how much you maintain a sense of self-control; it's synonymous with happiness.

Sustaining Self-Control Is Easy When We Eliminate Anger

Can someone or some event make you angry, cause you to lose control, or otherwise control your emotions? It's commonly believed that people and events can make us angry. But wait a minute. Let's stop and think about it. Is that really true? You may hear people say that all the time, but is it really true? Of course not! That would be real scary if someone or something had that kind of power over you, now wouldn't it?

Consider this example: What do you get when you cut open a lemon and squeeze it? Lemon juice! So, what do you get when you "cut open" and "squeeze" an angry person? What comes out of them? Anger! If there's no anger inside of them, no anger can be squeezed out!

People or events can't make us angry; all they can do is trigger the anger that's already inside. When we're self-responsible, we own all of our emotions. Nobody can do it to us. Self-responsible people don't put the burden of their happiness on someone else. They know it's a choice.

Anger can be an excuse to blame, rather than accept responsibility. Anger may be the attitude of a victim, with its root being unforgiveness. It often stems from harboring hatred, resentment, and disappointment, which can come from an unwillingness to let go of the past.

Anger is also used to dominate, control, or manipulate. When we honestly and openly communicate our needs, wants, and values to determine a mutually beneficial course of action, anger is less likely to be triggered.

If you easily get angry, you probably have some unresolved issues. You need to identify them, let go of them, and move on. Go back and re-read the first step, *Totally Forgive*. Forgiveness is the greatest way to eliminate anger and make sustaining self-control easy. When you have no anger inside you, no one can rattle your cage. You'll maintain your cool and sustain self-control.

A conscious show of anger, used in a deliberately proactive way to make a point or get someone's attention, is different. With some people, for example, it's sometimes necessary to raise your voice to get through to them. You are well aware of what's going on. You're not just reacting. Nobody triggered your anger. You're taking charge of the situation.

Are You a Doer or a Watcher?

Doers have a vision. Watchers just observe. Doers have a dream and act on it. Watchers toss and turn. To be successful, you need a vision. The *Bible* says, "Where there is no vision, the people perish." All successful people know where they're going, and they take action. When they are faced with a challenge, they are more likely to be clear and focused in their response and exert self-control.

When you have a challenge, look beyond it to what you want for yourself, your business or job, and your family. It's generally a mistake to just react to things. Your self-control is a measure of how well you respond to challenges; it has to do with responsibility.

Self-Control at Home

Of all the places in our lives, where do you think self-control is most important? At home! But is that where it's practiced most? We may be responsible to and for people all day long. We may put on a façade at work, even if we don't care for someone or something, just to keep the job or the employee. You might meet someone who behaves obnoxiously, but because you're at work you do your best to maintain a sense of professionalism and self-control.

We may be patient with co-workers or staff all day long, but what may happen when we get home? We may pull into the driveway, open the car door, and our self-control may fly right out the window. You get home and the last thing you may want to be is responsible. You've been responsible all day. You may feel you don't have any more self-control left. All you may want to do is go open that refrigerator, grab something to drink, sit down in front of the TV, and "zone" for awhile. The slightest interruption to this may set you off, no matter who does it. Boom! It may be just that easy to lose control.

It's difficult to justify losing control with your family. Self-control affects every part of family life. Maintaining integrity, sincerity, and maturity is essential so you can correctly communicate your feelings at home. It's hard to justify not doing that at home, while you may be doing it for a complete stranger at work. Why? Is money more important to you than your family? Only you can decide that.

If arguments and anger erupt every time a challenging situation occurs at home, it becomes more difficult to continue the relationship(s). It's far better to prevent the anger, so the relationships are not jeopardized. Who wants to be abused or accused? What would cause you to want to deal with that? Just avoid the anger. Resolve the situation with kindness and move on. If you have an occasional flare up, apologize and calmly work it out.

Self-Control at Work

Self-control in thought, word, and deed is fundamental for success. When you have a task at hand, do you have the discipline and desire to get it done? Can you maintain a sense of professionalism and control? Are you decisive? Self-control is essential because it affects every aspect of the operation of an organization. How does self-control affect your organization?

If your boss reacts with anger every time you present a situation to him, do you want to continue the relationship? Do you feel inclined to be as helpful to that person as you had in the past? If you're the boss and reacting angrily, how do you think you're affecting your relationships? Self-control deals with communication, either self-talk or with others, whether it's at home or at work. Think about it.

What if this would happen throughout the organization? If you don't communicate effectively with people by listening to them sharing their ideas and concerns, you're going to have unwanted situations. Most of the problems in an organization can be resolved by listening, asking questions, then listening again.

People who lack self-control don't listen or, at best, listen ineffectively. They may be more interested in what's on their mind rather than what the other person is saying. If anger erupts at work, use self-control to avoid fueling the fire and igniting the potential for emotional hurt and negative feelings. Listen to what people are saying. We need to be excellent listeners before we can lead to diffuse hot situations.

If you intervene, do so in a calm, soft tone of voice. Allow others to get it all off their chest, then ask if there is anything else bothering them. Continue maintaining self-control and keep asking if there's anything more they'd like to say. After they've had their say, you can go in and share what you believe would be helpful to resolve the situation.

Three Ways to Maintain Self-Control

How do you maintain self-control? At times it can be challenging. When you deal with the same people every day, your self-control is going to be tested. You could become a little "short-fused" if you aren't aware of this and don't develop the appropriate skills.

Here are three steps to help you maintain a measure of self-control in everything you do:

1. Listen before you think. The most effective salespeople, for instance, are those who listen the most. How can you sell a product or service to someone if you don't take the time to listen to their needs? If you are an employer and you don't listen to your employees before you make a decision, you may not know the whole story. You are reducing your chances of making an informed decision or developing the correct solution. You may need to ask questions to get more information. Carefully listen to the answers.

If you immediately let your emotions override practicality, how can you create an appropriate solution to a problem? If you short-circuit (interrupt) everyone along the way, you're likely to create *more* problems. Listen *before* you think. It is important to listen well and gather the information before your emotions and your self-indulgences can interrupt. Then you'll have a chance to think and decide how you're going to solve that problem. *Listen.*

2. Think before you assess. Collect the data, then assess the situation. If it's an emotional situation, separate emotion from fact. *Think.*

3. Assess before you act. After you collect the data, it's time to make an assessment. After that, implement whatever policy or action you're going to take. *Assess.*

There's nothing revolutionary here. We all need to remember these steps, as simple as they may seem. It's just that we may get so caught up in everything that's going on, we may need to remind ourselves.

When you come to the end of the day and go home and reflect on it, do you generally feel satisfied that you accomplished what you wanted? Were you focused and self-controlled? Do you feel each day you are making progress toward fulfilling your purpose? Are you working on fulfilling your definition of success and heading toward your dreams? How do you feel about yourself in these areas?

Do You Feel All Stressed-Out?

Did you ever watch a hamster running in a circular wheel? Is he going anywhere? He's running and working up a sweat. His eyes are bugging out, but he's going nowhere. Have you ever felt like that? If you have, you are not alone.

Where are people going during rush hour every day? They may be working hard, but where are they going? Are they heading toward their vision, or are they in a rut? Are they feeling all stressed out, just waiting for the weekend? What's the difference between a rut and a grave? You could almost think of a rut as a grave with no ends! Surveys show that at least 70 percent of the people hate their work or some aspect of it. No wonder many people aren't happy. Work is usually such a large part of life. If there's no fulfillment for you in your work, it can lead to problems. It can also affect your self-control.

Use your time wisely, investing it in things that are going to be productive for you. Self-control helps you stay on track to get the outcomes you want. It helps you maintain focus and a sense of direction. When you know where you're going and you work on it every day, you can avoid feeling all stressed out. Stress often results from lack of direction and self-control in life. Purpose gives your life meaning and makes it easier to maintain self-control.

Is Your Clock Too Fast?

A talented basketball player found success in his game when he learned to slow down. Before that, all his natural talent, plus years of excellent coaching, practicing, and playing, had not enabled him to reach his potential. He knew it was because, as he put it, "His clock was too fast." Some people call it hurry sickness.

He had developed the self-control which enabled him to focus his energies on the skills he needed to be a formidable player. He had the self-responsibility to maintain the physical conditioning that allowed him to come to every basketball game in peak condition. He was missing the ability to be on the court playing *his* game, to be proactive, to never let the game play him.

It all came together for this young man when he learned to let his clock tick slower. He learned to keep working the ball and scanning the court. He just looked for the right opportunity for that perfect pass to the free agent poised for a shot. He became an excellent point guard and led his team to championships by keeping his clock steady.

This timing factor is also true for other areas of your life. Some people confuse self-control with denial. *Equate self-control with your willingness to patiently await results.* Getting what you want is much sweeter when you know you had the wisdom, faith, and patience to wait (while diligently working) for the jackpot. This is far better than later realizing you cashed in your chips too soon for a minimal and often self-defeating payoff.

Self-Controlling a Crisis

The amount of self-control used in a real crisis, or a crisis created by someone out of control, often determines the chances for a desirable outcome. A person in control lays anger and frustration aside while the situation is studied. He evaluates the possible consequences of any remedial action. Finding the cause(s) can then help define the remedy. Measures may then be taken, if possible, to avoid a future occurrence.

Personalities become incidental when the search for meaningful response is led by a person with self-control. In fact, as in Patton's case, it is often a sign of burnout to have a normally capable leader lose self-control in a moment of crisis. Such behavior inevitably worsens any situation because the morale of the group being led is negatively impacted by this sign of weakness.

Like that basketball player, a leader needs to set his clock on slow to exercise an unusual amount of self-control. Gifted people are often impatient. They may be accustomed to quick results from their efforts. They may feel impatient when they experience a lag in time from when they want something to when they get it. An effective leader is patient; he gives people time to grow. Remember, you can't push a rope, but you can gently pull a wet noodle!

Patience Is One of the Greatest Virtues

Patience is another aspect of self-control. *Patience is a virtue, while haste makes waste.* These clichés are more important today than ever. Many people are looking for instant gratification. A couple of generations have grown up with TV, fast food, credit cards, and buy-now/pay-later thinking. Many do not exercise the self-control or self-restraint required to accept the delayed gratification necessary to achieve success.

True success takes time. It doesn't happen overnight. This is a *Staircase.* There's no elevator here. We climb it one step at a time. Patience is essential as we journey through life. For example, research shows that it takes an average of 15 years to be an overnight success.

Have the Self-Control to Think

The main purpose of this book is to help you think. It's to encourage you to open your mind more and remove yourself, just a little bit, from what's going on out there. This can be a time for you to take a look inside to reflect and review some of the principles of success that can make a difference in your life. Only you know what you could lose if you choose not to participate in the adventure of *No Excuse!* living.

You Need to Have a Dream

If you get all caught-up in reaching for the stars and think success is going to happen overnight, you'll probably be disappointed; you may then give up and do nothing at all. Have dreams. Dreams are powerful because those who conquer are those who believe they can. Emerson said, "Those who achieve, believe they can achieve." Having a dream will help you maintain self-control.

Maintain self-control and a sense of professionalism in everything you do, and you're likely to find that people will follow and respect you. To be an effective leader, you need to exercise self-control. As mentioned before, on rare occasions anger, or losing it (your temper), can be an effective tool, provided it's not done at the expense of other people. To be effective as a parent, a leader, and in your behavior in general, you need to maintain certain levels of consistency. If you're not consistent in your actions, people may be guarded around you and misunderstand your communication. Others may assume a defensive position. Your self-control can help you be consistent and better understood.

The greatest potential for control exists where action takes place. Internally we have great potential. When it comes to self-control, listen to that inner voice or gut feeling we all have. This is your intuition. Trust that voice. You'll find that experience validates it. With a sense of self-control and patience, you'll find that when you do make a decision, your intuition can have quite a favorable impact on your potential to succeed.

We Live in Acres of Diamonds

One of Earl Nightingale's most popular audio programs, *Lead the Field,* has a great little story called "Acres of Diamonds." Written by Russell Conwell, founder of Temple University, it's about an African farm owner back in the late 1800s. He heard of many other farmers all across the continent who became wealthy because of the diamond mines. There was a big diamond rush going on.

As the story goes, the farmer was so enthusiastic about making a fortune that he actually sold his farm and went on his merry way to search for wealth and happiness. Well, after years and years of searching for diamonds and not finding any, he gave up. He became so discouraged that he finally went into a river and drowned himself.

The main point of the story began when the gentleman who bought the farm was walking around the property one day and noticed a bright, shiny object in the creek. He picked it up and was amazed at its size and brilliance. He took it into his house and set it on his mantel.

A few days later a friend stopped by, saw the stone, and asked the farmer where he found it. He said he found the stone in the creek, where there were many others just like it. To the amazement of the farmer, his friend told him it was a diamond.

The farm was loaded with diamonds; all the resources were there. All the wealth the original farmer could have hoped for was right there in his own backyard. Instead of taking the time to look at what he had on his own land, he looked outside.

Success Is Primarily an Inside Job

We sometimes fail to look inside ourselves. Instead, we go outside searching for what we want. We look for the external things where we can make the quick buck or get a quick fix. We are tempted to look for success on the easiest and quickest path when, in all honesty, true success takes time.

Some of the greatest and most fundamental resources are right there within you. Take the opportunity to tap into them. Find those wonderful principles that you know are inside you. Success is primarily an inside job. It begins with you, even though people, places, or things can be helpful as you work toward what you want. Many people mistakenly think their success depends primarily on circumstances and other external factors, rather than what's inside themselves.

Someone wise said, "People quit five minutes before the miracle." Have you ever looked back and wished you had taken a little more time and not quit? Did you ever say to yourself, "If I had only exercised a little more self-control, I'd be further along"? Did you ever regret not having more patience with someone or some activity? Could you have achieved that dream or a success you desired, if only you had just kept going?

Success is mind-made not man-made. What your mind creates and how you perceive it is all based on how you think. The success you will achieve in your life will be based largely on how you think. Self-control and patience are virtues that make a big difference in determining whether or not you live the life you want. Look for the diamonds inside of you. Look for what you already have inside and run with it.

Bringing It All Home

When you give yourself time to succeed, and grow personally in the process, the skills you acquire along the way help you maintain that success. If you lose your success for some reason, these skills will help enable you to build success again.

Ending your frustration with other people is a glorious thing to do for yourself and them. Anything that helps you do that frees you from the fretting that so often accompanies failure. It makes your life so much easier when you are well prepared with a self-control mindset. You can then handle anyone or any adversity that may come your way.

Self-control is essential for a leader. Without it you'll lose credibility, and it is unlikely anyone will want to follow you. If you can't control yourself, you'll never be able to successfully lead. Since you lead by example, the best way to teach others self-control is to practice it yourself.

Say you are a parent who comes home from work exhausted. You need to know how well-equipped you are to deal with the demands of children who are genuinely in need. They need food, comfort, playfulness, attention, and love. And remember, your spouse is likely to need the same things as well.

Self-control is one of the most important qualities for parents to develop. Children gain many of their perceptions about life when they observe their parents. A parent in control of himself will make a positive difference in a child's life. So again, self-control becomes a matter of preparation and pacing. Come home with some reserve energy for this important time of day, this important time of life.

Use your self-control calmly; give fair warning to loved ones. When you hug someone say, "I've had a very busy day; it's good to be home. I'd love to spend a little quiet time with you." Or, you may want to tell your family that you need to take a short nap first. That's a lot different than saying, "Leave me alone. Can't you see I've had a rough day?"

If we, like the wise little pig, have done our homework in developing self-control, our home can be a secure haven where happiness abounds.

Chapter 9
ALWAYS BE HONEST
First Part of the Fifth Step of
the THESAURUS factor

And now we come to the A step—*Always Be Honest/Always Dream and Set Goals.* This is essential. I could have just discussed *Always Dream and Set Goals* and skipped *Always Be Honest,* but nothing in your quest for success will matter if you're not honest. No matter what you do on the rest of the *Staircase,* or how many attempts you make at achieving success, do it honestly. No matter how many people you deal with, or how many jobs or businesses you have, if you operate dishonestly you'll never feel respect for yourself or your achievements.

Emerson said, "You can't do wrong without suffering wrong." Honest success is crucial. What are you all about? When you're honest with yourself, you'll be honest with others. If you're dishonest with yourself, it's very difficult to be honest with others. Live honestly. *True success is honest success.*

The biggest failures that occur in life have not been in business itself; the real tragedies have been moral failures. People who have been at the top of their careers with everything they've ever wanted, everything society would consider success, like money, fame, prestige and power, have sometimes lost it all. How many people can you think of who have been at the top, who got there by either lying or cheating in some fashion or another, and then lost everything? That's why it's so important to always be honest. When you are honest with yourself and others, people are more likely to be comfortable in dealing with you because they're likely to trust you.

Have you set your goals honestly? Have you honestly acknowledged you've attained them or admitted you've failed? A satisfying life depends on honestly knowing what you want out of life for and from yourself and others. If you are unwilling to do the work of discovering that and stating it clearly, you'll probably find it difficult to be honest with yourself about other things. This implies your world will be one of constantly shifting values and desires. Dishonesty, with yourself as well as with others, can cause you to take many slippery roads. Dishonesty causes inconsistency, instability, and fear.

Most of us have dealt with people who were dishonest with us. When the truth is ultimately known, as it always is, we may feel like the rug has been pulled out from under us. Dishonest people slip and slide in many directions, avoiding the truth and evading people they are deceiving. There are no resting places for dishonest people.

This step on the *Staircase* is a resting place for those who understand the values and benefits of an honest life. You value it because you realize that the only way to stay honest is to stop and take stock from time to time. It is essential to honestly re-examine your goals and desired outcomes to see how close you have come to achieving them. Honest self-evaluation will tell you if you are on track in pursuit of them.

Do You Live by an Honor Code?

At West Point, the Honor Code says, "A cadet will not lie, cheat, steal, or tolerate those who do." Duty, Honor, Country. Those of us who adhered to that code, as nebulous as that may sound, felt quite satisfied when we accomplished something, because we were true to ourselves. We did it ourselves. We did not look on the outside. We did it in a way that was true to who we were and what we were about.

What a difference it makes, whether in business or family life, when you are honest. Whenever you complete a task or overcome a challenge honestly, you get a wonderful feeling. If you do it insincerely, dishonestly, or without integrity, you risk losing everything you accomplished. You are unlikely to feel the same gratification. You probably won't learn nearly as much either. Also, it may not stay done. It could be questioned later. You could lose what you dishonestly gained.

There are two principles I hold dearest in my heart with regard to dealing with people: honesty and integrity. By operating that way, you can rest assured people will be more likely to want to deal with you. If you treat them with respect, give them a fair price, and they know they can trust you and what you say, the chances are greater that they want to do business with you. However, if they detect any dishonesty or insincerity, human nature may cause them to back away from you because they may feel uncomfortable. When you don't trust someone, how can you communicate? How can you possibly relate with those people? If you need to deal with them, you would be cautious, to say the least.

Here's an interesting little story about three high school seniors. It was during the spring, right near graduation time, when they got a serious case of spring fever. One morning, they decided to skip school. When they returned to school, they told the teacher they had had a flat tire.

"Well," the teacher said, "you also missed a test. Therefore, I want to give it to you now. Why don't you all sit apart and take out a blank sheet of paper," she said. 'The first question I have is, which tire was flat?'"

See how dishonesty came back to haunt the boys? It always comes back to haunt us. We need to forgive ourselves for any past temptations to be dishonest, whether we gave in to them or not, and move on.

Be assured that most of us have been tempted at one time or another to be dishonest. The challenge you and I have is to remain true to our deepest values of integrity when temptation knocks at our door.

I see things (like TV solicitations) that point out how so many people are influenced by deception. We all need to be careful of such influences. One thing we want to be sure of before we decide to invest in or get involved with something: The opportunity is honest and the people behind it are of great integrity. Check things out before you invest your time and money in anything. Yes, be open-minded but cautious at the same time.

There's Always Hope

While many of us are hurting inside and faced with challenges, always remember there is hope. *Webster's Dictionary* defines hope as "to cherish a desire with expectations of fulfillment." Hope is wonderful and magnificent. It gives you something to look forward to. It keeps you going. It also can help you to be inspired. Make sure that your hope is not based on deception or lies. Be sure you're not being taken in by things that could cause internal destruction down the road. By simply watching, reading, and listening, you'll learn how people can get caught up in falsehoods of what could be. In many cases, the resources you have inside can provide you with all the hope you'll ever need. Add commitment and diligent effort to your hope and you'll be rewarded. Your reward may be financial or something else. Your honesty will pay off in dividends of peace of mind.

Always Be Humble

There's no room for false modesty on the *Staircase*. False modesty is dishonest. It's displaying an image of modesty when, in reality, that person is not modest; he's putting on a false front. It's just as dishonest to fail to acknowledge and appreciate your achievements as it is to fail to admit your shortcomings.

There's no room for bragging either. When you accomplish something worthwhile, people are likely to compliment you. That's fine. However, bragging is a sign of a lack of self-esteem, immaturity, and insecurity. It is based on feelings that no one will recognize you for what you have done. Bragging is an attempt at one-upmanship—blowing your own horn—trying to make yourself look better than the next person. Bragging is different than sharing. When you share ideas and information, it is generally because you are confident that what you have to say will help someone. Sharing is great; bragging is not!

People who have made significant contributions to the world tend to be humble, which *Webster's Dictionary* defines as "not proud or haughty...unpretentious." Humble people know, deep in their heart, that without the help of others it is unlikely they would have accomplished what they did. If they are people of faith, as they usually are, they generally give credit to their Creator as well. Always give credit where credit is due, and appreciate the assistance we received which supported our efforts.

Do You Know What You Want?

Let's face it. *You can never be satisfied if you don't know what you want.* Think about a two-year-old arriving in a room filled with toys. A few other children are playing there, more or less contentedly. Our new arrival studies the scene for a bit and then makes a move. Does he go toward a toy laid quietly in a corner? No! He heads toward a toy in some other child's hands—a toy that's being pushed, pulled, and enjoyed. That's what attracts his attention.

Wanting what someone else has is often the first reaction of inexperienced people. They may trust the other person's choice of the toys rather than their own untried choice. It eliminates the need to think and decide what is best for themselves.

When this little newcomer gets acquainted with all the toys in the room, he knows the potential for pleasure each offers. After the rules of the game have been explained, like no grabbing, the toddler will then have a way of setting goals. It may mean taking turns playing with the toy, but it will pay off in satisfaction. It is likely to put an end to wanting only what someone else has, while building respect for that other child's rights.

If you haven't found and committed yourself to your own goals, other people's pleasures will always have the potential to influence you enough to divert you from finding what's best for you. As a father said to his son in Shakespeare's *Hamlet,* "This above all; to thine own self be true, and it must follow, as the night the day, though canst not then be false to any man."

We can learn from other people by watching them achieve their goals; that's true. However, our admiration pays off best when we imitate their perseverance. We're not being honest with ourselves if we adopt *their* goals. It is, however, honest to adapt their determination to suit our own goals, which may or may not be similar to theirs.

Earl Nightingale identified being honest with ourselves as "the big thing." "The big thing," he said, "is that you know what you want."

"...That All Men Would Be Free."

If part of being honest is knowing what you want from life, and working tirelessly toward it, then Abe Lincoln once again proves the point by his example.

Lincoln's goal for himself was something that would benefit others, namely…that all men would be free. He spent his entire life striving to realize this outcome. His work manifested itself in two great achievements that would eventually change the course of a nation.

One was the *Emancipation Proclamation,* which confirmed that black men and women had the right to life, liberty, and the pursuit of happiness.

The other was keeping the Union intact, because "deference shall be paid to the will of the majority, simply because it is the will of the majority." In his famous *Gettysburg Address,* Lincoln's goal for preserving a government "of the people, by the people, and for the people," was never stated more eloquently.

Today, Americans concerned about their communities, as well as citizens of the world seeking freedom, are searching for leaders with Lincoln's qualities. He was political without being corrupt; calm without being lethargic. Lincoln was open-minded, yet didn't take unfair advantage of people and situations. He was tough, yet gentle. He was determined to get things done, yet he didn't abuse his power. He was a man of faith, without being overzealous. Lincoln believed in "the ultimate justice of the people."

When you're true to yourself, you're more likely to be true to other people. What you value is what you think about most. What you think about is what you become and what you attract. Hold dear to your heart the concepts of honesty and integrity, and they'll always guide you.

No matter what failures you encounter, no matter what you accomplish, when you're honest and sincere in everything you do, you'll always feel respect for yourself and how you got there. You'll also feel more deserving.

Chapter 9a
ALWAYS DREAM AND SET GOALS
Second Part of the Fifth Step of
the THESAURUS Factor

You had an opportunity to define success for yourself in the first part of this book. Now, with goal setting in mind, do you remember your definition of success? In general, remember it's the progressive realization of worthwhile dreams and goals. Without desired outcomes in mind, you don't know where you're headed. And if you don't know where you're headed, chances are you're already there!

In 1952, Florence Chadwick swam across the English Channel and back. After that, she set a new goal to cross the 21-mile long Catalina Channel off the coast of California.

When she started out that morning it was chilly and foggy. The men on the chase boat were even shooting sharks. The water was cold. As she neared the coast, a thick fog rolled-in. She couldn't see. She was tired and shivering. Even though her coach and her mother were vigorously encouraging her to keep on going, to not quit, she still gave up.

After she got in the boat and the reporters came over to her, they asked "Why did you stop?" She answered, "I couldn't see the shore. I could only see the fog." At that point, she realized that *one of the most important things in seeking something is to never lose sight of it.* This is true whether you can physically see it or not.

Florence's second attempt was successful, even though the weather was just as cold and foggy as the first time. The difference was she had already pictured in her mind what the shore would look like before she got there! Furthermore, she was so determined on her second attempt that she actually beat the men's time by about two hours. That's remarkable.

The point is, the power of the mind, the power of a vision, is amazing. Always keep in sight where you want to go. Where do you want to be a year from now, two years from now, three years from now? *Dreams and goals are essential; they literally define your success.*

Put Your Dreams in Concrete and Your Plans in Sand!

Once your desired outcomes are fixed firmly in your mind, they will assist you in reaching your dreams. Without goals, you have no direction. Dorothy, in the *Wizard of Oz,* took only one yellow brick road. When you have ten yellow brick roads, when you are straddling two different paths, you don't accomplish much. If you don't stay on track, if you don't have a one-track mind, so to speak, it's very difficult to get where you want to go. You need to be focused to achieve the results you want.

Hopefully, you have an unwavering vision of where you want to go or what you want to become. Along the way, however, you may need to change the plans you created to accomplish that outcome. You may have to deal with different forces, pressures, expectations, and challenges, depending on how things develop. Keep your focus on the outcomes you want. Be sure they complement your definition of success, your purpose, and what you want to be. You may surprise yourself and achieve outcomes beyond your wildest dreams.

Many years ago, I dreamed about being a motivational speaker and author. I didn't know if I'd ever achieve that outcome. Nevertheless, I always visualized it happening. That was a dream, not necessarily a goal.

Goals are more specific. *Goals help you realize your dreams.* A goal could be something like, "I want to present to over a hundred companies and see my book read by over one million people during the course of a year." To realize that, I needed a plan of action. Remember, *goals define your success.* Always reach for outcomes you feel will be helpful to others and have the most importance to you. Seek to make a difference.

Goals are the most tangible of all the steps along the *Staircase.* They're like type AB blood. If you have AB blood, your system will accept 0, A, or B and be "happy." Goals are the same way; they're the universal recipient. Your level of commitment in incorporating all the steps on the *Staircase* into your life will, in many cases, determine the degree of success you have in achieving your goals.

To be an effective leader, it's essential to elevate your attitude and enthusiasm. If you have the goal of confronting your boss with a problem, self-control is necessary. If your goal is to get over what happened a year ago or just last week, you need to totally forgive. The accomplishment of these goals is emotionally related, as is the achievement of most goals. Do you see the importance of employing one or more of the *Staircase* steps in each situation?

If you want to be a more effective salesperson, you need to set goals to reach certain quotas. You'll also need to use the principles of the *THESAURUS Factor* to assist you in your presentation and communication skills. All the principles intertwine to give you a strong foundation of knowledge and understanding.

When you have achieved your goals and have realized whatever you define success to be, you are successful. In turn, hopefully, you also become fulfilled along the way. If each success supports your purpose, you are more likely to be fulfilled.

Have You Written Down What You Want?

Goal setting can be challenging at times because of the many areas of your life that call for your attention. Your personal, family, professional and financial goals all require your time and energy. Physical and mental health goals—taking care of yourself physically, emotionally, and spiritually—also need attention. The key is to take some time to write all these things down and then strive to maintain a balance. Remember, it is OK to be out-of-balance temporarily, as you focus on an area that truly needs your attention. You can regain your general balance.

Lou Holtz mentioned that one time, when he was unemployed, he read *The Magic of Thinking Big* by Dr. David J. Schwartz. (It's a book I would recommend to anyone—a wonderful, motivational, inspirational book along the lines of *Think and Grow Rich by* Napoleon Hill.) During that time, Lou took the opportunity to write down 120 things he wanted to accomplish. After he completed this list, he got so excited that he ran over to his wife and said, "Look, look, I have all these great goals!" His wife said, "Why don't you put down number 121—'Get a job!'"

Write down your goals. It's a proven fact that you're four times more likely to achieve what you write down. The act of writing causes you to focus your attention. The process of writing causes those goals to be processed by your brain. If it's not important enough for you to write it down, it's not important enough for you to accomplish.

Do You Use Affirmations?

An affirmation is a statement of an outcome you desire, written in the present tense, as if you've already achieved it.

Once you have your goals written down, perhaps on a 3 x 5 card, I recommend that you post them in front of you, maybe on your bathroom mirror, and read them at least twice every day—once upon arising and once again upon retiring. These are two times when your subconscious mind is most receptive to new ideas. There's usually little or no interference from other thoughts or situations that require your attention. The subconscious also receives new input more readily when you talk to it with emotion. Read your affirmations with emotion. Reach down into the depths of your soul and pour your heart into it for best results.

Do this for 30 days straight and you will have put a new belief into your subconscious. *Repetition and emotion are how you access your subconscious.* Once the affirmation is accepted, your subconscious will then drive your conscious mind to direct you to do the things necessary for you to realize your desired outcome.

Make Each Day Count

Eventually, I developed a dream. I got a vision of what I wanted to do and how I wanted to contribute. I knew that every action, no matter what job I had or position I held, would contribute to the progressive realization of my goals, and eventually my dreams. That, after all, is the definition of success; it's *a progression and a journey,* not a resting place.

It's great to have a to-do list; it's an excellent start. You have a feeling of accomplishment when you have crossed off eighteen items on a twenty-item list. However the remaining items may be the most important. Sure, you feel satisfied about crossing off eighteen things, but did you really do those things that contribute the most toward realizing your goals? Or did you just open some junk mail and rearrange your files?

When you have an objective, it's essential that you work toward it every day! This means prioritizing your tasks and completing them in order, as much as possible. (If it's a work-related objective, you may want to take a day or two of rest on the weekend, e.g., Sunday.)

Make each day count toward your progress. We are all affected by factors that interfere with our daily schedule and to-do lists. However, those factors are not meant to be used as an excuse for not achieving your goals.

The things we want most in life tend to be the most difficult and take the most time to complete. As with electricity and water, it is human nature to follow the path of least resistance. If that path doesn't lead to where you want to go, you may need to change directions. Real success requires persistent, consistent, focused effort.

The Goal Prioritizing Grid

I want to share with you a way to help you establish and prioritize your goals. It's called the Goal Prioritizing Grid.

To use the Goal Prioritizing Grid effectively, first write down all your goals, then prioritize each one. Next, actually write in these quadrants what you want to accomplish day to day, week to week, month to month, and year to year to give yourself a larger picture of what you want to accomplish.

Priority One Items Are Both Important and Urgent. They are things you do every day to maintain the organization's integrity, vitality, viability, and operation. Without doing them, that company's productivity could falter.

The Goal Prioritizing Grid

URGENT

Priority #1
(Day-to-day Routines)

_____
_____
_____
_____
_____

Priority #3
(Interruptions—Reactive)

_____
_____
_____
_____
_____

IMPORTANT ———————————— **NOT IMPORTANT**

Priority #2
(Goals—Reactive)

_____
_____
_____
_____

Priority #4
(Don't Bother)

_____
_____
_____
_____

NOT URGENT

The same thing is true at home. We're focusing more on work when we talk about goals, but the same thing is true with family life. Do you have personal *and* family goals? You need to do certain things every day, week, or year to keep your home clean, organized, attractive, and in good repair. There are some basic things that need to be done. They are Priority Ones. If you don't do them, something or someone is going to suffer.

Priority Two Items Are Important But Not Urgent. This quadrant is critical; put your goals here. Remember that goal of wanting to present a seminar to a hundred different companies and organizations next year? That goes here. The items listed here aren't urgent; they're not right now, but they're so important to your success. List your goals here and invest some time in them daily, if possible. People who "live" in the Priority Two Quadrant are primarily proactive.

Proactive is a word that may not be found in some dictionaries, but it is common in management literature. According to Stephen R. Covey, author of *The Seven Habits of Highly Effective People,* "Proactive means more than merely taking initiative. It means that as human beings we are responsible for our own lives. Our behavior is a function of our decisions, not our conditions. We can subordinate feelings to values. We have the initiative and the responsibility to make things happen.... Highly proactive people recognize that...they do not blame circumstances, conditions, or conditioning for their behavior...it's a product of their own conscious choice, based on values, rather than a product of their conditions, based on feeling."

Priority Three Items Are Urgent But Not Important. This is a quadrant for things that just sort of happen for many people. For some reason, because of a day-to-day reaction to life's events, urgent things tend to take priority over important things. The people who live here are probably reactive.

Once again we look to Stephen Covey's book, *The Seven Habits of Highly Effective People,* where he says we are proactive by nature, however, "if our lives are a function of conditioning and conditions, it is because we have, by conscious decision or default, chosen to empower those things that control us.... Reactive people are often affected by their physical environment.... Reactive people build their emotional lives around the behavior of others, empowering the weaknesses of other people to control them."

Reactive people often exhibit a habitual robotic-like response to situations or events. For example, when the telephone rings, a reactive person automatically answers it. He's giving power to the person calling over what he's doing that instant. Remember, if it's important, they'll call back or leave a message. It's okay to let your answering machine or voice mail take calls and have them pile up. You can answer them later when the time suits *you!*

Oftentimes, the main factor that inhibits our achieving our goals is the conflict between Priorities Two and Three. It may look impressive to have a to-do list of 20 items and have 18 of them crossed out, but if you accomplished items that were urgent yet not important, did you spend your time wisely? As Peter Drucker, author of *The Effective Executive,* said, "It is often more important to do the right things than to just do things right."

What is easier? Rearranging your desk or starting on that sales report; finding new clients or associates, or stopping by the old ones to say "Hi"; working on a relationship or giving up; changing certain behavior patterns, like drinking, smoking, and overeating, or making excuses why you can't?

Once again, if you don't work toward accomplishing what you want most, the door of excuse-making and complaining is likely to swing wide open. You probably have the talent and desire to accomplish your goals. However, it also requires discipline, the proper use of time, and appropriate effort to achieve them.

What's the Catch Here?

The point is, we're talking about self-responsibility. When you are self-responsible, you tend to be in control of yourself. A problem may arise, however, when you want to do everything yourself. Self-responsibility, taken to an extreme, can actually get you in trouble when it comes to prioritizing goals. If you spend time on areas that are urgent but not important (Priority Three), if you fail to delegate or don't properly prioritize, it's going to be difficult to stay on track; it will take you longer to reach your goals, if you reach them at all. Once again, the major conflict is between Priorities Two and Three.

Here are some items that would fit into Priority One:

1. Making a new sales appointment. This is urgent and important, because without sales appointments you are unlikely to have any sales.
2. Planning is urgent and important. If you don't have a plan, you're unlikely to ever reach your goals.

Here are some items for Priority Two:

1. Your goals, both personal and career.
2. Writing your own book.
3. Building a new house.
4. Getting tenure.
5. Retiring from your job into your own business.
6. Becoming an accomplished speaker.
7. Earning $100,000 or more a year.
8. Doing $1,000,000 or more in sales.
9. Achieving a certain profit margin for a corporation.

In short, Priority Two items are goals. There could be a variety of things that are longer term. They're not urgent, but they're very important.

Many people certainly have things they feel are urgent (and easily done), but not important. Yet they may allow these things to get in the way of their goals. Remember, the path of least resistance may not be the path toward the outcomes we want.

To do the sometimes difficult things necessary to achieve your goals, you may need to get out of your comfort zone. It will help you grow personally. You need to stretch. You may need to take some sort of risk. You need to step out from where you are to get somewhere else. As long as you have something to grab onto, you can leave the comfort or familiar zone. Often this zone is more familiar than comfortable; you're just used to it.

Sometimes goals can be scary because if they're intangible—like personal growth, for instance—they're not right there in front of you. You seldom get immediate gratification and they're difficult to see. Such goals may require more imagination and faith.

What could be some goals for your children? How about setting some goals for your relationships? What might be some goals for the people who work for you or with you?

A mission statement is crucial and it's absolutely essential. If your company does not have any mission statements, there's probably no overall direction for people to follow. If you are in a position of management or supervision, it is vitally important to sit down with your people and find out what their goals and aspirations are. This enables you to work together to accomplish your company's goals while still meeting the desires of your staff as much as possible.

Suppose you begin training seven people, all of whom you believe want to be sales managers. Suppose further, that after a year goes by, you discover that six have absolutely no desire to be managers. What have you done? You have wasted a lot of time and energy trying to train people who have no interest. It never works.

The best way to avoid that situation is to sit down with your people, early on, and establish goals. Something wonderful is likely to happen. In most cases, team-building immediately begins to take place. Your concern and caring can help create a feeling of unity, where everybody's on the same sheet of music.

Can you imagine going to a symphony with half the orchestra playing *The 1812 Overture* and half playing Beethoven's *Fifth*? It would be a little confusing, to say the least! If an organization is not playing on the same sheet of music, it's very difficult to accomplish anything.

Finally, we come to **Priority Four Items Which Are Not Important and Not Urgent.** What's to be said about this quadrant? Not much, except ignore anything listed there. You would be spending time on things that are absolutely worthless to the accomplishment of where you want to be.

NOTE: I would not put vacations or recreation here. They are important to your well-being and maintaining a balanced life.

Invest time in your goals. Write them down. Every motivational speaker and success consultant will tell you that all great people have had clearly defined goals. They've taken the time to spell them out in detail. It would be an excellent investment of your time and energy for you to do the same.

What Can Hinder the Accomplishment of Your Goals?

What is it that could work against our being honest with ourselves when we are trying to determine just what it is that we want out of life?

Achieving goals can be hindered by the fear of being limited to getting only what you say you want. Specifying something defines desire and, in a way, sets a limit. Make room for increases in your goal statements. For example, you could say your goal is to earn $100,000 or *more* rather than limiting it to $100,000. State what you want and beyond. If you don't, you may run the risk of limiting your true potential, never becoming all you can be.

Naming something as your goal gives you a certain ownership. It is an excellent and essential beginning to getting what you want. It gives you a satisfaction that never comes to someone who gets something they didn't ask for. You've probably seen it happen. For instance, there are children who aren't given the chance to build up desire for something before it's handed to them. They could grow up unable to appreciate anything. These children may be accused of ingratitude by parents who have deprived them of a chance to know what it means to be grateful after working hard to achieve a goal. Their parents often don't know the difference between being a big spender and being generous. Big spenders give some of their surplus to those who happen to be around. Generous people offer to be a resource for others, and allow them to determine what they need or want.

We don't want to put down the effort of well-intentioned people. Most of us do have some difficulty sorting through just what our aims are when we give. Do we just want to be liked? Do we just want to assure we'll get a gift back when it's our turn? Do we just want to avoid the embarrassment of being the only person who didn't give? We may have some of these reasons in mind when we give. By honestly acknowledging that, we become more aware of our intentions. We also become stronger and can come closer to being the truly generous people we want to be.

Lack of imagination is another thing that can get in the way of writing down goals. We may not even let ourselves dream of things that seem beyond our reach. This is sad. Your dream is your vision for something better in your life. So dream as big as you can. It's people who see things as they could be and ask "Why not?" who bring about the changes that make life better for everyone.

A fulfilled human being is more likely to be a gift and resource to everyone around him, than is a disappointed and discouraged person. The world can benefit by your dreaming and your setting and accomplishing goals for a better life for yourself. In the process of pursuing your goals you are most likely helping others. Or, at a minimum, you are a happier person to be around. Everyone wins.

Most People Die with Their Music Still in Them—*Their Song Unsung*

Honesty and goal-setting can be challenging. While they normally involve patient processing of life's experiences, there are occasional moments when we suddenly realize a truth about ourselves. It could be that we're not doing what we really want to do most passionately in our lives. We may not be meeting our own expectations of ourselves in several key areas.

I had an experience like that when I was the officer-in-command of a funeral detail. I was a company commander in the Missouri Army National Guard, stationed in Carthage. The funeral was for a young soldier of mine, my jeep driver, who had been killed in a motorcycle accident.

When I stepped forward to present the flag to the soldier's mother, as required, I said: "This flag is presented on behalf of a grateful nation as a token of our appreciation for the honorable and faithful service rendered by your loved one."

I could barely say the words. They were suddenly so real for me.

There was a bigger truth than mourning the loss of a soldier and friend. I had to honestly admit I was mourning the loss of all who die too young. I mourned the loss of all the dreams that get cut down before they blossom. I mourned the loss of people who die with their music still in them, their song unsung. I was raging against not being able to control death, not being able to prevent what I didn't want.

I realized I was as powerless at this graveside as I had been at my father's. When it came to controlling the forces of death, I was no more able to do so now than I had been at eleven.

I knew that all any of us have is the present. We can choose to be all that we are meant to be. We can choose to make a difference each day, large or small, in the lives of others. We cannot change the past. We can change our lives today. We can set and achieve goals that are important to us, one step at a time. We can embrace the present and, through our contributions to life, leave a legacy for those that follow.

Chapter 10
UPGRADE YOUR KNOWLEDGE
First Part of the Sixth Step of
the THESAURUS Factor

K nowledge gives you the information you need to go forward so you can grow and become the best you can be. Helen Keller said, "The most pathetic person in the world is one who has sight but has no vision." Increased knowledge can help you have a clearer vision. Always take the opportunity to learn more about things that can help you move toward your dreams.

Every time you think, you form an opinion. That process causes you to look inside, perceive better what's going on outside, and make a decision. (Your decision could even be not to make a decision!) Every time you think deeply about something, you grow. Every time you exercise your mind you grow. Einstein said, "The average person uses less than ten percent of his brain power."

We've all heard the expression "mind over matter." It's so true. The power of the mind is phenomenal. In the area of health, for instance, it's well-known that people have recovered from illnesses that doctors said were beyond medical treatment. They made up their minds to overcome their medical condition and survived. In some cases they helped many others by sharing their experiences.

Are you spending time focusing on things that aren't necessary, applicable, or helpful to the realization of the outcomes you want? Watching the TV show *Sesame Street* is helpful to children. However, when they watch something negative or violent, is that benefiting them? When you participate in events and daily routines, ask yourself if they will contribute to your personal and professional growth. When you cease to learn positive beneficial things, you cease to grow; you're literally wasting your time.

Push the Outside of the Envelope!

Accept no limits for yourself. *The only limit we really have is our vision.* If it needs to be bigger, we can make it bigger. As test pilots say, "Push the outside of the envelope." They're referring to taking the aircraft to the edge of its performance capabilities. They want to see what it can ultimately do without breaking it. Push at the outer edges of your knowledge and you'll expand your vision. Did you stop doing that? Some people stop learning when they leave school. When did you first become aware of what you didn't know? When you discovered you needed knowledge in certain areas, did you take action?

Babies are born with the desire to know more. A healthy, growing child is interested in almost everything new that comes along. Kids grow by pushing at the outer limits of their knowledge, and that's how adults grow too.

Recall a child's total preoccupation with something new. When he's finished focusing, he'll often let out a sigh of satisfaction. How long has it been since you got satisfaction by learning something new? Explore the outer limits of your knowledge. Push at the edges of your interests and talents and you will grow.

Wise parents know boundaries are their children's learning frontiers. They guide each child's growth by enlarging boundaries as the child matures. Children given gentle but firm guidance can become strong adults capable of endless learning and growth.

In my travels consulting and giving seminars, I've found that many people who usually act bravely are often affected by *the fear of having no boundaries*. This is often a result of having lived under rigid limits in the past. But like many other obstacles in life, this too can be overcome. Once again, we need to let go of the old and embrace the new. A continuing educational program of personal and professional development books, CDs, and seminars can really make a difference in your understanding of your own boundaries and supposed limitations. As a result, you're likely to expand them tremendously.

Knowledge is virtually useless unless you use it or share it with others. Be generous with it. There's no need to hold onto it. When you share it you still have it! Besides, there's more where that came from. Knowledge is a powerful tool to help you and others when it's used or shared. Also, sharing it reinforces and may even deepen your understanding. When you teach others, you often teach yourself something in the process.

By its very nature the knowledge you already have is limited. On the other hand, the knowledge you don't have is virtually unlimited. Be courageous. Let go of your limits. Go to the edge and learn more. Don't settle for just what you have now. Pause on this step of the *Staircase* to *upgrade* yourself with new knowledge. Push the outside of the envelope that surrounds what you already know.

Do you equate learning only with formal education? If so, you may want to consider broadening your view to include other ways of learning.

Push at that edge. Thomas Edison had only three months of formal education. When he began, Henry Ford knew just a little about cars, but he knew enough to hire qualified people to design and build them. We can learn not only through our own experiences but also from others by reading, watching a presentation, observing, and listening.

Even if you have years of formal education and professional credentials, it's still important to be open and interested in the world around you. You may have been so focused on your specialty in your formal schooling, that you missed out on gaining a broad knowledge base. You may need to lighten up. You may have been taught to think in a way that no longer works for you. That way may not work for you any longer. You may be a perfect candidate for pushing the outside of the envelope that was given to you by your schooling. Be fearless on this step. Be glad for what you know, and open up your mind to learn more.

Tap into Your Brain's Enormous Capacity

The human brain, your brain, is incredible. About the size of two fists put together, it is capable of recording eight-hundred memories per second for a hundred years without exhausting itself! It can store somewhere between ten billion and one-hundred billion pieces of information. The brain records everything it takes in and always remembers it; even though we don't recall all the information stored, it's all on permanent file.

A True Warrior of Knowledge

Survival was more than just "hanging on for dear life" for Major Rhonda Scott Cornum. She's the U.S. Army flight surgeon who was in a helicopter that was shot down during the 1991 Persian Gulf War. She was then captured and held as a Prisoner of War.

When the time the enemy found her, they discovered she had already been shot in the shoulder. She also suffered two broken arms, a torn knee ligament, and a fractured finger. Somehow she still managed to pull herself clear of the burning wreckage. Her captors concluded that she was in so much pain it was hard to believe she was still alive.

Cornum's survival also meant she exhibited integrity and moral courage. She couldn't risk showing cowardice during her week-long interrogation. She received no medical treatment either, while being moved eleven times! She tenaciously held onto the determination that got her through medical school and then the army.

Cornum's life reveals a continual quest for knowledge. Cornell University was her first choice for college. But unable to afford it as a freshman, she enrolled at Wilmington College in Ohio, then transferred to Cornell. In 1975, at the age of 20, she earned her Bachelor of Science in microbiology and genetics. In 1979, she earned her Doctorate in biochemistry and nutrition.

Cornum never dreamed of having a military career. But during her second year of graduate school, she presented a summary report abstract on the metabolism of amino acids at a conference in Atlantic City. There she was approached by an officer from the Letterman Army Institute of Research at the Presidio in San Francisco. He invited her to attend the Institute so she could learn a technique related to her Cornell work. Cornum accepted the invitation because she was thirsty for more knowledge and enthusiastic about their laboratory and what it could offer.

True to form, Cornum grew from her learning. Soon she developed an avid interest in military life. She was even considered a candidate for astronaut training. In 1986, she earned her medical degree.

To make greater use of her knowledge, Cornum served as a flight surgeon assigned to the 22nd Battalion, 229th Attack Helicopter Regiment. This unit was one of the first deployed to Operation Desert Shield. Her primary duty was to provide medical care to the more than 300 members of the unit.

Cornum's helicopter was shot down February 27, 1991, the fourth day of the 100-day ground war. She was on a mission to rescue the pilot of a USAF F-15 who was shot down behind enemy lines. Five of the crew of eight were killed when the helicopter was hit by intense anti-aircraft and automatic weapons fire. Fortunately, Cornum survived and was released from captivity on March 6, 1991.

What Cornum learned from her experience was invaluable, not only to herself but to the entire country. It forced her to push to the edge of her own mental and physical endurance. In fact, as Cornum shared her knowledge, Americans learned more about the role more military women could have.

"It is important that everyone be allowed to compete for all available jobs, regardless of gender," she says. Also she noted, "The qualities most important in all military jobs, like integrity, moral courage, and determination have nothing to do with gender."

About herself, Cornum says, "A long life in and of itself is not my goal. I hope I have one, but not at the expense of a great life en route." She focused on quality rather than just quantity. No one could have spoken truer words than Cornum, whose contributions came from a life invested in consistently acquiring more knowledge.

How Do You Get Rid of Self-Imposed Limits?

Dance up a storm on this step! Your success is largely determined by your level of expectation.

Are unlimited expectations realistic? Yes, for you they could be! But remember, whatever you believe is what's likely to be realistic for you. Your expectations of others and what they will do for or with you needs to be limited. Believe in everyone, but count on no one other than yourself to be as committed to achieving *your* dreams and goals. *Anyone else's desire to meet your expectations will be limited by the outcomes they want.* To gain cooperation it needs to be a win-win situation. When it comes to what you expect of yourself, you can accelerate your success by getting rid of self-imposed limits, as well as the limits others may set for you.

Always be open to learning more. Look for an enthusiastic mentor who is teaching what he loves most. A friend who had received an excellent university education told me that was her secret. She figured she would probably be inspired most and learn best from committed educators who were passionate about their subjects. She was correct.

Inspired teachers may come to you through books, CDs, classes, seminars, and the people you meet. Follow up by obtaining additional materials to reinforce and supplement what you learned. In the great information age we are now in, there are plenty of resources for you to use to be on the cutting edge of your profession. If you're like most people, you probably know what you need to read, listen to, and attend to keep growing in your field. The key is—*do it!*

Be sure you are pushing at the many edges of your envelope. Keep your life interesting and your learning wheels turning by pursuing new interests. Remember, variety makes life more exciting.

This step also has room for the dance of self-knowledge. The sage advice, "Know thyself," is just as true today as it was for the ancient Greeks. It is an essential part of your journey along the *Staircase*.

The More You Know—*the More You Grow*

If you cease to learn, you cease to grow. Knowledge and experience go hand in hand. *Experience is the validation of knowledge.* Knowledge breeds understanding, and understanding breeds wisdom. Bergin Evans, educator and writer, once said, "Wisdom is meaningless until our own experience gives it meaning."

You may read all the books in the world on scuba diving, but if you don't get into the ocean, how can you expect to see any fish swimming around? Don't you dare say in an aquarium! Unless you take what you learn and apply it in actual experience in the environment, it's difficult to validate what you've learned.

There is not necessarily a correlation between formal education and success! Did you know that? Just because I graduated from West Point does not necessarily mean I will be successful. Abe Lincoln was self-taught. The Wright Brothers did not go to college. Sam Walton was not well-educated either. You could go on and on. You could list many people who had little formal education, but became very successful, powerful, and accomplished. Many college graduates cannot find a job in their field of study. In fact, 90 percent of them eventually won't be working in the area in which they earned their degree! Formal education can be wonderful, but it provides no guarantees. Many people, in the past as well as the present, became successful without it. Not having a formal education is *No Excuse!* not to be successful.

What's important is what you do with what you know. Are you adapting and applying what you learned to where you want to take your life and what you want to become? If you want to be the top salesperson, you need to invest time in learning about sales. If you want to be an excellent parent, read books and listen to CDs on how to be an effective parent. If you want to be a champion gardener, there are books and CDs that can teach you how. Get to know yourself, and learn what kinds of skills and knowledge you need and want to acquire. This is one of the keys to a more enjoyable life.

Give Yourself Time to Learn—*You Are Your Own Best Investment*
Did you know that four years after you plant a Chinese bamboo tree, there is still no visible growth? This is true no matter how much you nourish and water it. But, lo and behold, during the fifth year the Chinese bamboo can grow ninety feet tall! How did that happen? For four years it established a strong root system. In fact, it has one of the most extensive root systems of any plant. To support ninety feet it needs a lot of roots. The point is, anything worthwhile, like knowledge and education, takes time.

You may not see the results of your efforts right away. You may be planting the seeds day-in and day-out. For example, when you start your own business, define success in your life, establish a purpose, and start giving to other people, you're sowing the seeds. When you take in new knowledge, you're planting seeds for even more knowledge. You may not see the results immediately; it might take three or four years or more. You are establishing a root system. Once it's solid, nobody can topple your tree. Your tree is you. *You are your own best investment for the present and future.*

No matter what you want to achieve, you need information that can assist you. Make sure the knowledge you gain can help you get where you want to go and become what you want to be.

Knowledge can help you to be more effective and can contribute to the rate of your thinking and activity. The rate at which you gain knowledge helps to determine whether you succeed or fail. It can help give you the edge over your competition.

Apply your education to serving the needs of others. You'll find that when your intention is to serve others, it can make a significant difference in your ability to provide a useful product or service.

When you increase your knowledge, you'll have more information to take care of the people you live with, work with, and serve. It can make a major difference in both your business and family life.

Associate with People Who Are Knowledgeable in Your Field

Another important aspect of upgrading your knowledge is to associate with people who are knowledgeable in your field. One of the most beneficial things you can do is to be a part of a support group. Associate with people of like-mind with whom you can share ideas, dreams, and goals. It will empower you! If you're an educator, associate with other educators who are forward thinking and also want to increase their knowledge. If you own and operate your own business, mix with other business owners. If you want to market your business more effectively, make it a point to be with people who know marketing.

One mind is fine, but when you put two, three, or four minds together, what a difference it makes. It's the power of collective thinking. Two or more minds are better than one, in most cases. Associate with a group that is hungry for knowledge. You may be surprised to find there are lots of people like that who will take time to invest in themselves and you. Upgrade your knowledge. It's an investment that will last you a lifetime.

Chapter 10a
UNDERSTAND PEOPLE
Second Part of the Sixth Step of the THESAURUS Factor

Earl Nightingale said, "There is a direct correlation between communication and language and the degree of success you achieve." Think about it. As soon as someone begins talking, don't you immediately get a feel for where they are on the *Staircase*? You will probably get an instant impression of how educated they are by they way they pronounce their words, the effectiveness of their communication, and the extent of their vocabulary.

When you're dealing with people every day, who do you enjoy working with the most? Would you rather work with someone who expresses himself effectively or someone who doesn't? In sales, the person who can best express how the benefits of his company's product or service relates to the needs of the client will probably get the sale. Parents who can effectively express discipline to their children will be obeyed more often. The person who can communicate effectively with different types of people in his organization is likely to be more effective as a leader. Communication is the fundamental cornerstone of human relations. Without good communication skills, you cannot be an effective manager, leader, or parent.

A couple can develop true love when they understand and respect each other. You may have fallen in love and continued on to develop genuine love because you met a person who understood and respected you—no matter what you said or did—unconditionally. You communicated with each other. This type of relationship is to be treasured. I believe all of us want to feel like we're understood and respected.

Dale Carnegie, in his great book, *How to Win Friends and Influence People,* shared many ideas on how to get along with other people. The whole premise of the book is basically to show concern and respect for others—be interested in them and what they say and do.

When you show a *genuine* interest in the needs of other people, you'll be amazed at how rapidly a relationship can develop. Most people, however, tend to spend more time thinking about themselves. They would rather benefit from the interaction personally than give of themselves so others can benefit. When the person you're dealing with benefits from the interaction, the relationship is more likely to continue and grow. You'll have a better chance of communicating and developing understanding and respect.

Oftentimes people who need recognition the most get it the least, and that's many of us! Some people try to get recognition by calling attention to themselves. They are afraid no one will notice them if they don't blow their own horn. They fail to realize that we get what we give away. If you want more recognition, understanding, and love, give it away to others first. When you meet someone, pronounce their name correctly. It's a compliment to ask someone how to pronounce their name. Reach out and do your best to understand them, and it's likely you'll increase the effectiveness of your communication. You will eventually get it back; maybe not from them, but it will come back. They or someone else will strive to understand you, and you'll feel gratified that somebody cares.

People Will Often Like You When You Listen to Them

One of the keys to effective communication is listening; it helps you understand. Remember, Epictetus, the Greek philosopher said, "We were given two ears and only one mouth. We need to listen twice as much as we talk!" Very few people have had any formal training in listening. Yet it is important to do it every day. If you don't know how to listen, how can you expect to understand people? If you're thinking about what you're going to say while they're talking to you, how can you possibly understand them? How can you relate to them? *To be an effective communicator you need to listen.*

A wonderful colleague of mine, Jim Gallager, is one of the founders of the International Listening Association based at Ball State University. He once shared with me that "We listen through our feet!" When I first heard that it struck me as odd. What he meant was we listen based on our feelings, experiences, environment, and thoughts. Every day we have new feelings and experiences, and our environment may change. This all affects how we think, which largely determines how we listen.

When you interact with someone, your "feet" will probably have a major influence on how effectively you listen and how well you understand what is being shared. However, if you're focused only on your own feelings, thoughts, and experiences, you're not likely to invest time listening to the other person. Focus outside of yourself and on the other person.

Invest your time and energy in understanding other people's feelings. Do your best to get in touch with their experiences. What are they thinking about? How are they in their environment? Do we listen through our feet? The feet analogy gives us a simple way to understand how we could listen more skillfully with a stronger awareness of what we bring to the relationship.

Most speakers talk at the rate of 120-150 words a minute. An excited, motivated speaker talks at around 160-190 words a minute. We think at anywhere from 400-600 words a minute. For you to sit and listen while your mind is going at a different pace is a challenge. On average, you pick up only about 25 percent of what you hear.

To learn most effectively, it is necessary to reinforce what you've heard. This is the reason CDs have been so successful. Through repeated listening, you can learn the material much more thoroughly. Instead of always listening to music, which is nice to relax to once in a while, you could listen to something you'd like to learn or to help motivate yourself. When you don't need to relax, you could play a motivational or instructional CD in your car or home CD player. Listening to it can help you develop as a parent, salesperson, spouse, or something else that interests you.

Listen with your feet. Every time you share people's feelings and understand them and their thoughts, you'll listen better. Whenever you show respect, concern, and interest in them, you'll listen more effectively. They're likely to feel you understand them. You'll most likely have an instant relationship with them and their business. You've created a win-win situation.

When you listen, be sure to look into the other person's eyes. Ignore distractions like noises and other people walking by. It's not just what you hear with your ears that is important; it's also what you learn with your eyes. This is called empathic listening, and it shows people you care. Remember, *people don't care how much you know until they know how much you care.*

Mother Teresa was limited in her knowledge of science, but she was one of the world's most empathic listeners. If ever there was a person to ask, "What does it feel like to give of yourself to thousands of hurting people, day in and day out, showing empathy and compassion?" she would be the one! The lady knew how to listen.

How Do You Express Yourself?

When someone presents a talk, 58 percent of their impact is visual (what is seen), 35 percent is verbal (how it's said), and only 7 percent is content (what is said). In other words, we communicate primarily with feelings. Any presentation can be changed and given an entirely different meaning based on the way the speaker expresses his *feelings,* how he uses his *energy,* and how he expresses his *thoughts.* If you don't use inflection (change your voice tone and loudness), or look into the eyes of the person you're speaking to, the meaning of what you're saying may be communicated very differently than what you intended. When your voice and behavior are congruent, you communicate most effectively. For example, if you are saying you are absolutely certain about something, while looking scared and doubtful, you're incongruent; i.e., you're giving mixed messages.

How effective are you at expressing thoughts and ideas? How effective are you at sharing your products and services? If you are in sales and marketing, it is important to effectively express the benefits of your product and service and how they can satisfy your customer's needs. If you don't, you may not make many sales. You cannot be an effective manager, leader, or parent if you cannot express yourself effectively.

When you talk to others, whether you're sharing or seeking knowledge, be yourself; be real. Let people know you care about them and that you want to satisfy their needs. When you learn more about dealing with people, you'll be more able to help them.

Everyone Has a Dominant Learning Style

We all learn and experience our environment differently. We all see the world through a different pair of eyes. There are three learning styles: Some of us are primarily visual, some primarily auditory, and some primarily kinesthetic. So what does this mean?

When people go to a concert, what do they focus on? Sixty percent of the people are visual; they tend to focus on the lights, the environment, the seating, how the orchestra or band is arranged, how the entertainers are dressed, and maybe even the colorful clothing worn by the audience. They focus on the visual aspects because that's primarily how they communicate. They best perceive the world through *seeing*. Sight is their dominant sense. A visual may say, "I see what you mean." Some people, however, are auditory. When they go to a concert, they're not really concerned with how things look; they're more interested in the sound of the music. When auditories go to a concert, they listen for the exact notes and how precise they are. They hear the crowd and other environmental noises, like the sound of a siren sounding near the concert hall. These folks perceive the world primarily through *hearing*. An auditory may say, "I hear what you are saying."

Can you understand how relationships are affected by the way a person perceives what's going on? When you have a visual and an auditory together, and they aren't aware of each other's dominant sense, they probably won't communicate effectively. If one person relates best by seeing and the other by hearing, they would do well to know that about each other. When they are aware of this difference, it increases their chances of relating and understanding each other.

The kinesthetics perceive their world primarily by how they *feel*. What's the atmosphere like in that room? Is it exciting and friendly or unenthusiastic and cold? Does the music help to create sad or happy feelings? Do they feel comfortable in the environment? Does the program make sense? Are they feeling pleased about being there? A kinesthetic may say, "I feel the same way."

Everyone shares a little of all three learning styles. We are all visual to a degree. We are all auditory and kinesthetic to some degree as well. However, we all have one dominant sense. What is yours?

When students are learning in a classroom, the visuals are going to focus on the board; what it says and how it reads. The true auditory, however, will wait until the teacher explains what he just wrote or showed. The kinesthetic will ask, does it make sense? Does it feel right? Is it conceptually correct? Can you see how this impacts the way we communicate with other people?

Would You Like to Better Understand People?

Most of us come in contact with people every day. Everyone is different and we all have our own style of relating with others. How can we effectively deal with these various personality types? It takes versatility: That's the ability to adapt your own personality or temperament to that of others so you can satisfy their needs. It is the key to effective communication.

Many of us have a personality or temperament different than the people with whom we associate. We all perceive the world somewhat differently. You can verify that by asking two people who saw the same event to describe what they saw. You'll almost certainly get two different answers. We all have a dominant need. Unless you understand a person's personality and need, it's difficult to have a mutually satisfying relationship, make a sale, or lead effectively.

If you make sales calls or are responsible for managing and leading others, it's essential for you to learn more about the different personality types or temperaments. If you don't, it could be very difficult to get people to work with you. You want people to work *with* you, not just *for* you. Teamwork is more likely to be productive when people feel they are a bigger part of something, not just considered a hired hand. How can you interact more effectively to satisfy the needs of specific personalities?

The idea that people have different personalities and dominant needs was developed long ago by Carl Jung in his book, *Personality Types*. But to make it easier to understand these differences in people, we have adopted the approach developed by Dr. Robert A. Rohm in his book *Positive Personality Profiles*.

What Makes Up a Personality?

There are basically four types of personalities or temperaments, but no one is only one of them. While each of us is a unique blend of the four, we tend to favor one or two areas the most. In fact, 80 percent of us exhibit predominantly two temperaments. To help you better understand yourself and others, and why you think, act, and feel the way you do, let's approach this graphically with a pie chart of four quadrants.

To begin with, people are primarily either task-oriented or people-oriented, and either outgoing or reserved. The mix of these four characteristics, and the charts that go along with them, explain the great variety of personalities that exist.

To get a handle on all of this, let's split the pie horizontally and look at the upper and lower halves. The top half represents people who are outgoing and fast-paced. The lower half represents people who are reserved and slower-paced. Active and optimistic people are outgoing, while passive and cautious, "realistic" people are more reserved. One is not better than the other, just different. When we attempt to assess someone's personality, all we are doing is observing behavior. We are not passing judgment.

Outgoing People

You know people who predominantly tell and talk. All you need to do is go to a meeting and you'll soon know who does most of the talking and telling. Some of these people do not even pause or seem to take a breath between words. They just keep talking. They go, go, go!

People who tell and talk a lot tend to be more aggressive, anxious, and enthusiastic. They are more assertive than others and express themselves more. Their expressions and how they say something are more visual. Outgoing people show their emotions more. You know immediately how they are feeling by their facial expressions, how they move their hands, their arms, and the words they use. You know if they are happy, sad, angry, or upset. They don't hide anything.

Outgoing people are self-confident and always seem to be involved in something, usually in a leadership capacity. They like to be in charge of people, programs, and events and don't mind risk. Outgoing people can round out their personalities by being a little more cautious and steady.

Reserved People

Then you have other people who are not nearly as talkative. They ask and listen more and tend to be more supportive, respectful, and soft-spoken. They tend to control their emotions. They don't use nearly as many facial expressions or body movements. You often can't tell if they're happy or sad, angry or upset. They internalize a lot of their emotions and are usually polite and have lots of patience.

Reserved people are cautious and don't like getting involved in very many activities. They tend to analyze things longer and can be very critical. Quality is important to them and they tend to nit pick. They look for substance and are content to go through life with one or two close friends. They are homebodies and would sooner be alone rather than in a crowd. They are steady and reliable and don't care for surprises or risk.

Reserved people can round out their personality by tightening up, being more inspiring, and a little more assertive.

Now let's split our personality pie vertically and look at the right- and left-hand sides. The right half represents people who are primarily interested in relationships. They care most about people and how they feel and like to interact with others. The left half represents people who are primarily interested in things. They love planning, working on projects, and getting things done.

People-Oriented People

You know people who are predominantly interested in relationships. They are more concerned with touching and feelings. They are empathetic, open, and love to share with and care about others.

People-oriented people are good listeners and are concerned about how other people feel. They have a strong need to be accepted and therefore are tuned-in to the needs of others. People are more important to them than getting things done. People-oriented people can round out their personality by being more focused on their objectives.

Task-Oriented People

Task-oriented people are more focused on getting the job done. They like mechanical things to be in top running order and are very detail-oriented. They love to plan things out and make it happen. They are reliable and thorough.

Task-oriented people are often so hard-charging and direct that they can easily offend others. Their focus is so strong that they often are not empathetic or sensitive toward others needs. They just want to get it done, no matter what. Task-oriented people can round out their personality by listening and being more empathetic toward others.

Let's Put It All Together

Now let's put the horizontal and vertical lines onto one pie chart for a really simple and easy way to look at the four personality types. Let's also add the letters D, I, S, and C to label them, starting with the D and going clockwise around the pie.

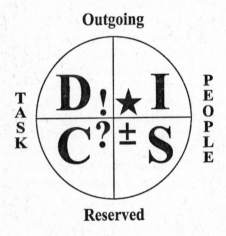

The D (Dominant) Needs to Be in Charge

The D quadrant represents a person who is both outgoing and task-oriented. The letter D is used because this personality type tends to be a **Dominant, Driving, Demanding, Determined, Decisive Doer.** The exclamation point symbolizes this is a person with a do-it-now attitude! About 10 percent of all people are Ds.

Ds (Choleric, according to Hippocrates) control, tell, and dictate. Their eye contact tends to be forceful and persistent. They are usually direct. Their body movements are very precise; they're in control. This is like the traditional style CEO sitting behind the desk giving orders. They need to be in control and in charge.

Ds are always moving forward, getting things done, and looking for something better. They're task-oriented. If you're a salesperson presenting a pharmaceutical product to a physician who is a D, he'll probably be more concerned about the effectiveness of the medication rather than its safety. Safety is important to them, but they primarily want to know that it works.

Ds are admirable in crises; they often handle things well. They're generally accurate in dictating instructions. However, let's say you want to make a proposal or a suggestion. If you do not understand his need to be in control and you attempt to dictate to him, you'll never get what you want. You are threatening his need to be in control.

So how do you deal with a D? How do you communicate with someone who's dictating to you all the time, telling you what he wants? How do you deal with someone who's very efficiency-oriented and wants it done now? How do you deal with a person who only looks at what is happening in the present and who may not be concerned about what happened yesterday or what will happen tomorrow?

What is the best way to deal with someone who wants to control? Let them control! If you want to propose an idea or sell a product or service, give the D *options*. When you give him, say, three *options* like a, b, or c, he still feels in control. In other words, you make recommendations, but you let him make the decision. You both win. It works—even with children.

The I (Inspirational) Needs to Be Noticed

The I quadrant represents a person who is both outgoing and people-oriented. The letter "I" is used because this personality type tends to be *Inspirational, Influencing, Inducing, Impressive, Interactive, Interesting,* and *Interested* in people. The star symbolizes that this is a person who likes to make it fun. About 25-30 percent of all people are "Is."

The I (Sanguine, according to Hippocrates) enjoys "show and tell." They are enthusiastic and talk through great hand, arm, and body movements. They smile and go on and on and on. You often can't get a word in edgewise. If you're a salesperson, they may not listen to you. When you try to provide information to them, you'll often find that as you attempt to communicate with them they're often thinking about something else.

It's often a challenge to get a decision from an I. When you do, it may be based on faulty reasoning. An I's dominant need is to be recognized. To win with them, provide an incentive. They like rewards and awards. If you provide them with an incentive to do something, they'll probably do it.

When you go into an I's office or home, you may find quite a number of trophies on display. You may immediately know he is an excellent soccer player. It may be quite obvious how much he likes sports and how many awards he has received. He probably has an I-Love-Me room. Have you ever been in a house where everything in one room obviously belongs to the owner? You've found an I!

If you have someone who is more focused on the future, as Is are, they want to be the best at something. They also want the best equipment and the best home. Provide them with incentives and let them talk. You need to be a good listener when you're around an I; they love it! Whenever you can, be sure to share in their enthusiasm.

The S (Supportive) Has a Need to Be Accepted

The S quadrant represents a person who is both reserved and people-oriented. The letter S is used to indicate a personality that tends to be a *Supportive, Stable, Steady, Sentimental, Shy, Status-quo, Specialist.* The plus-minus sign suggests they are flexible and have a more-or-less attitude. About 30-35 percent of all people are Ss.

S people (Phlegmatic, according to Hippocrates) tend to show their emotion rather than hide it. How can you tell? They smile more. Their facial expressions are brighter. They tend to use their arms a little bit more. They're not nearly as restrictive in their body movements as Cs. They relate to the world through feeling; they are kinesthetic.

Ss are people-oriented and not very assertive. They communicate how they feel by their body language. They feel, but are not necessarily taking that next step of talking with you to share what's going on. However, they are often enjoyable and pleasant to be around because of their feeling orientation. Ss are basically relationship-oriented, and their dominant need is to be accepted.

Most of us have a certain need to be accepted. However, depending on our position or what we do at work or in our business, for instance, we may have more of a need to be in control. When the need to be in charge is greater than the need for acceptance, our D qualities prevail.

Ss have soft facial expressions and tend to be more humble. Again, this is not a judgment; it's an observation. When you go into an S's office, there are often pictures of the family all around. You can spend time with an S talking about family and friends. When you share your product or service with them, they're not necessarily as concerned about its effectiveness or the statistics. They're more concerned that they are accepted if they use your product or service.

Today there are a lot more people with S characteristics moving up the corporate ladder. How come? Because when you take the time to understand and care for others, it makes a big difference in retention of people in an organization. This is one of the ways an S can shine.

When you have a D and an S together, who do you think wins? The D. Sure. Because the true S is not going to sacrifice the relationship just to be in control or get his way.

How do you satisfy the Ss with their great need for relationships? Help them feel accepted. When you visit or deal with an S, share things about your personal and family life. They enjoy that. That's how they relate to the world. If you're in sales, for example, provide them with information. More importantly, let them know that what they're getting involved in is just fine. They need to know so the other people they deal with will still like them. By doing this you can establish a relationship.

If the S person you're presenting to is a physician, he wants to know if his patients accept what he is doing for them. Is the medication, for example, safe? The S's primary concern is that it's safe. He wants to be sure his patients accept *him*.

The C (Cautious) Needs to Be Accurate

The C quadrant represents a person who is both reserved and task-oriented. The letter C is used to indicate a personality that tends to be *Cautious, Competent, Calculating, Concerned, Careful,* and *Contemplative.* The question mark symbolizes a person who asks questions because he has a need to know. About 20-25 percent of all people are Cs.

The C (Melancholy, according to Hippocrates) is task-oriented and has a need to be accurate. What do you give him? How do you satisfy his needs? Give him lots of information. If you determine that a client is a C, be sure to bring along a truckload of material the next time you call on him. Just put it on his desk, and chances are he'll be as happy as a lark. It may take him a year or two to make a decision, but at least you're satisfying his need. You're providing him with the information he needs to make a decision. Be sure to provide a summary sheet to give him the opportunity to move more quickly.

When an I salesperson deals with a C, it can be a real challenge. Can you imagine what happens when the I, who is primarily interested in recognition and telling, but not accuracy, tries to sell something to or relate with a C? It is not likely to work unless the salesperson understands the other person's needs and meets them. That's why understanding how to relate to each personality is so important. And it's true at home as well as at work.

What kind of behavior would you observe in a C? He asks and controls and doesn't say much. He may have a "closed" personality, and he's likely to be worried about something. An enthusiastic I salesperson going into a C's office is one of the most difficult situations you can encounter. Why? Because you often can't tell how Cs are feeling. You probably won't know if they're happy or sad. You may not know if they care about what you're saying, and they're often not about to tell you either. They're unlikely to express how they feel about it because that's not their need. The C isn't so much concerned about being assertive; he controls by exercising his need for accuracy.

If you are in sales and marketing, and you don't know what personality your prospect is, you could be headed for trouble. If he's a C and you come into his office enthusiastically talking about your family and friends, you'll probably turn him off. You need to provide him with the necessary information to make a decision. Otherwise, there's no relatability, and the sale is probably lost.

As an example, the C doctor wants to know that every study available, "from Harvard to Yale" supports the medication that the salesperson is showing him. He wants to know that what he is reading is statistically accurate, informative, and as foolproof as possible.

What Happens When Two of the Same Type Are Together?

In some cases, like attracts like. We may tend to like people who are like us because our similarities often breed mutual understanding, which can lead to a relationship. As long as you are aware of the dynamics of such a relationship, you can prepare to handle it. Here are some examples:

When two Ds are together, they may leave their discussion with anger. One may even be on the floor because of the fight that just happened! They both have a need to control. To "win" they need to give each other options.

When you have two Is together, just pull up a chair, sit back, and watch. If they're at a party together, for instance, they are often clowning around or the center of attention. They want everybody to look at them. They both need recognition. To "win" they need to recognize and compliment each other.

Two Ss together would likely come out of their discussion either hugging each other or crying. They are so relationship-oriented that they readily accept each other. They easily win with each other.

When two Cs are together, you probably have a more serious situation. For instance, engineers and scientists are typically Cs. They are analytical and tend to focus on numbers and things. They both need to be accurate. To win they need to give each other information; they want the facts.

My Style

You may think that, as a motivational speaker, I'm an I. But after I was tested, I was categorized as a D/S (Dominant/Supportive). It meant my dominant need was to be in control, while I also had a high need to be accepted.

How does this fit into the workplace? This personality combination can lead to indecision. Being interested in relationships, I need to be accepted, which can cause me to be somewhat indecisive. I don't want to jeopardize the relationship, even though I have a need to be in control. Sometimes making an unpopular decision can be a challenge to the S part of my personality.

How About Spouses?

In marriage it's the same way. At home I truly believe I tend to be more D, while my wife tends to be more S. That makes us compatible until she goes up into the D quadrant. I need to understand that.

At home, like Noni and I, both spouses often have different temperaments. It's less typical, for instance, to have a C living with another C. Therefore it is particularly essential that both spouses learn about the personality types, so they can best deal with the one they married.

It has often been said that opposites attract. And that certainly seems to be so in many cases. With the personality types, we often find that Ds attract Ss, while Cs attract Is. Let's consider why that is.

A D normally attracts an S because Ds like to be in charge while Ss like to support. The Ds confidence is reassuring to the S whose dominant need is to be accepted.

A C typically attracts an I because Cs tend to be cautious, while Is are supportive. The serious C looks for the I whose dominant need is to be recognized. The C would like to have more fun.

Notice in both cases that a task-oriented person tends to attract a people-oriented person. The effect is that opposites tend to attract because they complete each other. One makes up for what the other lacks.

Putting It All Together

Yes, we're all different. People behave and express themselves differently. Take time to learn about other people. Listen to them and you can communicate more effectively. Shakespeare said of listening, "Give every man thy ear but few thy voice." When you understand someone's personality, you can relate with them better.

We all fit in somewhere. By using the Personality/Temperament Indicator, you can increase your chances for success in your relationships. This is not manipulation. It is a tremendous tool to help you communicate more effectively with people to create win-win results.

Chapter 11
REMEMBER TO HONOR FAMILY AND FRIENDS
Seventh Step of the THESAURUS Factor

If I could spell thesaurus by making the first letter R I would; it's that important. How many people do you know who, in their search for glory, fame, and wealth, aren't rich at all? They've stepped on everybody important in their life along the way. You can have all the money in the world, but if you don't honor those who supported and assisted you, you will not be truly successful or happy.

A house without caring inhabitants is not a home. Life can be much more satisfying when you enjoy it together with loved ones. And the extent to which you love, honor, and respect others is based on how much you love, honor, and respect yourself. To honor someone is to value them. If you don't have those feelings toward yourself, how can you expect to have it for others? As mentioned before, you can only give something you already possess. A house becomes a home when the inhabitants honor each other.

Your family and friends help define your success in life. Once you leave this earth, what can you take with you? You're born with nothing material, and you can't take anything material with you when you pass away. Your material possessions are not important. Life is an opportunity to create a legacy of who you are and what you are about to the people around you and others you have influenced along the way. As Bill McGrane, II, said, "Leave something behind to grow."

Aren't your children and friends a reflection of who you are? Of course! They know both your weaknesses and strengths. It's likely they know almost everything about you; it's one thing that makes them so special. When they comment on your unskillful behavior, or show an interest in you as a person, sometimes it can be difficult. Perhaps they are helping you confront issues instead of hiding or running away. As you grow personally, they may too. Or, they may not grow, which can present even greater challenges. As they become more knowledgeable, they may understand more about who you are and appreciate you more.

Honor one another. That's the key for excellent relationships. Henry Wadsworth Longfellow said, "The best portion of a good man's life is his little, nameless, unremembered acts of kindness and love." When we give to each other unconditionally (expecting nothing in return), that's when family and friends truly become a part of our lives. It is then that we can be truly successful and happy.

When you leave this earth, all you leave behind is what you've contributed. Yet many people, on their climb toward success, squash those around them. Unfortunately, it just doesn't seem to make any difference to them.

As I have watched my children grow, I've seen a little more of my wife and me in them. It's been rewarding. Every time I share with them, or experience them, it means more to me than earning any amount of money. If my children grow up feeling a loving respect for and value who they are and where they came from, I will consider myself successful. It doesn't matter whether they live under the same roof with me or not. As they become older, I expected them to leave home. In today's society it may be difficult, and even undesirable, to remain living with the same people with whom you started your life. But it doesn't matter. The strength of the loving bond can reach beyond the boundaries of what they once called home.

What matters most is what you give of yourself to your children; this reaps the greatest rewards. It's what you take for granted that can create the greatest losses in your life. As I saw my children grow, I realized that, over the years, they have gotten to know who I am, and that's just as important as what I did for anyone outside the family.

After I lost my dad, I was hurting for awhile. Not having him to lean on was tough. It was difficult not having a father I could ask, "Hey, am I doing okay?" Let's remember forgiveness; we all need to forgive and let go. Let go of the excess baggage if you really want to move on. Most of us are going to lose some of the people we care about as we grow older. Treasure the time you have with them now, rather than waiting five or ten years!

Honor Your Family and Friends Today

When Eric Clapton, the great guitarist, lost his little boy in a tragic accident; he wrote a song, *Tears in Heaven,* to honor him. Part of the lyrics went like this: "Would you know my name, if I saw you in heaven?" If you lost a loved one today, would they have known who you really are? Would they have known what you're about? Take time to share who you are with them, and honor them today. Tomorrow may be too late.

This step of the *Staircase* is an excellent place for you to discover the gift most worth giving and receiving: the gift of honoring people. Remembering to honor family and friends is, for me, the most serious step of all. This is what St. Paul meant when he warned that, "If you have not charity, all else is as a ringing emptiness."

169

Native Americans measured a leader's greatness by his generosity of mind and spirit. Their culture did not keep score on getting just for the sake of getting. Everything was meant to be shared. In other words, what and how much you *gave away* determined your reputation as an honorable, admirable person. The person of distinction was the one whose talents brought them rewards, yes, but also whose generosity prompted them to share their rewards with others. A hunter bringing back food for the tribe is an excellent example. The Native Americans knew the value of giving.

When we live a life of sharing, we are naturally led to gain another piece of wisdom; giving thanks and honoring people is the most excellent gift of all. The greatest gift of thanks is to remember to honor someone with gratitude, to appreciate what they have done for you.

Many of us have family and friends who deserve to be honored for the love and support they have given us. Remembering the kind things they have done has another benefit. Martial, the Roman poet, said, 'To be able to enjoy one's past life is to live twice!" Memories of honoring those closest to us can be a real joy.

When my daughter Nicole was seven, I invited her (for the first time) to hear me speak. It was at Union College in Schenectady, New York, where I presented to about ninety sorority sisters. Of all the seminars my daughter could experience first, I felt this would be a good fit for her. She would be in the audience with the sisters and I hoped she would enjoy herself.

To my surprise, she managed to sit through the whole thing. She may not have listened to all of it, but she was there. She watched what I did and gained an appreciation for what I was about.

As I drove home with her, she turned to me and said, "Dad, don't stop what you're doing. It seems to help a lot of people." I felt incredibly honored.

How can you put a price tag on kind words of appreciation, especially from a child? When you see your child developing and maturing, reflecting your values and skillful behavior, isn't that success? Then she turned to me and said, "How about that 'Happy Meal' from McDonald's you promised me?" I felt happier than I had in a long, long time. Whether or not I got paid for speaking that night didn't matter. Nicole's gift of appreciation was so much more important to me.

Robert Louis Stevenson said, "A friend is a present you give yourself." True friendship is rare. Unconditional love and honoring people for who they are is also rare. Giving to other people without expecting anything in return may be a challenge at first. However, it is the essence of friendship and kindness in general. Learn to give for the joy of giving. It is fun! Smile without expecting one back. Share who you are with other people without expecting them to share themselves with you. Honor others without expecting honor in return. I believe you'll be happier because of it.

When you honor others outside your circle of family and friends, do you get a warm and loving feeling inside? When you give to a homeless or needy person, you can also feel warm inside. So why is it so difficult sometimes for us to do that? Could it be that some of us lived in homes where we weren't honored? Maybe we were criticized or belittled, or a giving spirit was never demonstrated to us. It is a learning process to honor family and friends, and others as well. Be patient with yourself as you do.

How we treat our family and friends often determines our happiness. Happiness, with your family and life in general, is something you cannot buy. No matter how many material things you may buy, they can't create happiness. Yet look at the families that are destroyed by searching for happiness in all the wrong places. They need to look inside themselves and at the actions they take. When more people honor each other, many arguments that are detrimental to living a successful life can be avoided.

The *No Excuse!* philosophy is meant to help people understand that the principles of success can be used not only in your business life, but to enhance your personal life as well. When you employ techniques and skill in communicating a more positive attitude, your life will gain new meaning. How can you justify throwing self-control out the window when you get home, after maintaining it all day at work? Aren't your family and friends most deserving of your honor and patience?

No Excuse! is a philosophy for everyone. When you employ its principles, you'll feel more respect for who and what you are. You can only contribute significantly to your family and friends when you feel respect for yourself. Living by the principles of *No Excuse!* will help you do that as you develop your vast potential.

Gratitude—*A Gift of Attention You Can Give*

Many people long to be honored or appreciated for the contributions they make as they go through life. And it's always a pleasure to return to a place and find someone glad to see you again. Most people appreciate such kind attention. We give that gift to others when we honor and greet them with obvious pleasure. Honoring others for the gifts they give *us* increases our capacity for a fulfilling life—whether the gift is years of devotion by a loving spouse, an affirming word, or the innocent smile of a child.

We enrich both ourselves and others when we give thanks. We lift ourselves and others when we honor family and friends. We can be so happy that we feel encouraged to continue honoring people. Our memories of these times are so sweet.

To have gratitude for the things, opportunities, and people in our lives requires a certain level of maturity. As we grow, we are more likely to realize we have been enriched by them. Like that child in the hospital, it would honor the giver if we can honestly say, "It's just what I've always wanted," even for the most surprising gift. We may need to open our eyes and recognize the gifts we received. We may not have been paying attention. Or perhaps we took the gifts for granted. Appreciate all gifts, large and small, for they represent the fullness of life, both in the giving and receiving.

Appreciate Tough Love

By honoring others, we fill ourselves again with the gifts they gave us. Give is a powerful word. I suggest you add *to give* to your list of desires, and be specific about what and to whom you'd like to give something.

If giving is the mark of those truly rich in spirit, showing appreciation is the mark of the rich and wise. Richness, in this case, may not be related to money or possessions. These people have appreciation for everyone and everything around them. Most of all, they have a deep appreciation for those they love most.

Stay close to those you love. Appreciate them. This is how you can keep love fresh. Express how much you love your family and friends through words and deeds. You'll want to do this now, for later on they may no longer be able to receive it.

Sometimes we need to show gratitude for having learned a difficult but valuable lesson. Always appreciate what a challenge it can be for a loving person to correct you when they feel in their heart they need to do so. The greatest value a friend or family member can give us is to respect us enough to risk our rejection or anger. This is called tough love. Sometimes we need to be told what we may not want to hear so we can move on.

How to Make Friends

In *How to Win Friends and Influence People,* Dale Carnegie wrote, "You can make more friends in two months by becoming interested in other people than you can in two years by trying to get other people interested in you." To drive home his point, Carnegie shares how dogs can easily make friends: "When you get within ten feet of a friendly dog, he will wag his tail. If you pet him, he may lick and jump all over you. The dog became man's best friend by *being genuinely interested in people.*"

Be Courageous and Honor Someone by Telling Them the Truth About Their Behavior

I want to share with you a little note my daughter wrote to me many years ago. It is one of my greatest treasures, and it taught me more about being a parent than any book or expert ever did.

One morning I got angry with her. And because I'm part D, I pointed a finger at her while I disciplined her. Here's what she wrote:

Dear Dad,

I'm sorry if I get you upset but please don't poke your finger at me when you are angry. I will try to do better, but you must understand I am only eight years old and that I am trying to learn from your example, but sometimes it is hard.

I love you,
Nicole

I've been told before about my behavior and how others felt about some actions I took in the past. However, no one ever left a more lasting impression on me than my daughter, not even my superiors at West Point! You can feel truly loved when you know that someone cares about you enough that they'll tell you the truth about your behavior towards them. They'll let you know what's acceptable to them.

Develop a Family or a Personal Mission Statement

In Stephen Covey's *The Seven Habits of Highly Effective People,* he shared that he had a family mission statement. We've all heard of corporate mission statements: A company owner gives direction to employees not only to meet quotas, but hopefully to encourage a sense of values, purpose, and contribution to society. Have you ever thought about having a family mission statement, or a personal one if you live alone? Would you consider including some language that encourages your family to honor each other as well as friends and other people? To give you an idea of how to do a family mission statement, I'll share ours with you in a moment.

First, though, I want to interject something about humor. Some of the funniest times we have had as a family were when we are sitting around the dinner table. All of a sudden the children would start laughing. It was contagious. It could start with my son or wife making a funny face. Soon everybody started laughing, and it went on for several minutes. It's a time when we forgot all the stresses of the day. It was fun and relaxing.

So there we were, sitting around the dinner table, all laughing. After we got settled, we decided to come up with a family mission statement, the

Rifenbary Family Mission Statement. Each of us thought of something we felt was most important for our family, and then we wrote it down. (If you're alone, what's important to you?)

The first thing we wrote was "to demonstrate courtesy to each other and other people." If my children can grow up being courteous and kind to others, I'll feel I succeeded as a parent. It's easy to be kind to a king. It takes a truly caring person to be kind to a beggar. If my children are courteous and thoughtful of other people—regardless of who they are, the color of their skin, or what their occupation is, they have given a gift to them. This would be a gift of honor.

If we communicate our feelings in an open, loving relationship with one another, the children are more likely to come to us when they get into trouble. They are less likely to want to hide anything from us.

The second statement of our mission is "to do the very best in everything we do, no matter what. It doesn't matter if you fail, as long as you give it your all." That can help you feel respect for yourself (self-esteem), regardless of your outcomes.

The final statement is "be truthful in all you say and do. Be honest with one another so that if something is bothering you, you won't beat around the bush. Don't try to deceive." *If you deceive, you'll never truly achieve.* Be open and direct. Communicate your feelings. Be honest.

Respect in the Workplace Can Lead to Greater Productivity

It is also important to remember to honor the relationships with people at our place of work. The United States is no longer a melting pot; it's really more like a salad bowl. We all come from many backgrounds and cultures, often with different ideas. Many of us need to learn to appreciate and respect each other, as everyone is a person of worth and has something of value to contribute.

What do I mean by salad bowl? A salad may be made with ripe red tomatoes, fresh green peppers, fresh lettuce, maybe some crisp spinach, onions, and mushrooms. When they're all mixed together, they make a delicious salad. Each vegetable has something to offer.

We need to understand this in the workplace. We live in a multi-cultural world. We cannot afford to be biased, prejudiced, or judgmental of other people.

I have taught my children to always respect people for who they are. I never want them passing judgment. Who are we to pass judgment of others? We need to observe behavior, as we do when we are assessing personality type; but we don't need to, nor is it recommended, that we pass judgment.

Families, businesses, and other organizations are systems. A country is a very complex system, much like a car. If the transmission goes out, the car won't go. If one element of the family, business, or other organization is out of balance or missing (like a lack of communication, respect, or courtesy), the system doesn't work correctly.

In the workplace, how can people work together if some are resentful, power-hungry, blaming each other, or circulating rumors? If people are always trying to look good, be right, and cover themselves, how can much of anything get done? If people don't show respect for each other, how can they be an effective team? It cannot happen. What's happening in your workplace? What can you do about it? Are you willing to address these issues?

Let's talk about courtesy. We're all from many different cultures and races, that's true. But the sooner we can accept that we're all in the *human* race, the better off we'll be. Remember, we all have something to offer. Most of us want to be honored and contribute something to the world; we want to make a difference. We need to honor others and encourage them to contribute to the world as well.

In an organization, most people want to contribute in some way to the others. Most have a specific talent or skill and a need to be productive. They may not be at the same level of proficiency as someone else, but that doesn't matter. As long as they have an opportunity to contribute, we can all learn from them. We live in a society of systems: a salad bowl. Each of us has a part to play. The happiest people are those who play their part from the heart and in line with their purpose. This would be someone who loves what he does.

Do You Appreciate Others?

When was the last time you showed those closest to you that you really care about them? How do you do that? It could be through a phone call, a letter, a gift, saying thank you, a greeting card, or perhaps treating them to a meal at their favorite restaurant. It doesn't need to be fancy. Something as simple as giving an unexpected hug, coupled with a few kind words, can make all the difference in the world.

I wrote my sister a letter one time when she was struggling with her career. She didn't know what to do or where to go. In my letter I said, "Look. Whatever you do, I'm behind you. You have the experience and knowledge. You've done so much in your life that, no matter what you do, it's OK." I supported her, affirmed her experience, knowledge, and what she had done, as well as gave her unconditional love.

Most parents would treasure a letter. They might read it a hundred times if you wrote them a letter saying, "Thanks for just being there."

Why are some families are in such disharmony when they get together, especially during the holidays? It's simple; the people closest to you think they know you and your behavior. They probably don't realize how much you may have developed, while they may not have, since the last time you were together. Therefore, they tend to treat you as they knew you before, and this can cause friction.

Fortunately, the more you personally develop, the more accepting you are likely to be of the people closest to you. Growing up, I can remember my mom disciplining me. I would say, "Oh, no, I don't have a bad temper. I have lots of patience. I'm not dependent on you." I would resent any constructive comments she made about my behavior. As I grew, however, I discovered most of what she said was true. Did you ever come to the conclusion that the older you get, the more you appreciate your parents' wisdom? That's a sign of your personal development.

The more you show appreciation for other people, the happier you're likely to be. Show it at home, as well as at work, and to the people you encounter outside of home and work. Your personal growth is the key. The more you grow, the more you are likely to be appreciative as your understanding increases.

Be Open and Shed the "Makeup" on the Inside

If we allow ourselves to get caught up in what society dictates success to be for us, we may begin to lose touch with who we really are. Facial makeup may be acceptable for a performer, or a woman striving to enhance her appearance, but what about using "make up" on the inside? How much make up are we using to cover (not reveal ourselves to others) our true thoughts and feelings? Are we dishonoring ourselves as well as others?

Are we willing to remove the emotional makeup that's inside to let those people closest to us see who we really are and what we're really about? When we do, we're better able to share with others everything that we are. It takes concentration, confidence, and self-esteem. It takes a positive mental attitude and self-control. It takes the understanding that we are all different and we grow differently. Therefore, we need to know that we are all okay so that we can accept ourselves and others unconditionally. Honor people by being who you really are. It is one of your greatest gifts.

You also need to know that people have specific needs that may be different from yours. You may choose to sacrifice what you want for the wants of others if it's for results that benefit all! That can be a challenge, but it's essential if you want to be a leader who honors others.

Chapter 12
UPRAISE YOUR DETERMINATION
Eighth Step of the THESAURUS Factor

D oes the word determination scare you? If so, that's okay! With seven steps behind you now, you've made some real progress and you've got a strong footing.

How you feel about determination depends on your attitude. When I first opened my retail business, I can't tell you how many times I wanted to throw in the towel. My desire was tested every day by people telling me, "You'll never make it." My determination was challenged by the media saying it was a difficult time economically for the business world. Desire comes from within, and I had a strong desire to succeed, despite the obstacles. Without this desire, it would have been difficult, if not impossible, to establish the determination to succeed.

"Never, Never, Never Give in..."

The opposite of determination is discouragement. It pays to be aware of our options and to periodically reconsider certain aspects of our lives. Changing circumstances often demand changed perspectives in order for us to keep our determination. You could feel compelled to reconsider your goals because someone else's action or something else impacted your life. Maybe your partner leaves the relationship or your company shuts down. Maybe as a child you wanted to be a jockey, but you grew to be 6'2"! At times like these, we need to know the difference between changing goals and quitting. We need to be flexible. Flexibility is one of the most important keys to maintaining your determination and leading a less stressful life.

Staying with a goal that can be attained with perseverance is the objective of *No Excuse!* living. Some people quit five minutes before the miracle. They may live with regret. Some keep going until they win. They can say, "No excuses, no regrets." Grab hold of your dream and go for it!

Sir Winston Churchill's determination made him a leader of unusual distinction. He spoke against appeasement when it was his nation's policy with the Nazis. If he had been in power at that time, perhaps the horrors of World War II would not have been so great. It was when Germany went to war with its neighbors and England that Churchill's party was elected to power. He assumed leadership of a nation as Prime Minister of Great Britain.

He offered the English his determination to continue the fight. That, and the inspiration of the blood, sweat, and tears of his famous speech, was all he could offer. Churchill's early life had taught him some valuable lessons in not quitting.

Churchill had his share of strike-outs, as most successful people do. His nine years of boarding school were marked by extreme academic difficulty, including repeated failures. But through those years he kept his determination intact. He was not satisfied to just be an observer of history; he chose to be a participant and leader. He sat for the entrance exams for Sandhurst, the West Point of Britain, three times before he was admitted.

Years later, he returned to the Harrow School, his prep-school alma mater, to speak to a graduating class. It is one of the shortest commencement speeches in history: "Never give in! Never give in! Never, Never, Never, Never—in nothing great or small, large or petty—never give in except to convictions of honor and good sense."

Now, as that speech demonstrates, never quitting doesn't mean never resting. There are times to rest, and excellent reasons for interrupting and re-evaluating any course of action that isn't bringing you the desired results. The difference between quitting and resting is this: With quitting the dream often dies; with resting the dream can be more easily rekindled, if necessary. Never quitting means keeping your dreams alive, even if you need to regroup and increase your determination.

Overcoming Challenges Makes You Stronger

If you feel you don't have options, in most cases you are just a prisoner of your own thinking. Or you may not have a dream.

A teenage boy who believes he can't go to school unless he wears the correct clothes or sneakers to fit in makes a big mistake. If he spends time and money buying them instead of investing in his future, it may be because he has no dream. He may be caught up in trying to please others in an attempt to be accepted. He may be living out a dream or image fashioned by others (probably the clothing and shoe manufacturers that seek to sell their products). He may have let others manipulate his behavior, at the sacrifice of both his own dream and of being his own unique self.

Parents may suffer while watching their children try to find their own dreams. And sometimes it's the parents' dreams that threaten to have an entrapping influence on their children. Parents may try to achieve their own dreams vicariously through their children. This is harmful unless the children truly share the same dream. Guiding your children to find what is best for them is very different from insisting, for instance, that they fulfill *your* dream to be a super athlete, scholar, or something else.

Difficulties most often trigger the temptation to quit, to give up on a dream. Yet difficulties are as much a normal part of life as a butterfly breaking out of its cocoon. Overcoming difficulty builds strength. If we were to cut the cocoon open instead of letting the butterfly break out on its own, it would emerge with wings too weak to fly, and it would soon die. Much the same can be said for a chick in an eggshell; it gets strong by hatching on its own!

Successful people often welcome difficulty. For example, a math whiz may get very excited tackling a challenging problem. Difficulties can stimulate our creative instincts. We can experience tremendous growth while overcoming challenges. And remember this, behind every adversity is a seed of an equal or greater benefit. It may not be immediately obvious, but the benefit will become evident at some point.

What's the Relationship Between Desire and Risk?

Living a *No Excuse!* life requires responsible behavior. And while it means you may need to take some calculated risks, it does not mean doing something foolish or dangerous. Calculated risks are often necessary when we're faced with difficulties, or when we pursue a goal based on a big dream. Lindbergh took a calculated risk when he flew solo across the Atlantic; the potential reward was too great not to do so.

His daring not only changed his life but also the lives of millions! His accomplishment brought him more notoriety than any human being has ever had, which led to his writing books and pioneering the airways. His achievement excited the people of the world because he bridged nations together like no one had ever done. The world was forever changed because one man had a dream and was willing to take a calculated risk to make it come true.

Let's consider the relationship between desire and risk, quitting and change. Have you ever quit something and within a year regretted it? Did you quit because you didn't have enough patience? Why didn't you stick it out just one more day?

Sometimes people quit just as they are about to achieve the outcome they want. It may look a little bleak, so they give up. People who win go the extra mile, take the extra step, take that calculated risk. There's a direct correlation between risk and success. How can you grow if you don't take risks? This is true for many aspects of life.

You take a risk every time you try to understand who you are. You are risking when you try to close a sale. It is a risk every time you meet a new person. You take a risk every time you attempt to resolve a conflict. Every time you risk, you have an opportunity to learn and expand your horizons. Every time you take a risk, although you may increase your possibility of failure, you also increase your potential for success. A failure is actually a learning experience; it's not a negative. Without risk there is little chance to achieve the success you've always wanted.

If you believe something is *too* risky to break through, maybe you could go around it. Danger and drudgery are enemies of accomplishment. You may need to cut back on the risk some to lessen your fear. Then you can let go of much or all of your fear, renew your strength, and let your strong desire carry you through the rest of the way.

Remember the child learning to ride a two-wheeler? If all he hears are cries of, "You're going to fall," he'll probably hear, "You're going to fail," when he tries something new later in life. If he hears instead, "You're going to love this when you've learned how," his determination to ride is likely to outweigh the risk of falling.

Take swimming, for example. Telling a child to stay in shallow water is wise if he doesn't know how to swim. But you can cut the risk of him going into deep water by giving him a life jacket and swimming lessons, assuring him of the joys of swimming. Now you've brought the risk to a manageable level and the child can get on with developing the determination to succeed.

Your Life Is Structured by Your Will

Back in the 1800s, a philosopher named Arthur Shopenhower wrote a book entitled, *The World as Will and Idea.* Initially, his philosophy was not widely accepted. He believed that *your life is structured by your will.* God's greatest gift to man is free will—the gift of choice.

Let's think about that for a minute. Your desire to succeed, your desire to grow, and your life, in most cases, is structured by your will. If you don't have a will to achieve, risk, and grow, you won't grow; you won't move forward.

Reflect on your life for a minute. Who made your decisions? Ultimately, wasn't it you? Aren't you the one with the choice, the final say? Aren't you responsible for almost everything that has structured your life? *Everything you've done in the past, whether you've succeeded or failed, has been like a story. You've basically created your own story. There's no one to blame. You are wiser not to make excuses because, for the most part, you have created your own plot in life, your own circumstances. Your will, your desire to grow and succeed, has largely determined what that story is all about.* Your will primarily determines the pattern, format, and structure of your life.

My desire to grow and share these ideas with others is very important to me. Whether they succeed or fail, they influence how I view and express myself to others. Whenever I reflect on the past, I always ask myself what, where, and how have I contributed to others and how I can improve my skills. The power of my will, my internal desire to serve and make a difference, is an important part of who I am. How about you?

If Your Desire Is Great Enough—*the Risk Doesn't Matter*

The conflict between quitting and change is the conflict between desire and risk. When desire outweighs risk, you continue on. As long as the dream is viewed as bigger than the price, you'll be more likely to pursue it. You may consider quitting but you won't; you'll persist. If you love what you're doing and what it can do for you and others, quitting could be eliminated from your vocabulary. If this is not true for you, you may want to do something you love. If risk outweighs desire, maybe a change is necessary. You may think it through with the help of a mentor, but ultimately it's your decision.

Shakespeare said, "We are such stuff as dreams are made on." History is full of people who believed in their dreams and persevered to see them come true. Will you be one of those people? You can, you know.

Plato labored intensely over his *Republic* masterpiece. In fact, he rewrote the first sentence nine different ways before he was satisfied. As famous author Mario Puzo said, "Rewriting is the whole secret to writing."

As a young boy, Jesse Owens went to hear the speedster, Charlie Paddock, speak. Young Jesse approached Paddock after the speech and said, "Sir, I've got a dream! I want to be the fastest human being alive." Developing his scrawny legs, Owens persevered to become, at that time, the fastest man ever to run the 100-meter dash, as well as the 200-meter dash. He won four gold medals. His name was inscribed in the charter list of the American Hall of Athletic Fame.

Franklin D. Roosevelt was struck down by polio, but he persevered. Even though he was unable to walk, he proved to people across the world he could lead as President of the United States. FDR never made excuses because of his disability. He just kept pressing on.

Adam Clark labored forty years writing his commentary on the Holy Scriptures. Milton rose every morning at 4:00 a.m. to write *Paradise Lost.* *The Decline and Fall of the Roman Empire* took Gibbon twenty-six painstaking years to complete. Ernest Hemingway is said to have reviewed *The*

Old Man and the Sea manuscript eighty times before submitting it for publication. It took Noah Webster thirty-six years to compile *Webster's Dictionary.*

As a boy, he dreamed of drawing comic strips. As a young man, he was advised by an editor in Kansas City to give up drawing. He kept knocking on doors, only to be rejected. He persevered until finally a church hired him to draw publicity material. Working out of an old garage, he befriended a little mouse who ultimately became famous. The man was Walt Disney, and his friend became Mickey Mouse. A nervous breakdown in 1931, and many rejections and setbacks, could not steal Disney's dreams. Walt Disney said, "All of our dreams can come true if we have the courage to pursue them."

Totally blind and deaf, Helen Keller became a famous author and lecturer. Instead of wallowing in grief, she lived life fully, in spite of her handicaps. She even graduated *cum laude* (with distinction) from Radcliffe College. Helen Keller had perseverance.

Leonardo Da Vinci spent ten years perfecting *The Last Supper*. He reportedly became so engrossed in his work he would forget to eat for several days.

The Last Judgment, considered one of the twelve master paintings of all time, consumed eight years of Michelangelo's life.

The Chicago fire of 1871 inspired Dwight L. Moody to build a school that would train young people to know the *Bible* and spread the Word.

Then there was Fritz Kreisler. As a young boy, he wanted to play the violin. His parents encouraged his interest by paying for his lessons. Kreisler didn't progress as he had hoped and finally quit. He tried to study medicine and failed, then joined the army and wasn't successful there either. He tried and quit many other pursuits. Desperate for a successful experience, he went back to his violin instructor. "I want to play," he told her. "Fine," she responded. "But you must acquire one irreplaceable quality. You must exhibit undefeatable determination." Fritz Kreisler persevered until his music filled Carnegie Hall.

Finally, here's a couple of people whose desire was so strong they overcame great risks; they put their lives on the line!

Imagine Neil Armstrong, in the middle of his astronaut training saying, "Well, this could be one small step for man, one giant leap for mankind, but I'm not taking it. I'm too scared. I'm too nervous. It's not for me." Instead, he said, "No matter what the risk, no matter what the sacrifice, I'm going to take that first step. I'm going to be the first man on the moon." Powerful!

What if Dr. Martin Luther King Jr., had said in the middle of his "I Have

A Dream" speech, "I'm getting out of here? I better not say any more. I could get hurt"? Of course he knew the risks involved, but his desire to make a difference, his desire for world peace, his desire for equality surpassed his fear of failure and even death.

How about the Wright Brothers' courage and commitment in inventing the airplane? They designed, built, tested, and experimented for four years under almost unbearable conditions: enduring high winds, hordes of mosquitoes, and numerous, potentially life threatening accidents. What if they had said, "This is too tough; let's go home and forget it"? They jeopardized and lost their bicycle business while risking their lives to follow their dream. What if they had said, "It's not worth losing the business"? Their willingness to risk everything changed the world, bringing us all closer together.

Desire. Risk. How strong is your desire to make a difference? Is it worth the risk? How much do you want to improve your family life? What sacrifices will you make? What price will you pay?

How much do you want to improve your business skills, your selling skills? How much do you want to improve your leadership skills, your communication skills?

What risks are you going to take to get what you want? Are you going to change jobs? Will you change careers? Do you plan to start your own business? Or do you plan to build the business you already have to make it bigger and more productive? Are you going to leap off your current path onto another? What risks are involved? Whether you'll take action depends on your desire to grow and become the best you can be, and to serve others in the best way you possibly can.

Stay Motivated by Taking the V.I.P. Approach

Some of us get hit with negatives nearly all the time. How do we maintain our motivation if we're constantly bombarded by other people and the environment saying, "You can't do that"? How do we handle people who say the steps we're taking will not give us the results we want? First we need to examine whether they're qualified to give us recommendations. If they are well qualified, we need to consider whether they are correct. If they are poorly qualified, we can choose to prove them incorrect. If they are not being helpful and are consistently demeaning our efforts, it might be wise not to associate with them. We can choose, instead, to be around people who support us. We can find a mentor who offers us wise choices to consider.

Some people say motivation is shallow, and they're right. That's why you need it every day, much like a shower or a bath. Furthermore, real motivation comes from within. If you're not self-motivated, you'll probably have little desire to sustain the determination you need to succeed. Motivation can be stimulated externally, but it's your internal drive that keeps you going. *Unless you believe in who you are and what you're doing, it's difficult to be self-motivated. How can you have any desire if you don't feel you are important?*

How do you enhance self-motivation? I've structured something called V.I.P., "Very Important Person." I've also filled the acronym with a few other words that can enhance your ability to stay self-motivated. The **"V"** stands for *value.* You need to put value on yourself and your goals. When in your heart and mind you feel you are a valuable person, and that your goals are valuable, you'll have a greater desire to achieve them. When you feel worthless or undeserving of your dreams, your desire to achieve them diminishes. Value yourself, the people around you—and your goals. You'll find it makes a big difference in your self-motivation.

"I" is for *integrate.* Integrate with people who have dreams similar to yours. Allow those who share in what you want to achieve to be incorporated into your life, your business, and your family. When you associate with a group of people with common dreams and goals, you're likely to be more self-motivated because their energy will affect yours. You can support one another. This is one of the greatest secrets of success. When you find those people, it can make a tremendous difference in how you feel about life; you realize you're not alone in your quest and you have support

In a lot of ways, we're all basically in the same boat. Sure, some of us are more challenged in certain areas. Yet all of us have many of the same situations just because we're human. When you find people who understand you, your difficulties, and what you want, it can be uplifting and rewarding to be associated with them. Today there are many networking organizations and support groups that offer this kind of camaraderie.

The **"P"** means *participate.* Participate in events and seminars that support and reinforce your desires. If you have a desire to be one of the top salespeople in your company, participate in events that can teach you how. Get involved in activities that can help trigger your motivation.

If you want to be a more skillful and loving parent, participate in workshops, read books, and listen to audios that can help you enhance your parenting skills. This approach works across the board, regardless of your area of interest. The more you dream and do the correct things, the quicker you're likely to accomplish what you want.

You become and attract what you think about most. (Remember to think about what you want rather than what you don't want!) All of this will occur when you *value* what you think about, *integrate* with other people, and *participate* in appropriate activities. Remember to V.I.P.

The other step on the *Staircase* that dramatically affects your desire and self-motivation is your self-esteem, the Second Step. If you don't feel respect for yourself, if you don't believe in who you are, your determination to succeed will be severely affected. You need to feel enough respect for yourself to do whatever it takes to give yourself what you want, within the mission of your life.

Time Management and Desire Destroyers

What does time management have to do with desire? What is time management anyway? Can anyone manage time? No, not really! You can only manage activities. In other words, you manage yourself. Time never stops. It's managing activities within a certain time frame that enables you to move forward. When you ineffectively manage activities, your desire is severely hampered. Why? Because it causes disorganization and problems. When you're disorganized, it's difficult to stay on your path of success. We'll cover more on that later.

Here are some key factors associated with time/activity management that can interrupt or destroy your desire. I call them Desire Destroyers.

The first Desire Destroyer is Procrastination. Why does putting things off have such a significant impact? If you procrastinate, how can you possibly get where you want to go? Procrastination hinders your determination to succeed. Procrastination is generally the result of lazy behavior or fear of failure and the unknown. Lazy behavior usually means that there is a lack of a dream or goal, and thus a lack of desire. The cure for this, of course, is to find a dream big enough so that you are motivated to do whatever it takes to get the outcome you want. If you're feeling unsure, you may put off doing what you need to do. If you need to take a risk, and you fear failure and the unknown, you may procrastinate to the degree of your fear.

There are four solutions to procrastination. One—*find your dream.*** Focus on something you want very much. Two—***begin.*** Just get started. Getting started is half done. **Three** *the cold-cut technique.* Say you've got a big salami. Obviously you can't eat the whole thing at once, so you cut it up into small slices. In other words, break a task into small, manageable chunks. If things are perceived as too big or too difficult, we tend to procrastinate. This is similar to the fears of risk, failure, and the unknown. The key is to complete one small piece at a time. You'll feel encouraged, and eventually you'll get the whole job done. Inch by inch, anything's a cinch! The key is to get out of your inertia and set things in motion to gain momentum. Once momentum is gained, it's easier to do than not to do your task.

Once, while I was on a radio talk show, I got a call from a woman who wanted to clean her basement. She said it had been bothering her for the last eight months; it was filled with all kinds of old stuff. I responded, "Well, why don't you rope off just a small corner of the basement and clean that first?" Two weeks later, I got a note from her saying she did that and it worked. I don't know if she moved everything into that corner or just cleaned it out, section by section. However, tackling a small chunk first enabled her to get the job done. It didn't seem so overwhelming. Instead, it seemed like a more possible task.

One day you may decide to paint a room, but you may keep procrastinating because of all the preparation required before you can even begin painting. The solution is to take it one step at a time. Develop an action plan. The first week go ahead and pick the color. The second week buy the paint and the brushes. The third week paint one wall. Eventually what happens? Before you know it, the room is painted. You may have been so excited that you went ahead of your own schedule!

The cold-cut technique works with getting almost anything done. The things we want most in life may take the most time and/or may be the most difficult. Just break the task down into small chunks, and you are less likely to procrastinate; your desire will remain.

You may be familiar with the 80/20 rule; the Preado Principle. In retail, for example, I made 80 percent of my profit from 20 percent of my product. In sales, you're likely to make 80 percent of your quota based on 20 percent of your clients. It applies to almost everything, especially in time/activity management. You'll probably spend 80 percent of your time and energy on 20 percent of your tasks. That 20 percent is the most difficult and takes the most time.

The fourth solution for overcoming procrastination is—*provide yourself with incentives.* Reward yourself along the way. Don't work just to work. After you eat that small piece of salami, give yourself a pat on the back. Say, "Hey, I did it!" When you provide a little bit of positive reinforcement, you'll find it inspires you to eat that next piece of salami, paint another wall, or clean out another corner of the basement. After you've finished a challenging task, it's important to reward yourself with something like a movie, a new outfit, a book you've wanted, or something else you would enjoy. In other words, enjoy the trip.

The second Desire Destroyer is Disorganization. This occurs predominantly in meetings, with paperwork, and your environment. When you walk into an office and it's a complete mess, with papers all over the place, doesn't that have a negative impact on you? It makes it more difficult for you to focus on the task at hand.

What about meetings? When you don't have an agenda, you have disorganization, which leads to an ineffective meeting. It has a significant negative impact on your desire, especially once you leave the meeting; you may feel disheartened, having gotten little or nothing from it. Disorganized meetings inhibit activity almost more than anything else. Generally, meetings can enhance your desire only when they're conducted effectively.

How do you handle disorganization? What's the relationship between that and activity management? *First, assess the situation.* For example, if your office is a mess, look at it and assess it. What do you have to do to get it organized? *Secondly, prioritize. Third, implement.* Look at your office, prioritize the things you have to do, then do them. It'll have a major impact on your degree of organization and allow you to be more productive.

Success-oriented people don't like disorganization. If you're disorganized when you work with and express yourself to other people, you won't get much done. If your organization or company is disorganized, it can have a major negative impact on your desire to be motivated to accomplish the tasks at hand.

You might want to think of yourself as your own business. No matter what your environment is or what you do, you are, in fact, your own business. For best results, you need to be organized. You might even think of yourself as "Me, Inc." Conduct yourself and your life in a businesslike, organized manner.

The third Desire Destroyer is Interruptions. And, of course, the major interruption for most people is unscheduled visits from others. The second interruption is telephone calls. The third is crisis situations.

Did you ever consider that it's actually valuable to be interrupted? If your phone didn't ring or you didn't have any memos coming across your desk, you might get the idea you weren't needed. You may ask, "Am I valuable to this organization?"; "Am I valuable to this family?" If you were never interrupted, that would probably mean no one needed you.

Interruptions are a fact of life. How do you deal with them? First, manage your people, your environment, and your office. Second, instruct people on when you may be interrupted. Third, delegate activities that would take you from your main focus and that someone else could do. It takes self-esteem to do this, and it's well worth the results.

You can spend more or less time on time/activity management; it's completely up to you. Even a little management of your activities can go a long way and can be an excellent start. No matter what's going on around you, it's your responsibility to deal with it so you can be most effective with the time, energy, and resources at your disposal.

Upraise your determination. The more you organize and manage your activities, the greater desire you'll have to continue your quest because of the clarity of mind you will have achieved. Eliminate clutter in your life. The greater your desire to accomplish your dreams, the more self-motivated you are likely to be in general; and specifically, to control how much you'll allow yourself to be interrupted.

Determination Is the Key to Realizing Your Dreams

The relationships you have with your teachers, mentors, and leaders impacts the strength of your determination to accomplish what you want. Are they encouraging or discouraging your determination? Consider shying away from relationships with people who discourage your precious determination. Choose these key people carefully.

The dream of democratic self-rule, that began with the signing of the Magna Carta in 1215, was finally realized by the 18th Century. However, it was threatened in England, as well as in Europe, with the rise of Fascism in the 1930's. Churchill sparked the British people's determination to keep on going so they could maintain their freedom.

When you dream, have determination, and take the appropriate action to go where your dream leads you, you'll know one of life's greatest joys. If you give up too easily on your dream, your purpose, you'll never have a fulfilling life. You can choose to become whatever you desire to be. If you're filled with determination, you'll attract friends who share your dream; you'll find people who will support you.

By now I believe you are wise enough to understand that what you have means nothing next to who you are. (Unfortunately, in this world where material goods are often the focus, many people don't realize this important fact.) Who you are is with you wherever you go. Your determination can lead you to take the necessary action to take you to your dream. What you become along the way is what it's all about!

Here's an interesting poem I want to share with you. It's called "Mr. Meant To":

Mr. Meant-To had a friend, and his name was Mr. Didn't-Do. Have you ever had the chance to meet them? Did they ever call on you? Well these two I hear they live together, in a house called Never-Win. And I hear this house is haunted by the Ghost of Might-Have-Been.

—Marva Collins

Always think about what you can do, rather than what you could have done. Remember, the desire from within can enable you to do what is necessary to realize your dream.

Think of your life as a giant 1,000-piece jigsaw puzzle of a beautiful landscape. One of the first things you would do is take the lid off and turn the box over to empty the pieces. This is like being born. One of the earliest major accomplishments is complete when you turn the pieces over. It's like an infant going from its stomach to its back. Then, like the foundation of your life, you begin to put the frame of this puzzle together. You put that together first because it's easier, fundamental, and important. It's like when you first walked, talked, and graduated from high school.

As life goes on, you reach the half-way point, say 500 pieces, and all that's left is blue sky. You look at all those similar-looking pieces and ask, how in the world am I going to get it all together? How am I going to become what I was created to be and live the life I imagine? Just keep going! Never quit. Success is a journey, not a destination. Some pieces are put in place easier than others, but you need to persevere. You may never get all the pieces of your puzzle of life together, but as long as you "keep on keeping on," giving of yourself, your feelings, ideas, talents, and skills, you'll grow and become the best you can be; you'll make a difference.

Walt Disney failed in business five times before he saw his dream come true. He just wouldn't quit. Once during a student tour of Disney World, one of the children raised a hand and said to the guide, "Wouldn't it have been great if Walt Disney was here to see this?" The guide responded, "He already has. That's why it's here." Disney had the vision before it became reality. He believed it before he could see it.

Always keep sight of what you want to become and where you want to take your life. When you have the desire to achieve, everything you do can have value. You know you will make a difference in this world if you just keep moving on toward your dreams. Be strong and stay determined. You can do it!

Chapter 13
SUCCEED AND BALANCE
YOUR LIFE
Ninth Step of the THESAURUS Factor

With this final step, we want to tie it all together so it is really clear that success is a journey, not a destination. All the principles of the *Staircase* are interwoven and interdependent. To be truly successful, you need balance in your activities. They all affect each other in determining how successful and balanced your life is or can be. Also, you can go up and down the *Staircase,* dwelling on one step if necessary, depending on your needs at that point in time. It is a back-and-forth process. You may want to refer to this book many times as you seek new understanding in any area covered.

Your thoughts are the only things you can have absolute, total control over. Once you understand that, you can become liberated. Unlike animals, which live by instinct, God gave us a free will so we can make choices. The power to choose releases you from idle hope and lets you open your life to healthy expectation. It enables you to rely on your inborn resources and abilities, as well as on the skills you have developed.

Your journey along the *Staircase* sets the stage for a life of great adventure and achievement. By reading and studying *No Excuse!* you have had an opportunity to open your mind to ideas and principles that can help you create a successful, happy, and fulfilling life. Keep them fresh by daily application, and you can eliminate any habits and excuses that could prevent you from fulfilling your destiny.

Mark Twain said, "Habit is habit and is not to be flung out the window but coaxed down the stairs, one step at a time." You can avoid new excuses just as you can eliminate old ones. With *No Excuse!* living, you can guard against the negative thinking that may threaten to undermine your efforts.

One of the first things we addressed was how to define success. Remember, whatever you define success to be, as you achieve it you're successful! Then you can come up with something new and exciting to achieve. It's all part of your journey. It's a progressive realization. Again, my definition of success may be different than yours. That's okay! You and I may experience happiness in different ways. That's okay, too! Happiness comes from within. What's happiness to one person may not be to the next.

You may go to work in the morning and usually come home at night. Or maybe you work later hours or travel out of town. If you are a parent, student, or retiree, and you don't work outside your home, it is still likely you have a daily routine. Life is very much a full circle. *No Excuse!* as a philosophy for success is also a full circle. Without the integration of all the other steps, your chances of being happy, fulfilled, and purposeful are reduced.

If you keep making excuses, how can you expect to have a rich life experience? Is there any excuse not to achieve success? How can you blame lack of time for not accomplishing things when it's probably your inability to effectively manage activities? How can you blame other people for misunderstanding and not giving you the outcomes you want, when it may be your inability to communicate effectively with them that caused the situation?

Whenever you have a task or situation that you need to handle, and you have an excuse, think again. Remind yourself that you are responsible for your decisions, and you're likely to find these excuses irrelevant. *As a result of being a student of the* No Excuse! *philosophy, I recommend that one of your major goals be to eliminate excuses from your life.*

Succeed and Balance Your Life is the integration of all the other steps. Without self-esteem it's very difficult to believe in yourself. Without purpose, without having any idea of why you are here, it's very difficult to define success for yourself. They're all interconnected and interdependent.

Are you willing to take responsibility for the decisions you are going to make now and in the future, regardless of their outcomes? They are all going to make at least some impact on your life and the people around you. When you take responsibility for your decisions, you'll grow from the experience whether you receive the outcome you want or not!

Create Your Own Declaration of Independence

Back in 1776, the *Declaration of Independence* proclaimed the beginning of a great Republic. Fifty-six men put their lives on the line to be free. They didn't make any excuses and they were ready to take responsibility for their actions. Today, *No Excuse!* living prepares *you* to sign your own declaration of independence for a life of personal freedom and enterprise.

Why did our forefathers create the *Declaration of Independence?* They had reached such maturity and self-reliance by the end of Britain's successful struggle against France that they were no longer willing to tolerate England's control. The Americans had become self-responsible to the point where they no longer needed outside influence for support.

May I suggest that you consider this text from the *Declaration of Independence* as your own personal declaration of freedom:

> *We hold these truths to be self-evident, that all men are created equal, that they are endowed by their Creator with certain unalienable rights, that among these are life, liberty, and the pursuit of happiness. That to secure these rights, governments are instituted among men, deriving their just powers from the consent of the governed That whenever any form of government becomes destructive to these ends, it is the right of the people to alter or to abolish it and to institute new government, laying its foundation on such principles and organizing its power in such form as to them shall seem most likely to affect their safety and happiness.*

When you are empowered by *No Excuse!* living, you are, in effect, your own independent state. You have the right to make peace, establish alliances, conduct business, and do all those things that independent states do. On July 4, 1776, fifty-six men secured a future of self-determination and changed the course of history.

Right now you can boldly pledge your own independence. I suggest you write the date and this affirmation in your personal diary, planning book, or on a calendar: "From here on out, I'm more self-responsible and self-assured than ever. I am exercising my own inalienable right to life, liberty and the pursuit of happiness."

Where Does Success Come From?

Recently, I went to the dictionary to see what it said about success. Much to my surprise, one of the definitions was, "Success is the outcome of an event whether positive or negative." Does that intrigue you like it did me? It means that even a negative (unwanted) outcome can be viewed as a success because, hopefully, you *learned* something from it. Ideally, you gained some new understanding and wisdom; you grew. Your perception and attitude has a lot to do with how you interpret the event. Remember, *behind every adversity is the seed of an equal or greater benefit.* In effect, you could say *there's no such thing as failure! There is only the opportunity to learn.*

How do you deal with failure? Life is always up-and-down, ebb-and-flow. If you worry about failure, it's more difficult to overcome; a lot of your energy is wasted worrying. Einstein said, "Men worry more about what they can't see than what they can see." If you're always concerned about your outcomes being negative, you're setting yourself up for failure. A constant negative focus makes it difficult to overcome failure and look beyond it. *You get what you focus on.*

Democracy and Free Enterprise Provide the Environment for a Happy, Productive, Fulfilling Life

You now have the tools to help yourself and those around you lead a better life. There's *No Excuse!* not to do so. When you integrate forgiveness, self-esteem, attitude, enthusiasm, self-control, honesty, dreams, goal setting, knowledge, understanding people, honoring family and friends, and determination so you can grow, you'll have a wonderful life. The combination makes it almost inevitable that you'll succeed, live a balanced life, and be happy and fulfilled.

Years ago, Mikail Gorbachev, Premier of the former Soviet Union, addressed the crowd at Founder's Day ceremonies at the University of Virginia. Ironically, the campus was founded by Thomas Jefferson, chief architect of the *Declaration of Independence.* Jefferson's thoughts about democracy continue to have a profound effect on American life. In fact, his ideas are inspiring leaders all over the world who are still working to instill democratic reforms. Jefferson left a legacy that opened the human spirit to change. It would no longer be confined to the hopelessness and disrespect of unacceptable situations. Part of this change was reflected in the fact that Gorbachev spoke at this campus.

A government needs to provide its citizens with an environment to support life, liberty, and the pursuit of happiness. We personally have a responsibility to embrace life, cherish liberty and free enterprise, and to pursue our dreams while encouraging others to do the same. Happiness is a byproduct of pursuing our dream, i.e., going toward our vision. In the process, we can learn to know ourselves better while giving of our skills and talents to contribute to the world.

One of my favorite quotes of all time, by Ralph Waldo Emerson, describes a life of success and balance:

> *To laugh often and much; to win the respect of intelligent people and the affection of children; to earn the appreciation of honest critics and endure the betrayal of false friends; to appreciate beauty; to find the best in others; to leave the world a little better place than we found it, whether by a healthy child, a garden patch or a redeemed social condition; to know even one life breathed easier because you lived. This is to have succeeded.*

How can success be more special than that? We all have the opportunity and potential to make a difference in the lives of other people. *It's easy to make a dollar, but it's more important to make a difference.* There is truly *No Excuse!* not to be successful.

Get Ready to Fly—*Start Living Your Dreams*

Like *The Knight in Rusty Armor* at the end of his journey, are you ready to embrace life and its opportunities? Your training on the *Staircase of Success* has given you an opportunity to be more aware of the simple joys of daily life. There's a poster that shows a butterfly soaring from his cocoon. The caption says, "You can fly, but that cocoon has to go." May I suggest that you let go of your cocoon, and get ready to fly!

People who *receive* without effort often end up *having* without appreciating. When you work for something, you are more likely to realize its value and be grateful for it.

Those not content to rest on their laurels, and be satisfied with what they've done so far, are inspired to know they can live the life they want. They just need to define what success means to them.

We will not scoff at people who don't know what they want; we can help them find it. We can show them the satisfaction that comes from deciding on a dream and going for it. This is critical because, as it says in the Scriptures, "Where there is no vision, the people perish." As a bonus, happiness comes as you pursue your dream.

As you live the *No Excuse!* life, you can experience success with balance. Just as West Point produces leaders, *No Excuse!* living helps you become successful. You can achieve the outcomes you want because you now have the principles you need to develop your skills and help other people.

No Excuse! living is exciting! Your mind has now been exposed to the opportunity for positive living and the healthy accumulation of wealth in *all* areas of your life. You now know that you can open your life to the adventure of living your dream. As you apply these principles, your life can become more exhilarating than you ever imagined.

Why Is It Necessary to Live a Balanced Life?

To live a happy, fulfilling life, we need balance. What good would it be to achieve success, while totally disregarding how you treat other people? What good would it be to achieve success while ignoring your family? You probably wouldn't enjoy your success much, not to mention all the enemies you'd make and the heartache you'd cause! Of all the ideas discussed, balance is critical. The environment, the eco-system we live in, is in a state of balance. Do you know what happens when something gets out of balance? Something else is negatively impacted.

THE WHEEL OF LIFE
All spokes need to be of equal length for your life to be balanced.

The world was not created out of balance, and neither were you. Take a look at all seven areas of your life: Social, Physical, Mental, Spiritual, Family, Career, and Financial. Ask yourself if you're spending too much time in any one particular area. Is your life in balance? Or is your life like a car with an out-of-balance tire—a little shaky? For example, are you spending too much time at work and leaving your family or your spiritual well-being behind? Are you spending too much time on household or other responsibilities while letting your health deteriorate? Are you doing too much volunteering while your income suffers? It may be necessary to be out of balance for awhile to accomplish something. Remember though, "All things in moderation" is an excellent rule to live by in general. You may want to consider examining your life and balancing things out, if necessary.

Take time for fun. If all you do is work and never play, you may create a pretty dull life. Pace yourself. You'll accomplish more in the long run.

Sit down and analyze exactly where you're spending time and energy. Eventually you get a clearer picture of what's happening in your life, and be better able to make appropriate adjustments. If you discover that you spend too much time at work and are almost never home for your family, you could lose your most precious relationships. You could take action to perhaps delegate some work to your staff and go home earlier. Or you could explain to your boss that you need an assistant.

If you don't take care of your physical and mental health your system will have to work that much harder to maintain itself. You may get away with it for awhile and not notice the decline but, eventually, it'll catch up with you and your body may say, "No more!" That's where physical and mental breakdowns can come from—too much stress and not enough regard for your health. Whatever you don't take care of eventually goes away. As the dentist jokingly said to the patient with a toothache, "Don't take care of your teeth, and they'll go away! The pain will be gone but so will your teeth!" Don't take care of your health and it will go away too.

You may not think much about your spiritual life either, but it's so important. It gives you that something extra. It helps give you a vision and an understanding of why you're here to begin with. Why were you put here on this earth? The spiritual aspect of your life is vitally important in helping you determine your purpose. Life is really about serving. Find out how you can best serve, then do it. When you serve, success will follow.

You've probably heard the expression "Money is the root of all evil." Is that true? Of course not! The actual words are, "The love of money is a root of evil." Money pays for food, shelter, clothing, heat, transportation, education, schools, churches, and many other things. Without money, it would be almost impossible to live and participate in today's society. If you neglect the financial aspect of your life, it's probably out of balance. Did you know that arguments and situations that arise from lack of (or mismanaged) money are a major cause of family challenges?

After they finish school, some people have a tendency to neglect the mental aspect of life. They may stop reading, learning, and growing. There are so many excellent books and other resources available today, there is *No Excuse!* for not growing. If you want a richer, fuller, more rewarding life, you need to learn and grow. The mind is like a muscle. If it's not exercised, it will atrophy. Einstein once said that we use less than 10 percent of our brain! Just think of the untapped resource that resides in your head. You probably eat three times a day to nourish your body. Could you read 15 to 30 minutes a day from a personal development or educational book to enrich your mind?

The Little Boy in the Park
I will leave you with one final story. A little boy was walking through the park. He looked down and found a shiny penny in the grass. He picked it up and was very excited and pleased. He was so energized by finding the free money that every time he went outside his head would be down as he looked for more. Over the course of his lifetime he found many nickels, dimes, quarters, and even a few dollar bills. They totaled $12.96.

That money hadn't cost him a thing, or so he thought. In reality, though, it did in what he missed—about 30,000 sunsets and over 300 rainbows, his children growing up, birds singing and flying in the sky, sunshine, laughter, and so many other beautiful things. The lesson here is to remember to look beyond day-to-day activities; pick your head up and look at the true riches and splendor life has to offer. Live fully and enjoy your journey.

The Rewards of *No Excuse!* Living

West Point and the Army were magnificent experiences—*No Excuse!* experiences! They taught me to live a *No Excuse!* life, which led to developing this program and writing this book.

The Army did many great things for me. I'm especially thankful for learning the value of family, friends, God, country, and myself. The greatest gift the Army gave me, however, was teaching me to accept responsibility for my own life. The Army also taught me to move on to a new challenge when my purpose indicated it was necessary—when it was the *No Excuse!* thing to do.

Embrace the *No Excuse!* lifestyle, practice self-responsibility, and take care of yourself, your family, and your career. Follow the dream in your heart and become the best *you* you can be. When the going gets tough just say, "No excuse!" and get on with your pursuit. *No Excuse!* can help you overcome obstacles and achieve personal excellence as you incorporate core values, accountability, and balance into your life and career.

* * *

Who Is Jay Rifenbary?

Jay Rifenbary, husband and father, is a professional speaker, trainer, and consultant, and founder and president of the Rifenbary Training and Development Center. He is a graduate of the United States Military Academy at West Point and was a qualified Airborne Ranger and Military Commander. He was also a top ranking sales professional, corporate manager, and entrepreneur.

Jay brings a unique background of interpersonal skills, military experience, and business acumen to each of his speaking and training engagements. He is sought after as a speaker and author on personal development/success, motivation, leadership, communication, team building, and family and interpersonal relationships. Jay speaks for Fortune 500 companies, direct sales/network marketing conventions, associations, government, and schools across the U.S., and is also available internationally. He and his wife, Noni, have two children and live in New York.

THE NO EXCUSE CREED

66*I am a No Excuse person. I live self-responsibly and I am accountable for everything I say and do. I know what it means to be alive, and my direction is clear. I understand my purpose in life, and do things with a sense of mission. I act with integrity, own all my decisions, and always do the best I can. I forgive myself and others for what was or was not done that may have caused heartache and failure in the past. I forgive my environment and I overcome obstacles. I let go of the past and move on to achieve excellence. I have intact self-esteem and maintain it by value judging no one. I give everyone total unconditional acceptance, because we are all equal in the eyes of God. I am no better than anyone else, and no one is better than I am. However, as a No Excuse person, I am always confident of my talents and skills. I maintain excellent health, feel energetic, and carry a cheerful countenance. I maintain self-control in thought, word, and deed, and I have the patience to see things through. I am always honest with myself and others, and set goals which are true for me. I have a dream big enough to overcome my fears, handle risks, and live the life I choose. I am always learning and growing—ever expanding my mind and learning new skills. I care about people and encourage them to be all they can be. I understand and communicate effectively with others. I honor my family and friends and realize how important they are to me. I respect others, appreciate their talents and skills, and have love and compassion for everyone. I have a strong desire to serve others and make a difference. I balance my activities among the seven key areas of life: Physical, Mental, Spiritual, Family, Career, Financial, and Social. My life is a product of the decisions I make, and I am in charge of it. I have No Excuse—all my excuses are gone. No Excuse living is for me. I am a No Excuse person.*"

—JAY RIFENBARY

Copyright © 2008 Jay Rifenbary